Access 97 For Windows For Dummies

D0517390

Field Types to Know and Love

Each field (or column) of your datasheet can hold only one type of information. Here are the basic Access information types:

Text: Stores any kind of text (letters, numbers, and even letters *and* numbers)

Memo: Holds really long text entries (such as descriptions, reports, and such)

Number: Holds any number you intend use for counting or doing math

AutoNumber: Automatically fills in a unique number for every record

Currency: Stores numbers and symbols that represent quantities of money

Date/Time: Contains dates, times, or both

Yes/No: Holds two-option logic values such as Yes/No, True/False, or Male/Female

Hyperlink: Contains clickable links to World Wide Web pages on the Internet or your company's intranet

OLE object: Contains highly technical, complex objects that can do everything but wash your car

Online Support for Access 97

System	Access Command	Notes
America Online	keyword PC Applications	Look for *MS Access Q&A* in the message boards under Database Use and Development
CompuServe	go MSACCESS	This whole area is devoted to Access; lots of good stuff
GEnie	move to page 505	Includes the Microsoft Roundtable and knowledge base
Newsgroups	comp. databases. ms-access	Requires access to Internet newsgroups
Prodigy	jump MICROSOFT	Offers support forums and the knowledge base
World Wide Web	http://www. microsoft. com/Support/	Requires access to the Web

Access 97 Telephone Support Numbers

When all else fails, there's nothing like picking up the phone and yelling *help me!* at some innocent soul on the other end of the connection. Here's where to dial for assistance:

Number	Who You Reach
800-936-4100	The FastTips hotline for free recorded help 24 hours a day
206-635-7050	(United States) Access 97 phone support; you pay for the call, but the first two answers are free
905-568-3503	(Canada) Access 97 phone support; you pay for the call, but the first two answers are free
800-936-5500	(United States) Fast answers to your Access 97 problems, 24 hours a day — $55 per incident
800-668-7975	(Canada) Fast answers to your Access 97 problems, 24 hours a day — $55 per incident
800-426-9400	General, nontechnical questions about Microsoft Access
206-635-4948	(Hearing Impaired) Support for all Microsoft Office 97 products for hearing-impaired individuals who have a TDD or TT modem

...For Dummies: #1 Computer Book Series for Beginners

Toolbars for Every Occasion

In Access, your toolbar changes depending on what you're doing. So how do you keep track of so many different buttons? Simple: If you want to know more about a particular button, choose Help⇨What's This? and then click on the button in question.

Here are some of the more common Access 97 toolbars:

The Database toolbar:

The Table Datasheet toolbar:

The Formatting (Datasheet) toolbar:

The Table Design toolbar:

The Query Design toolbar:

The Report Design toolbar:

The Filter/Sort toolbar:

The Form View toolbar:

IDG BOOKS WORLDWIDE

...For Dummies: #1 Computer Book Series for Beginners

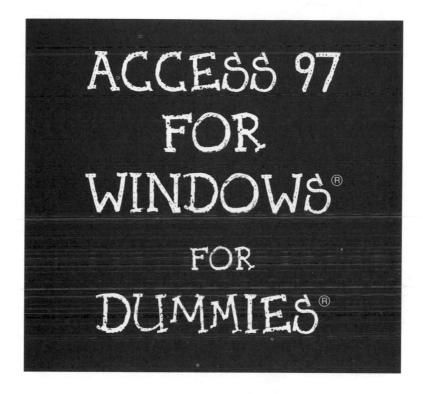

ACCESS 97 FOR WINDOWS® FOR DUMMIES®

by John Kaufeld

IDG Books Worldwide, Inc.
An International Data Group Company

Foster City, CA ♦ Chicago, IL ♦ Indianapolis, IN ♦ Southlake, TX

Access 97 For Windows® For Dummies®

Published by
IDG Books Worldwide, Inc.
An International Data Group Company
919 E. Hillsdale Blvd.
Suite 400
Foster City, CA 94404
http://www.idgbooks.com (IDG Books Worldwide Web site)
http://www.dummies.com (Dummies Press Web site)

Library of Congress Catalog Card No.: 96-79271

ISBN: 0-7645-0048-1

Printed in the United States of America

10 9 8 7 6 5 4 3 2

1E/RZ/QT/ZX/IN

Distributed in the United States by IDG Books Worldwide, Inc.

Distributed by Macmillan Canada for Canada; by Transworld Publishers Limited in the United Kingdom and Europe; by WoodsLane Pty. Ltd. for Australia; by WoodsLane Enterprises Ltd. for New Zealand; by Longman Singapore Publishers Ltd. for Singapore, Malaysia, Thailand, and Indonesia; by Simron Pty. Ltd. for South Africa; by Toppan Company Ltd. for Japan; by Distribuidora Cuspide for Argentina; by Livraria Cultura for Brazil; by Ediciencia S.A. for Ecuador; by Addison-Wesley Publishing Company for Korea; by Ediciones ZETA S.C.R. Ltda. for Peru; by WS Computer Publishing Company, Inc., for the Philippines; by Unalis Corporation for Taiwan; by Contemporanea de Ediciones for Venezuela. Authorized Sales Agent: Anthony Rudkin Associates for the Middle East and North Africa.

For general information on IDG Books Worldwide's books in the U.S., please call our Consumer Customer Service department at 800-762-2974. For reseller information, including discounts and premium sales, please call our Reseller Customer Service department at 800-434-3422.

For information on where to purchase IDG Books Worldwide's books outside the U.S., please contact our International Sales department at 415-655-3023 or fax 415-655-3299.

For information on foreign language translations, please contact our Foreign & Subsidiary Rights department at 415-655-3021 or fax 415-655-3281.

For sales inquiries and special prices for bulk quantities, please contact our Sales department at 415-655-3200 or write to the address above.

For information on using IDG Books Worldwide's books in the classroom or for ordering examination copies, please contact our Educational Sales department at 800-434-2086 or fax 817-251-8174.

For press review copies, author interviews, or other publicity information, please contact our Public Relations department at 415-655-3000 or fax 415-655-3299.

For authorization to photocopy items for corporate, personal, or educational use, please contact Copyright Clearance Center, 222 Rosewood Drive, Danvers, MA 01923, or fax 508-750-4470.

is a trademark under exclusive license to IDG Books Worldwide, Inc., from International Data Group, Inc.

About the Author

John Kaufeld got hooked on computers a long time ago. Somewhere along the way, he discovered that he really enjoyed helping people resolve computer problems (a trait that his Computer Science pals generally considered a character flaw, but that everyone else seemed to appreciate). John finally achieved his B.S. degree in Management Information Systems from Ball State University, and he became the first PC Support Technician for what was then Westinghouse outside Cincinnati, Ohio.

Since that time, he's logged nearly a decade of experience working with normal people who, for one reason or another, were stuck with a "friendly" personal computer that turned on them. He's also trained more than 1,000 people in many different PC and Macintosh applications. The vast majority of them not only survived the experience, but thrived on it. Today, John is president of Access Systems, a computer consulting firm. He still does troubleshooting, conducts technical and interpersonal skills seminars for up-and-coming computer gurus, and writes in his free moments.

John's other IDG titles include *FoxPro 2.6 For Windows For Dummies, Paradox 5 For Windows For Dummies,* and the best-selling *America Online For Dummies* (he regularly uses AOL, where he's known as Jkaufeld, and he loves to get e-mail, answering every message he gets). John lives with his wife, two children, one overbearing canary, and a lovable American Eskimo puppy in Indianapolis, Indiana.

ABOUT IDG BOOKS WORLDWIDE

Welcome to the world of IDG Books Worldwide.

IDG Books Worldwide, Inc., is a subsidiary of International Data Group, the world's largest publisher of computer-related information and the leading global provider of information services on information technology. IDG was founded more than 25 years ago and now employs more than 8,500 people worldwide. IDG publishes more than 275 computer publications in over 75 countries (see listing below). More than 60 million people read one or more IDG publications each month.

Launched in 1990, IDG Books Worldwide is today the #1 publisher of best-selling computer books in the United States. We are proud to have received eight awards from the Computer Press Association in recognition of editorial excellence and three from *Computer Currents'* First Annual Readers' Choice Awards. Our best-selling *...For Dummies*® series has more than 30 million copies in print with translations in 30 languages. IDG Books Worldwide, through a joint venture with IDG's Hi-Tech Beijing, became the first U.S. publisher to publish a computer book in the People's Republic of China. In record time, IDG Books Worldwide has become the first choice for millions of readers around the world who want to learn how to better manage their businesses.

Our mission is simple: Every one of our books is designed to bring extra value and skill-building instructions to the reader. Our books are written by experts who understand and care about our readers. The knowledge base of our editorial staff comes from years of experience in publishing, education, and journalism — experience we use to produce books for the '90s. In short, we care about books, so we attract the best people. We devote special attention to details such as audience, interior design, use of icons, and illustrations. And because we use an efficient process of authoring, editing, and desktop publishing our books electronically, we can spend more time ensuring superior content and spend less time on the technicalities of making books.

You can count on our commitment to deliver high-quality books at competitive prices on topics you want to read about. At IDG Books Worldwide, we continue in the IDG tradition of delivering quality for more than 25 years. You'll find no better book on a subject than one from IDG Books Worldwide.

John Kilcullen
CEO
IDG Books Worldwide, Inc.

Eighth Annual Computer Press Awards ≥1992   *Ninth Annual Computer Press Awards ≥1993*   *Tenth Annual Computer Press Awards ≥1994*   *Eleventh Annual Computer Press Awards ≥1995*

IDG Books Worldwide, Inc., is a subsidiary of International Data Group, the world's largest publisher of computer-related information and the leading global provider of information services on information technology. International Data Group publishes over 275 computer publications in over 75 countries. Sixty million people read one or more International Data Group publications each month. International Data Group's publications include: **ARGENTINA:** Buyer's Guide, Computerworld Argentina, PC World Argentina; **AUSTRALIA:** Australian Macworld, Australian PC World, Australian Reseller News, Computerworld, IT Casebook, Network World, Publish, Webmaster; **AUSTRIA:** Computerwelt Osterreich, Networks Austria, PC Tip Austria; **BANGLADESH:** PC World Bangladesh; **BELARUS:** PC World Belarus; **BELGIUM:** Data News; **BRAZIL:** Annuário de Informática, Computerworld, Connections, Macworld, PC Player, PC World, Publish, Reseller News, Supergamepower; **BULGARIA:** Computerworld Bulgaria, Network World Bulgaria, PC & MacWorld Bulgaria; **CANADA:** CIO Canada, Client/Server World, ComputerWorld Canada, InfoWorld Canada, NetworkWorld Canada, WebWorld; **CHILE:** Computerworld Chile, PC World Chile; **COLOMBIA:** Computerworld Colombia, PC World Colombia; **COSTA RICA:** PC World Centro America; **THE CZECH AND SLOVAK REPUBLICS:** Computerworld Czechoslovakia, Macworld Czech Republic, PC World Czechoslovakia; **DENMARK:** Communications World Danmark, Computerworld Danmark, Macworld Danmark, PC World Danmark, Techworld Denmark; **DOMINICAN REPUBLIC:** PC World Republica Dominicana; **ECUADOR:** PC World Ecuador; **EGYPT:** Computerworld Middle East, PC World Middle East; **EL SALVADOR:** PC World Centro America; **FINLAND:** MikroPC, Tietoverkko, Tietoviikko; **FRANCE:** Distributique, Hebdo, Info PC, Le Monde Informatique, Macworld, Reseaux & Telecoms, WebMaster France; **GERMANY:** Computer Partner, Computerwoche, Computerwoche Extra, Computerwoche FOCUS, Global Online, Macwelt, PC Welt; **GREECE:** Amiga Computing, GamePro Greece, Multimedia World; **GUATEMALA:** PC World Centro America; **HONDURAS:** PC World Centro America; **HONG KONG:** Computerworld Hong Kong, PC World Hong Kong, Publish in Asia; **HUNGARY:** ABCD CD-ROM, Computerworld Szamitastechnika, Internetto online Magazine, PC World Hungary, PC-X Magazin Hungary; **ICELAND:** Tolvuheimur PC World Island; **INDIA:** Information Communications World, Information Systems Computerworld, PC World India, Publish in Asia; **INDONESIA:** InfoKomputer PC World, Komputek Computerworld, Publish in Asia; **IRELAND:** ComputerScope, PC Live!; **ISRAEL:** Macworld Israel, People & Computers/Computerworld; **ITALY:** Computerworld Italia, Macworld Italia, Networking Italia, PC World Italia; **JAPAN:** DTP World, Macworld Japan, Nikkei Personal Computing, OS/2 World Japan, SunWorld Japan, Windows NT World, Windows World Japan; **KENYA:** PC World East African; **KOREA:** Hi-Tech Information, Macworld Korea, PC World Korea; **MACEDONIA:** PC World Macedonia; **MALAYSIA:** Computerworld Malaysia, PC World Malaysia, Publish in Asia; **MALTA:** PC World Malta; **MEXICO:** Computerworld Mexico, PC World Mexico; **MYANMAR:** PC World Myanmar; **NETHERLANDS:** Computer! Totaal, LAN Internetworking Magazine, LAN World Buyers Guide, Macworld Netherlands, Net, WebWereld; **NEW ZEALAND:** Absolute Beginners Guide and Plain & Simple Series, Computer Buyer, Computer Industry Directory, Computerworld New Zealand, MTB, Network World, PC World New Zealand; **NICARAGUA:** PC World Centro America; **NORWAY:** Computerworld Norge, CW Rapport, Datamagasinet, Financial Rapport, Kursguide Norge, Macworld Norge, Multimediaworld Norge, PC World Ekspress Norge, PC World Nettverk, PC World Norge, PC World ProduktGuide Norge; **PAKISTAN:** Computerworld Pakistan; **PANAMA:** PC World Panama; **PEOPLE'S REPUBLIC OF CHINA:** China Computer Users, China Computerworld, China InfoWorld, China Telecom World Weekly, Computer & Communication, Electronic Design China, Electronics Today, Electronics Weekly, Game Software, PC World China, Popular Computer Week, Software Weekly, Software World, Telecom World; **PERU:** Computerworld Peru, PC World Profesional Peru, PC World SoHo Peru; **PHILIPPINES:** Click!, Computerworld Philippines, PC World Philippines, Publish in Asia; **POLAND:** Computerworld Poland, Computerworld Special Report Poland, Cyber, Macworld Poland, Networld Poland, PC World Komputer; **PORTUGAL:** Cerebro/PC World, Computerworld/Correio Informático, Dealer World Portugal, Mac*In/PC*In Portugal, Multimedia World; **PUERTO RICO:** PC World Puerto Rico; **ROMANIA:** Computerworld Romania, PC World Romania, Telecom Romania; **RUSSIA:** Computerworld Russia, Mir PK, Publish, Seti; **SINGAPORE:** Computerworld Singapore, PC World Singapore, Publish in Asia; **SLOVENIA:** Monitor; **SOUTH AFRICA:** Computing SA, Network World SA, Software World SA; **SPAIN:** Communicaciones World España, Computerworld España, Dealer World España, Macworld España, PC World España; **SRI LANKA:** Infolink PC World; **SWEDEN:** CAP&Design, Computer Sweden, Corporate Computing Sweden, Internetworld Sweden, it.branschen, Macworld Sweden, MaxiData Sweden, MikroDatorn, Nätverk & Kommunikation, PC World Sweden, PCaktiv, Windows World Sweden; **SWITZERLAND:** Computerworld Schweiz, Macworld Schweiz, PCtip; **TAIWAN:** Computerworld Taiwan, Macworld Taiwan, NEW VISION/Publish, PC World Taiwan, Windows World Taiwan; **THAILAND:** Publish in Asia, Thai Computerworld; **TURKEY:** Computerworld Turkiye, Macworld Turkiye, Network World Turkiye, PC World Turkiye; **UKRAINE:** Computerworld Kiev, Multimedia World Ukraine, PC World Ukraine; **UNITED KINGDOM:** Acorn User UK, Amiga Action UK, Amiga Computing UK, Apple Talk UK, Computing, Macworld, Parents and Computers UK, PC Advisor, PC Home, PSX Pro, The WEB; **UNITED STATES:** Cable in the Classroom, CIO Magazine, Computerworld, DOS World, Federal Computer Week, GamePro Magazine, InfoWorld, I-Way, Macworld, Network World, PC Games, PC World, Publish, Video Event, THE WEB Magazine, and WebMaster; online webzines: JavaWorld, NetscapeWorld, and SunWorld Online; **URUGUAY:** InfoWorld Uruguay; **VENEZUELA:** Computerworld Venezuela, PC World Venezuela; and **VIETNAM:** PC World Vietnam.   2/14/97

Dedication

To Jenny, because without you I'd be completely nuts.

To J.B. and the Pooz, for reminding Daddy to smile when all he could do was write.

To IDG Books, for the opportunity of a lifetime.

My sincere thanks to you, one and all.

Acknowledgments

Another one's out the door. . . .

As with any good magic trick, there's more to putting out a book than meets the eye. Kudos and candy (lots of chocolate!) to my Project Editor, Shannon Ross, and Copy Editors Joe Jansen and Christine Meloy Beck for their diligent efforts in making my ramblings follow commonly accepted semantic guidelines. An equally significant quantity of thanks (and chocolate) are thrown in the direction of my Technical Editor at Publication Services, Inc., for making sure that I'm not making this stuff up.

Special thanks to Anne in Microsoft Outside Sales for having *information at her fingertips* when I needed to know about the impending release of Access 97. I can't tell you anything more about her because she's a Microsoft Trade Secret and I'm under nondisclosure. It's a legal thing.

Cindy in Microsoft's Access Support Group gets a special tip o' the hat for helping me track down a particularly irksome *feature* with a beta release of Access 97. Without her help, I'd have even less hair than I currently have (and these days, every hair counts).

Publisher's Acknowledgments

We're proud of this book; please send us your comments about it by using the Reader Response Card at the back of the book or by e-mailing us at feedback/dummies@idgbooks.com. Some of the people who helped bring this book to market include the following:

Acquisitions, Development, and Editorial

Project Editor: Shannon Ross

Assistant Acquisitions Editor: Gareth Hancock

Product Development Director: Mary Bednarek

Media Development Manager: Joyce Pepple

Copy Editors: Christine Meloy Beck, Joe Jansen

Technical Editor: Publication Services, Inc.

Editorial Managers: Kristin A. Cocks, Seta K. Frantz

Editorial Assistants: Constance Carlisle, Chris H. Collins, Michael D. Sullivan

Production

Project Coordinator: Valery Bourke

Layout and Graphics: E. Shawn Aylsworth, Brett Black, Cameron Booker, Linda Boyer, J. Tyler Connor, Dominique DeFelice, Angela F. Hunckler, Todd Klemme, Jane Martin, Drew Moore, Elizabeth Cardénas-Nelson, Laura Puranan, Anna Rohrer, Thereesa Sánchez-Baker, Brent Savage, Kate Snell, Michael Sullivan

Proofreaders: Christine D. Berman, Joel Draper, Henry Lazarek, Rachel Garvey, Nancy Price, Robert Springer

Indexer: Sharon Hilgenberg

General and Administrative

IDG Books Worldwide, Inc.: John Kilcullen, CEO; Steven Berkowitz, President and Publisher

IDG Books Technology Publishing: Brenda McLaughlin, Senior Vice President and Group Publisher

Dummies Technology Press and Dummies Editorial: Diane Graves Steele, Vice President and Associate Publisher; Judith A. Taylor, Brand Manager; Kristin A. Cocks, Editorial Director

Dummies Trade Press: Kathleen A. Welton, Vice President and Publisher; Stacy S. Collins, Brand Manager

IDG Books Production for Dummies Press: Beth Jenkins, Production Director; Cindy L. Phipps, Supervisor of Project Coordination, Production Proofreading, and Indexing; Kathie S. Schutte, Supervisor of Page Layout; Shelley Lea, Supervisor of Graphics and Design; Debbie J. Gates, Production Systems Specialist; Tony Augsburger, Supervisor of Reprints and Bluelines; Leslie Popplewell, Media Archive Coordinator

Dummies Packaging and Book Design: Patti Sandez, Packaging Specialist; Lance Kayser, Packaging Assistant; Kavish+Kavish, Cover Design

♦

The publisher would like to give special thanks to Patrick J. McGovern, without whom this book would not have been possible.

♦

Contents at a Glance

Cartoons at a Glance

By Rich Tennant • Fax: 508-546-7747 • E-mail: the5wave@tiac.net

page 45

page 277

page 129

page 203

page 323

page 7

Table of Contents

· ·

Introduction

· ·

*B*eing a normal human being, you probably have work to do. In fact, you may have *lots* of work piled precariously around your office or even stretching onto the Internet. Someone, possibly your boss (or, if you work at home, your Significant Other), suggested that Access 97 may help you get more done in less time, eliminate the piles, and generally make the safety inspector happy.

So you picked up Access 97, and here you are. Whee!

If you're confused instead of organized, befuddled instead of productive, or just completely lost on the whole database thing, *Access 97 For Windows For Dummies* is the book for you.

This is a book with a purpose: to explain Access 97 without turning you into a world-class nerd in the process. What more could you want? (Well, you *could* want a chocolate malt, but Marketing said that I couldn't package ice cream beverages with this book.)

You Don't Need to Be a Nerd to Use This Book

Becoming a nerd is totally out of the question. In fact, you need to know only a few things about your computer and Windows 95 to get the most out of *Access 97 For Windows For Dummies*. In the following pages, I presume that you

- ✔ Have Microsoft Windows 95 and Access 97 for Windows 95 on your computer (if you have the whole Office 97 suite, that's fine, too)
- ✔ Know the basics of Windows 95
- ✔ Want to work with databases that other people have created
- ✔ Want to use and create queries, reports, and an occasional form
- ✔ Want to make your own databases from scratch every now and then
- ✔ Have perhaps used other versions of Access (although this is certainly not a requirement)

The good news is that you don't have to know (or even care) about table design, field types, relational databases, or any of that other database stuff to make Access 97 work for you. Everything you need to know is right here, just waiting for you to read it.

Sneaking a Peek at What's to Come

To give you an idea of what's ahead, here's a breakdown of the six parts in this book. Each part covers a general topic of Access 97. The part's individual chapters dig into the details.

Part I: Which Came First: The Data or the Base?

Right off the bat, this book answers the lyrical question "It's a data-*what?*" By starting with an overview of both database concepts in general and Access 97 in particular, this book provides the information you need to make sense of the whole database concept. This part also contains suggestions about solving problems with (or even *without*) Access 97. If you're about to design a new Access database to fix some pesky problem, read this section first — it may change your mind.

Part II: Truly Tempting Tables

Arguably, tables (where the data lives) are at the center of this whole database hubbub. After all, without tables, you wouldn't have any data to bully around. This part gives you the information you need to know about designing, building, using, changing, and generally coexisting in the same room with Access 97 tables.

Part III: Finding the Ultimate Answer to Everything (Well, Not Everything)

If tables are at the center of the Access universe, then queries are the first ring of planets. In Access, queries ask the power questions; they unearth the answers you *know* are hiding somewhere in your data. In addition to covering queries, this part also explains how to answer smaller questions using Find, Filter, and Sort — Query's little siblings.

Part IV: Turning Your Table into a Book

Seeing your data on-screen just isn't enough, sometimes. To make your work *really* shine, you have to commit it to paper. Part IV covers the Access report system, a portion of the software entirely dedicated both to getting your information onto the printed page and to driving you nuts in the process.

Part V: Wizards, Forms, and Other Mystical Stuff

At some point, technology approaches magic (one look at the control panel for a modern microwave oven is proof of that). This part explores some of the mystical areas in Access, helping you do stuff faster, seek assistance from the wizards, and even venture into a bit of programming. If the Internet's limitless possibilities pique your online fancy, look in this part for info about the new connectivity features in Access 97. They're really amazing!

Part VI: The Part of Tens

The words ". . .*For Dummies* book" immediately bring to mind the snappy, irreverent Part of Tens. This section dumps a load of tips and cool ideas onto, and hopefully *into,* your head. You can find a little bit of everything here, including time-saving tips and the solutions to the most common problems awaiting you in Access 97.

Appendix: Installing Access 97

Because none of the information in this book really helps unless you actually have Access 97 loaded on your computer, the appendix explains precisely how to accomplish this. Don't worry, though — this section gingerly walks you through the whole process.

What the Funny Text Means

Every now and then, you need to tell Access to do something or other. Likewise, there are moments when the program wants to toss its own comments and messages back to you (so be nice — communication is a two-way street). To easily show the difference between a human-to-computer message and vice-versa, I format the commands differently.

Here are examples of both kinds of message as they appear in the book.

This is something you type into the computer.

> This is how the computer responds to your command.

Because this *is* a Windows 95 program, you don't just type all day — you also mouse around quite a bit. Although I don't use a cool font for mouse actions, I *do* assume that you already know the basics. Here are the mouse movements necessary to make Access 97 (and any other Windows 95 program) work:

- ✓ **Click:** Position the tip of the mouse pointer (the end of the arrow) on the menu item, button, check box, or whatever else you happen to be aiming at, and then quickly press and release the left mouse button.

- ✓ **Double-click:** Position the mouse pointer as though you're going to click, but fool it at the last minute by clicking twice in rapid succession.

- ✓ **Click and drag (*highlight*):** Put the tip of the mouse pointer at the place you want to start highlighting and then press and hold the left mouse button. While holding the mouse button down, drag the pointer across whatever you want to highlight. When you reach the end of what you're highlighting, release the mouse button.

- ✓ **Right-click:** Right-clicking works just like clicking, except that you're exercising the right mouse button instead of the left mouse button.

Of course, the Access 97 menu comes in handy, too. When I want you to pick something from the main menu bar, the instruction looks like this:

Choose File➪Open Database.

If you think that mice belong in holes, you can use the underlined letters as shortcut keys to control Access 97 from the keyboard. To use the keyboard shortcut, hold down the Alt key and press the underlined letters. In the example above, the keyboard shortcut is Alt+F, O. Don't type the comma — it's just trying to make the command easier to read.

If you aren't familiar with all these rodent gymnastics, or if you want to learn more about Windows 95 in general, pick up a copy of *Windows 95 For Dummies* by Andy Rathbone.

Finding Points of Interest

When something in this book is particularly valuable, I go out of my way to make sure that it stands out. I use these cool icons to mark text that (for one reason or another) *really* needs your attention. Here's a quick preview of the ones waiting for you in this book and what they mean:

Notes are things I just want to make sure you see — little tidbits that may otherwise vanish into the text.

Tips are *really* helpful words of wisdom that promise to save you time, energy, and perhaps some hair. Whenever you see a tip, take a second to check it out.

Some things are too important to forget, so the Remember icon points them out. These items are critical steps in a process — points that you don't want to miss.

Sometimes, I give in to my dark, nerdy side and slip some technical twaddle into the book. The Technical Stuff icon protects you from obscure details by making them easy to avoid. If you're in an adventuresome mood, check out the technical stuff, anyway. You may find it interesting.

The Warning icon says it all: *Skipping this information may be hazardous to your data's health.* Pay attention to these icons and follow their instructions to keep your databases happy and intact.

The wheel on the new Microsoft IntelliMouse adds some interesting innovations to Access 97. This icon marks time-saving tips featuring the newest addition to the bag of mousey tricks.

Setting Sail on the Voyage

Now nothing's left to hold you back from the wonders of Access 97. Cleave tightly to *Access 97 For Windows For Dummies,* consign the Microsoft manuals to a suitable dark hole, and dive into Access 97.

- ✔ If you're brand-new to the program and don't know which way to turn, start with the general overview in Chapter 1.
- ✔ If you're about to design a database, I salute you — and recommend flipping through Chapter 4 for some helpful design and development tips.
- ✔ Looking for something specific? Try the Table of Contents or the Index, or just flip through the book until you find something interesting.

Bon Voyage!

Part I

Which Came First: The Data or the Base?

In this part . . .

*E*verything starts somewhere. It's that way with nature, with science, and with meatballs that roll down your tie. So what more fitting way to begin this book than with a look at where databases start — as a glimmer in someone's mind.

This part opens with a heretical look at problem-solving, and then moves along to cover the new Access 97 program itself. A little later in the part, you discover the secrets of good data organization and where to find help when the world of Access 97 has you down.

All in all, this part is a pretty good place to start — whether you're new to the whole database concept, or just to Access 97. Either way, welcome aboard!

Chapter 1

The 37-Minute Overview

*I*t's confession time. This chapter probably takes longer than 37 minutes to finish, if you read the whole thing. Then again, you may spend *less* time than that if you're already somewhat familiar with the program, or if you're a speed-reader. Either way, the chapter *does* give you a good overview of Access 97 from start to finish (and I mean that literally).

Because the best way to get into Access 97 is to literally *get into* it, this chapter leads you on a wild, galloping tour of the software, covering the highlights of things you and Access 97 probably do together on a daily basis. This chapter is something of a "Day in the Life" story, designed to show you the important stuff while pointing you to other areas of the book for more information.

If you're new to Access 97, this chapter is a good place to start. If you're already familiar with the older versions of Access, I recommend that you skim through this chapter anyway to see how things have changed. Enjoy the trip!

In the Beginning, There Was Access 97 (But It Wasn't Running Yet)

The machine is quiet, the screen sits dark and devoid of image, and you aren't getting much work done. Nice as it is, the situation can't go on forever — the time has come to start Access 97.

You can't run the software if it isn't installed. If Access 97 is still sitting on your desk, encased in plastic wrap, flip to Appendix A, at the back of this book, for help installing the program. When you're done, return to this chapter and carry on.

Unlike in the old days (way back in the 1980s), when waking up your computer and running a database program could be terribly complicated, starting Access 97 is simple. Here are the steps:

1. **Mentally prepare yourself for the task at hand.**

   If it's before lunch, have a cup of coffee. After lunch, try chocolate.

2. **Turn on the computer, monitor, printer, and any other devices that look interesting.**

   With luck, your computer hums, beeps, and generally comes to life. Shortly after that, Windows 95 should start automatically.

   If you flip the power switch on the computer and nothing happens, your computer may be attached to a power strip or uninterruptible power supply (also known as *UPS,* just like the shipping company). In that case, turn on the power strip or UPS itself, and the computer should start just fine.

3. **Click on the Start button and then click on Programs on the pop-up menu.**

   So far, so good. But now comes the tricky part: finding Access 97 itself.

4. **If the Programs menu has an entry for Access 97 (see Figure 1-1), click on that entry to start the program.**

   If your Windows screen doesn't look anything like Figure 1-1, you probably have the old version of Windows or Windows for Workgroups. In that case, contact your company's computer support people and find out when you're upgrading to the current version of Windows.

   When you start the program, the Microsoft advertisement — er, logo — screen appears, followed shortly by the friendly dialog box in Figure 1-2. If you see this dialog box on-screen, Access is successfully running, so go on to the next section.

   If you can't find the Access 97 icon in the Programs menu, then your company's computer people apparently hid the icon somewhere else on the menu. Look for a special program group named something like `Applications` or `Microsoft Office` (as in Figure 1-3). If you *still* can't find Access 97, or if the program won't start, invest in a box of brownies and then bribe your favorite computer guru for help.

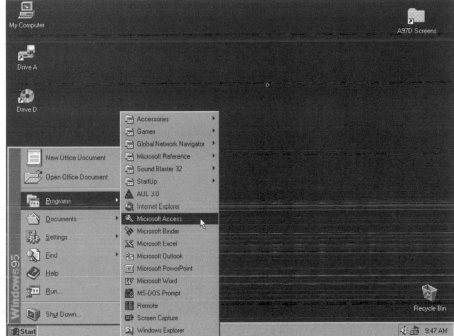

Figure 1-1:
For a smart program, Access 97 doesn't hide very well.

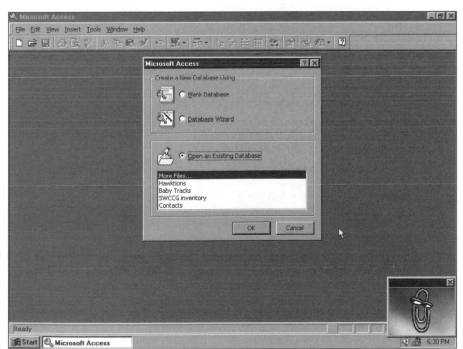

Figure 1-2:
Success at last — Access 97 is running.

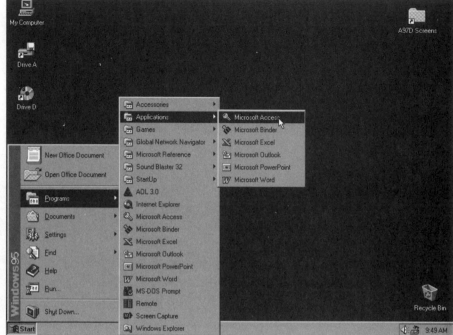

Windows 95

Figure 1-3:
Sometimes,
Access 97
makes you
look a little
harder.

Opening an Existing Database

Bringing the program to life is a good start, but it isn't the ultimate goal. After all, Access 97 without a database file is like a CD player without a CD: Nice to look at, but you can't dance to it. Loading your database is next on the hit list.

Database files fall in two distinct categories: those that already exist and those that don't. Odds are that you're working with a database that someone created for you. If so, read on — this section is for you. To create a new database from scratch, though, flip to Chapter 4.

If you just started Access 97 and your screen looks like Figure 1-2, opening a database only takes a moment. If the database you want to use is listed at the bottom of the dialog box, just double-click on the database name.

If the database you're looking for isn't in the introductory dialog box, then follow these steps:

1. **Double-click on the More Files option in the introductory dialog box to see a list of the databases in the current directory folder.**

   The Open dialog box appears, looking much like Figure 1-4.

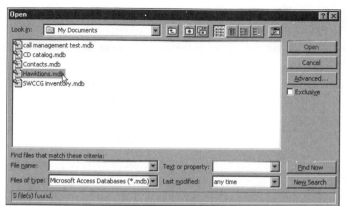

Figure 1-4:
The Open
dialog box,
in all its
glory.

2. **Double-click on the database you're interested in.**

   After a moment, the database loads into Access, and you're ready to work.

If the database you want to use isn't listed in the Open dialog box, either, it's probably in some other directory folder. Skip to Chapter 6 (the sidebar called "Bo Peep needed the Find File option") for help with tracking down the database in your hard disk or network.

If you've already been working with Access for a while (printing reports, checking out a form or two, and generally keeping yourself busy), and now you want to open another database, follow these steps:

1. **Choose File⇨Open Database or click on the Open Database button on the toolbar.**

   The Open dialog box (still appearing for your viewing pleasure in Figure 1-4) pops onto the screen.

2. **Double-click on the name of the database you want to use.**

   If the database isn't listed, you may need to go on a quick hunt for the little fellow. Skip to Chapter 6 and check out the sidebar called "Bo Peep needed the Find File option" for help with the Open dialog box's database search functions.

Touring the Database Window

When a database opens, it usually appears on-screen looking like Figure 1-5. The tabs across the top of the window display the various parts of your database: tables, queries, forms, and so on. The rest of the window lists the tables in the current database.

Figure 1-5:
A normal
database
appears,
looking, um,
normal.

After opening the database, you can fiddle with the parts inside:

✔ To open a table, click on the tab marked Tables and then double-click on the table you want to see.

✔ To run a report, query, or form, click on the appropriate tab and then double-click on the item you want to work with.

✔ When you get tired of this database, close it by clicking the Close Window button (the X box in the upper-right corner of the window) or by choosing File⇨Close. If you're a keyboard fan, Ctrl+W does the deed without disturbing the mouse.

✔ If you want to know more about working with the cool Access 97 interface (and all the wonderful ways you can play in it), check out Chapter 2.

If some kind soul invested the time to make your life a little easier, a start-up screen (or *switchboard*) resembling Figure 1-6 appears automatically when you open the database. Don't panic — this is a good thing. The only downside is that your switchboard is probably unique to your company, so I can't tell you anything about the options on it. (Sorry, but my crystal ball broke some time ago.) Find the person responsible for creating or maintaining your Access switchboard and offer to trade some cookies for help.

If your start-up screen does have options like the ones in Figure 1-6, you're in luck. I *can* help you make sense of this start-up screen because it was created by the Database Wizard (and he's very consistent). Look in the Database Wizard section of Chapter 21 for more information about the start-up screen's options and how the whole thing came into being.

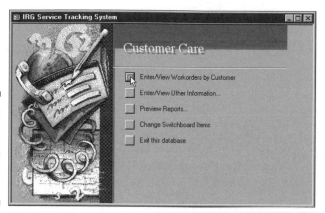

Figure 1-6:
A database
fronted by a
fancy
switchboard
screen.

Finding Candy amongst the Grass Clippings

I don't understand what the big deal is about getting kids to eat stuff. If you want preschoolers to eat something, just let them take it outside and drop it into the yard first, preferably right after you cut the lawn with a mulching mower. For some inexplicable reason, covering food with freshly cut grass seems to make it all the more appetizing to youngsters.

Finding specific records in your Access table is a little like a toddler's method of whittling through sticky grass in search of candy. Whether you're looking for last names, first names, part numbers, or postal codes, Access 97 makes finding your target records a whole lot easier — and infinitely less messy.

Here's one way to find records:

1. **Open the table you want to search.**

   If you don't know how to open a table, flip back to the preceding section.

2. **Click in the field you want to search.**

 3. **Choose Edit⇨Find or click on the Find toolbar button.**

   The Find dialog box appears (see Figure 1-7).

   Access 97 displays the name of the field in which you're searching in the title bar of the dialog box. If the title bar is proudly displaying the _wrong_ field name, press Esc or click on Close to make the Find dialog box go away, and then try Step 2 again.

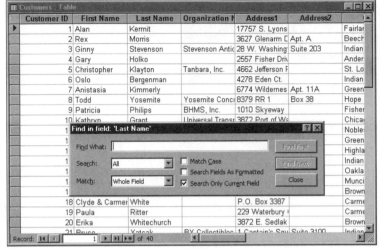

Figure 1-7:
The Find
dialog box,
at your
service.

4. **Type whatever text you're looking for in the Fi̲nd What text box (see Figure 1-8) and then press Enter or click on the F̲ind Next button.**

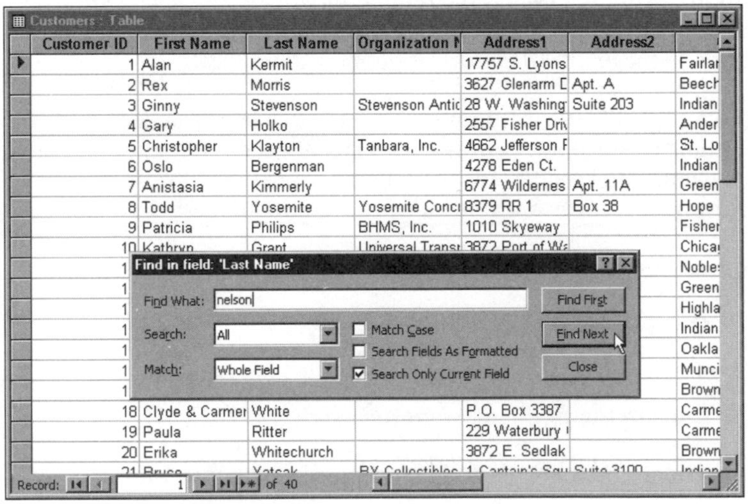

Figure 1-8:
Ready to
seek out a
record.

The search begins — and probably ends before you know it. If the program finds a matching record, Access 97 highlights the data (see Figure 1-9).

Customers : Table						
Customer ID	First Name	Last Name	Organization N	Address1	Address2	
9	Patricia	Philips	BHMS, Inc.	1010 Skyoway		Fisher
10	Kathryn	Grant	Universal Transp	3872 Port of Wa		Chica
11	Travis	Cooksey		5807 Layman A		Noble
12	Kevin	Davis		5646 Candelite		Green
13	Jack	Laux		25 Lower Bay L		Highla
14	Vincent	Steffers	Cardinal Antique	6917 N. Meridia		Indian
15	Edward	Anderson		431 Brentwood		Oakla
16	King	Daniels	Baystorm, Inc.	9 Graceland Pl.		Munci
17	Lindsay	Travers		102 Windsor Dr	Apt. F	Brown
18	Clyde & Carmer	White		P.O. Box 3387		Carme

Find in field: 'Last Name'

Find What: nelson

Search: All

Match: Whole Field

☐ Match Case
☐ Search Fields As Formatted
☑ Search Only Current Field

Find First
Find Next
Close

26	Clarence	Micy		385 Carlton Arm		Newto
27	Mario	Schussler		1625 Euclid Ave		Fortvil
28	Harry	Nelson		19474 Vermeer		Carme
29	Collie	Logan	Eye 4 Antiques	227 Polk		Zionc

Record: 28 of 40

Figure 1-9: Customer Nelson is found — hooray!

If no record matches your criteria, a big, officious dialog box informs you that `Microsoft Access finished searching the records. The search item was not found.` If this message appears, click on OK and smile as the dialog box disappears; then double-check what you typed in the Find What text box. You probably just mistyped the entry. If so, fix it and try the search again. If you *still* can't find the record, either look in Chapter 10 for more details about the Find dialog box or grab a nearby guru and seek personal guidance.

5. **Click on Close or press Esc to close the Find dialog box when you're done.**

You can do many more tricks with the Find command, so be sure to look in Chapter 10 when you're ready to impress the coworkers.

The right mouse button also provides some tricky ways to find records, but I'm saving those tricks for Chapter 10.

Making a Few Changes

Unfortunately for fruit growers and dairy farmers, life isn't always peaches and cream. Your customers move, the phone company changes an area code, and the digital gremlins mess up your typing skills. Whatever the cause, your job is to fix the problem in your database. Lucky you.

Changing the stuff in your tables isn't hard. In fact, it's almost too easy. I outline the precise steps in the following list. Keep in mind that your changes are *automatically* saved. When you finish working on a record, Access writes the new information to the database *right then.* If you make a mistake, *immediately* press Ctrl+Z to undo your changes — don't put it off until later.

Here's a quick word from the Society of the Perpetually Nervous: Be *very* careful when changing the records in your database. Making changes is easy; recovering from them can be tough. Access 97 can only help you undo the *last thing you changed.*

When you're ready to change a record, follow these steps:

1. **View the table on-screen as a data sheet or in a form.**

   Either way, your data is hanging out on the monitor and looking cool.

2. **Click in the field you want to change.**

   A flashing toothpick cursor appears in the field, and the mouse pointer changes to an I-beam.

3. **Perform whatever repairs the field needs.**

   All the standard editing keys (Home, End, Backspace, and Delete) work when you're changing an entry in Access 97. See Chapter 6 for the key-by-key details.

4. **When the field is *just right,* press Return to save the changes.**

   As soon as you press Return, the data is saved — and I do mean *saved.* If you immediately decide that you like the old data better, press Ctrl+Z or choose Edit⇨Undo Current Field/Record.

Reporting the Results

Capturing all those wonderful details in your tables is nice, but what's even *nicer* is seeing those records fill a printed page. That's where the Access 97 report system comes in.

Making your database look wonderful on paper is a cinch with Access 97. The program has all kinds of report options, plus a reasonably strong Report Wizard to walk you through the hard stuff. Check out Part IV for more about all the really cool report features.

Because printing a report is one of the most common things people do with Access 97 (who said computers would bring on the paperless office?), the following steps show you how to do it:

1. If your database display looks like Figure 1-10, click on the Reports tab.

If you're working with a custom form or a custom-built Access application
that's unique to your company, click on the Reports option (or whatever
option sounds like that) and follow the system's instructions. Because
systems vary so much from company to company, I can't really be more
specific. Sorry!

2. Right-click on the report you want to print.

A menu pops up wherever your mouse pointer is.

3. Choose Print on the pop-up menu (see Figure 1-11).

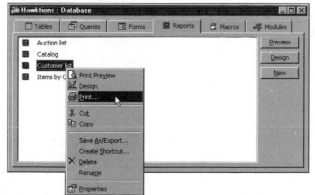

Access 97 puts a little dialog box in the middle of the screen to tell you
how the print job is going. When the print job is complete, the dialog box
vanishes without a trace.

If you change your mind while the report is printing, click Cancel on the so-how's-the-print-job-going? dialog box to stop the process.

Saving Your Hard Work

Actually, I don't have much to say on the topic of saving — Access 97 saves your work for you. This feature is both good and, well, not so good.

The Access 97 automatic save feature is good because it's one less detail left lying around to clutter up your life. Whether you entered a bunch of new records or simply fixed a couple that were ever so slightly wrong, your work is automatically safe and sound.

On the other hand, the automatic save feature *isn't* such a good thing because Access 97 doesn't pay any attention to what it's saving — it just saves everything that's there. If you accidentally wipe out 237 records and then make a couple of errant clicks, you can say *good-bye records, hello backups*.

I said it in a previous section, but it bears repeating: When you're changing the records in your tables, *please* be careful. Messing up a record takes only a second. Don't let this tragedy happen to you. (This has been a public service announcement from your author.)

Help is always just a few clicks away

No matter where you are in Access 97, help is always nearby. Chapter 3 covers all your help options in gory detail, but here's one to get you started.

If you're stumped for what to do next, press the F1 key at the top of your keyboard. This is the Windows universal *help me* key. It brings up a dialog box that's jam-packed with help topics ranging from an overview of the newest, coolest things about Access 97 to phenomenally trivial explorations of macros.

Unless you're in the mood to browse, click the Find tab at the top of the window and search for your topic of interest. You can also try your luck with the Answer Wizard, who listens to your questions and comes up with the darndest answers.

The Great Backup Lecture

I know you've probably heard this before, but the PC support nerd in me won't let the chapter close without a few words about backing up your databases. Even though I joke about it, doing regular backups is a *vital* part of using Access 97 (or any program, for that matter).

Why is backing up so important? Take a minute and imagine life without your computer. Don't reminisce about business in the Good Old Days of the 1970s — think about what would happen if you walked in one morning and found *no* computer awaiting your arrival. None. Zippo. The desk is empty — no business letters, no receivables, no customer list, no nothing. Everything was on the computer, but now the computer is history. (It certainly sounds like my definition of a bad day.)

Unless you want to look at your business, raise your hand, and wave good-bye, you need a formal backup plan. Even if it's just you and your computer, write down some notes about how your backup process works. Some specific things to include:

- **How often is the computer backed up?** A better way to ask this question is "How much data can you afford to lose?" If your information changes daily (like an accounting system, for example), you need to make backups every day or two. If you mainly play adventure games on your machine and use Access 97 as infrequently as possible, back it up every week or two. No universal rule is right for everyone.

- **Where are the back-up disks or tapes stored?** If the backups are stored right next to the computer, they'll be conveniently destroyed along with the computer in the event of a fire. Keep your backups in another building, if possible, or at least in another room.

- **How do you back up the data?** Write down a step-by-step procedure, along with a method for figuring out what tape or disk set to use in the back-up process.

- **How do you *restore* the data?** Again, create a step-by-step process. Your mind won't be particularly clear if tragedy strikes and you have to restore destroyed data, so make the steps simple and understandable.

Having a procedure is good; actually *making* the backups is better. After you settle into the back-up routine, try restoring your data once to make sure that your system works. If the program has a problem putting the data back onto your hard disk, you're *much* better off finding this out before the disk dies rather than afterward. Set aside a couple hours of your copious free time to ensure that your efforts will pay off on that fateful day when the disk drive dies. You'll thank me later.

If you're in a corporate environment, it's possible that your local Department of Computer People automatically backs up your data. To find out for sure, give them a call and ask.

Making a Graceful Exit

When you're done, you're done — but remember to give Access 97 a break, too. When it's time to shut down for the day, do so the right way:

1. **If you have a database open, choose File⇨Close or click the Windows 95 Close Window button in the upper-right corner of the database window.**

   Technically, you don't need to do this step, but I'm old-fashioned enough not to trust my program to close everything by itself without screwing something up. Whenever possible (and when it doesn't make me look *too* much like a nerd), I close my files manually before shutting down the program.

2. **Close Access 97 by choosing File⇨Exit.**

   Nighty-night, Access!

Go ahead and shut down Windows 95, as well, if you're done for the night. To do so, click on the Start button and then click on Shut Down. When Windows asks whether you're serious about this shut-down thing, click on Yes. After Windows 95 gets done doing whatever it is that software does just before bedtime, turn off your computer and make your escape to freedom.

Chapter 2

Finding Your Way Around like a Native

In This Chapter

▶ What's what with the new interface?

▶ Looking at the pretty windows

▶ Checking out the toolbars

▶ Ordering from the menu

▶ Doing tricks with the right mouse button

*C*ruising around an unfamiliar city is fun, exciting, and frustrating. Seeing the sights, recognizing famous landmarks, and discovering new places to exercise your credit card make it fun. Finding yourself lost deep within a neighborhood that's "in transition" makes it, uh, exciting. Being unable to find your way back in either case makes it frustrating.

If you're comfortable with earlier versions of Access, then driving your mouse through Access 97 is much like steering your car through your home town — twenty years later. The terrain looks somewhat familiar, but you're in for some surprises — things like "*where'd they move that menu item?* It used to be right over, um . . . oh geez, the whole *menu* is gone."

I know the feeling. Nothing is worse than having a lot of work to accomplish while trying to decipher a new program. This chapter helps you out of that trap by presenting a tour of the sights and sounds of Access 97. It covers the common things you see and deal with on-screen, from the main window to the toolbar and beyond. Kick back and enjoy the jaunt — it's a great way to get comfortable with Access 97.

Making Sense of the Sights

Because Access 97 is, after all, a Windows 95 program, the first stop on this merry visual jaunt is the program's main window. Figure 2-1 shows Access 97 in a common pose, displaying a database window (which I cover later in this chapter).

To make the most of Access 97, you need to be familiar with nine parts of the main window. I describe each part briefly in the paragraphs that follow. If you're *really* new to Windows 95, consider picking up a copy of *Windows 95 For Dummies* by Andy Rathbone (published by IDG Books Worldwide, Inc.). Having that book will make your life with Windows 95 a *lot* easier, I promise.

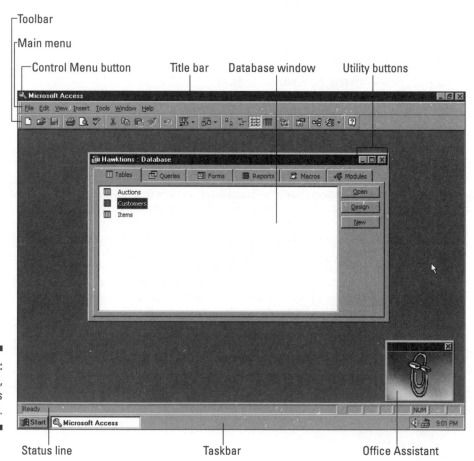

Figure 2-1:
Access 97,
in all its
glory.

✔ **Control Menu button:** Click on the Access "key" to open the Control Menu. Frankly, this menu is mostly for doing nerdy stuff. But because you *can* make Access 97 go away by double-clicking here, I suppose that this button has some redeeming value for the rest of us, despite its nerdy tendencies. In Windows 3.1, the button's picture was a box with a horizontal bar in it. These days, it looks spiffier.

✔ **Title bar:** Every window comes complete with a space along the top for the title. This space has a second purpose, too: It changes color to let you know which program is currently active in Windows.

✔ **Main menu:** Between the title bar and the toolbar sits the Main menu, Keeper of the Digital Peace. Aside from preventing fights between the two bars, this menu is also your main stopping point for Access 97 commands and functions.

✔ **Toolbar:** Think of the toolbar as an electronic version of Lon Chaney, the Man of a Thousand Faces. Just about every time you do something in Access 97, the Toolbar does a quick change. You can read more about this slippery character later in this chapter.

✔ **Utility buttons:** These three buttons appear on every window. From left to right, these buttons reduce the current program to a button on the Taskbar, make the current program either fit in a window or take up the whole screen (one button, two tasks — pretty cool, eh?), and close the current window.

✔ **Status line:** Access 97 is a talkative system, with words of wisdom to share about every little thing. Whenever Access wants to tell you something, a message appears on the Status line. On the far right of the Status line are indicators for keyboard settings such as Caps Lock. In Figure 2-1, the NUM indicator appears down there, telling me that my Number Lock is turned on.

✔ **Database window:** In the midst of this maelstrom sits a serene database window, explained in the next section.

✔ **Taskbar:** Across the bottom of the screen is the Windows 95 taskbar, Microsoft's quick-and-easy tool for switching among programs. Each running program has a button on this bar. To use another program, just click on its button.

✔ **Office Assistant:** This fellow is new to Office 97. He's everywhere you turn, showing up in all Office 97 products, including Access 97. When you have a question or want some help, give him a click and ask away.

Windows Shopping for Fun and Understanding

There's more to Access 97 than the big picture window. The program is chock-full of little windows for every need and occasion. This section looks at four of the most common ones: the database window, datasheet window, form window, and query (you guessed it) window.

For details on how these windows work, what to do with them, and why you should even care, keep trekking through this book. Databases and datasheets appear in Part II, queries star in Part III, and forms have a supporting role in Part V.

The database window

Most of the time when you open a database, it appears in a window like Figure 2-2. This window gives you access to all the cool stuff in your database, provides tools to change things or create new items, and generally helps you manage your database stuff. And it looks cool. Who could ask for more?

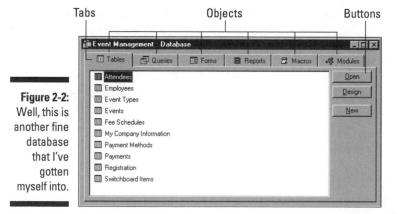

Figure 2-2:
Well, this is another fine database that I've gotten myself into.

The *tabs* across the top of the window switch between lists of the *objects* (tables, queries, reports, and so on) that make up the database. Along the right side are three *buttons* for working with the database's objects: Open displays the current object, Design lets you change the object, and New creates a new object.

Your database *might* start up looking like Figure 2-3. Don't let the pretty face fool you, though — this window is just a fancier front hung onto Figure 2-2's database. Seeing something like this window is a clue that you're working with a formal Access 97 application. The form may be something created with a wizard (like the one in Figure 2-3), or perhaps one of your in-house nerds whipped it up just for you. This special form is called a *switchboard*.

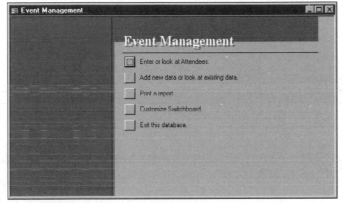

Figure 2-3:
A wizard-
created
switchboard.

The datasheet window

Is it a table or a spreadsheet? Only its owner knows for sure! Such are the traumas of the modern database. Being mistaken for a spreadsheet, for goodness sake! What's the world coming to?

Looking at Figure 2-4, it's easy to see why people may confuse the two. Yes, that's a *table.* Looks kinda like a spreadsheet, doesn't it? In *datasheet view,* an Access 97 table appears (and arguably acts) like a simple spreadsheet. The resemblance is only skin-deep, though — it's really a very different animal.

The datasheet window shows the *table name* across its top, just as it should. Right under that, the table's *fields* are arrayed across the window. The table's *records* are laid out in rows. Don't worry if you're not exactly sure about the difference between a record and a field. Chapter 4 has all the details about that.

On the right side and lower-right corner are a pair of *scroll bars,* which make moving through the table a real breeze. The *navigation buttons* are hanging out in the window's lower-left side. These buttons are a lot like the controls on a compact disc player or VCR (videocassette recorder). The buttons that have arrows pointing to a bar take you to the first or last record of the table. The arrow-only buttons move you to the next or previous record. Clicking on the arrow and asterisk button adds a new record to the table.

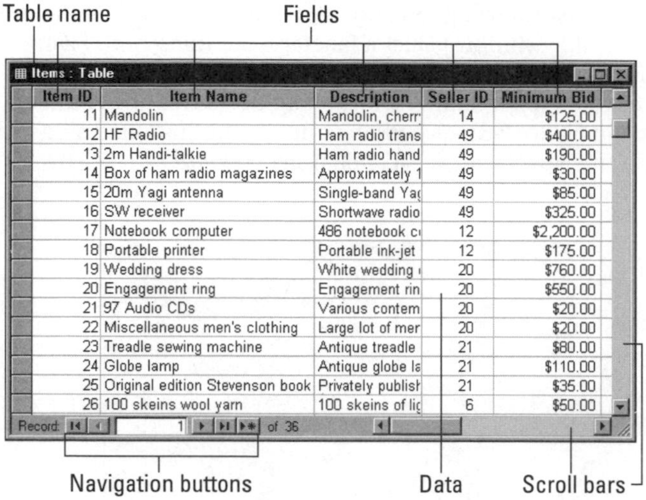

Table name   Fields

Item ID	Item Name	Description	Seller ID	Minimum Bid
11	Mandolin	Mandolin, cherr	14	$125.00
12	HF Radio	Ham radio trans	49	$400.00
13	2m Handi-talkie	Ham radio hand	49	$190.00
14	Box of ham radio magazines	Approximately 1	49	$30.00
15	20m Yagi antenna	Single-band Yag	49	$85.00
16	SW receiver	Shortwave radio	49	$325.00
17	Notebook computer	486 notebook c	12	$2,200.00
18	Portable printer	Portable ink-jet	12	$175.00
19	Wedding dress	White wedding	20	$760.00
20	Engagement ring	Engagement rin	20	$550.00
21	97 Audio CDs	Various contem	20	$20.00
22	Miscellaneous men's clothing	Large lot of mer	20	$20.00
23	Treadle sewing machine	Antique treadle	21	$80.00
24	Globe lamp	Antique globe la	21	$110.00
25	Original edition Stevenson book	Privately publish	21	$35.00
26	100 skeins wool yarn	100 skeins of lic	6	$50.00

Record: 1 of 36

Figure 2-4:
The Items
table,
dressed in
spreadsheet
drag.

Navigation buttons   Data   Scroll bars

The form window

Form view is the other popular way to look at Access 97 tables. With forms, the data looks more, well, traditional — none of that sissy spreadsheet-style stuff. A form usually shows the data in a table at the blinding rate of one record per screen, the same way that the nerds of the 1970s worked with their data, using million-dollar computers that had all the intelligence of today's microwave ovens.

Figure 2-5 is a very simple but classic example of an Access 97 form. Along the top is the ever-anticipated *title bar.* The table's *fields* take up the middle of the form. In the lower-left corner are the same *navigation buttons* you saw and fiddled with in the datasheet window.

If forms really pique your interest, check out Chapter 22 for more information.

The query window

The heart of any database program is its capability to search for information. In particular, the heart of Access 97 is the query system. And sitting at the heart of the query system is the *query window,* lovingly reproduced in Figure 2-6.

The top of the window displays the *title bar,* showing the query's given name. The window's top half shows the *tables* involved in the query. If the query uses more than one table, this section also shows how the tables are linked together (or *joined*). The lower half displays the *query criteria* — the instructions that make the query work. Because all this stuff can get large and complicated, the window has several *scroll bars* to help you see everything clearly.

Fields   Title bar

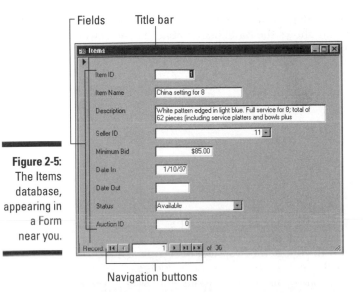

Figure 2-5:
The Items
database,
appearing in
a Form
near you.

Navigation buttons

Title bar   Tables

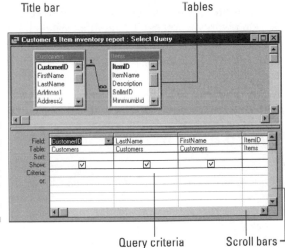

Figure 2-6:
The digital
Holmes at
your
service.

Query criteria   Scroll bars

When you run a query, Access 97 usually displays the results in a datasheet.

Belly Up to the Toolbar, Folks!

Toolbars are the Office 97 equivalent of sliced bread — they're *that* useful.
Access 97 has a bunch of them, too. You won't ever find yourself without a
toolbar around to help.

So what *is* a toolbar? It's that row of cool buttons just below the menu at the top of the screen. Figure 2-7 shows the Database toolbar in action (well, in as much action as any inanimate object ever shows).

Figure 2-7:
The Database toolbar, just sitting there.

The toolbars give you single-click access to the best features of Access 97. The engineers designed the toolbars to contain the most common functions you need when working with your data. The Datasheet toolbar, for example, includes three buttons that control the Filter tools (tools that help you quickly find things in your database). Instead of working your way through a menu to find these Filter tools, they're out in the open, just a mouse click away.

Because a toolbar exists for literally every occasion, I describe the toolbars throughout the book. Don't worry if you can't remember what all the buttons do — neither can I. If you're button-challenged, too, check out the following sidebar for a useful word about *ScreenTips,* Access 97's built-in toolbar button-reminder system.

Quick — what does that button do?

Access 97 has 22 different toolbars. (Okay, it's a nerd statistic, but I'm building up to a point — trust me.) Each toolbar has, um, lots of buttons on it. There's no way that anyone, not even the programmers, can remember what all the buttons do. Besides, who'd want to try?

Unfortunately, toolbars are pretty useless if you don't know what the buttons do. To resolve this problem, Microsoft came up with *ScreenTips* — little pop-up descriptions that appear when you point the mouse at a toolbar button.

To see a button's ScreenTip, just aim the mouse pointer at the button in question. Hold the pointer there for a second, and {poof!} the ScreenTip

appears. If you position your mouse, wait patiently, and nothing happens, your ScreenTips may be turned off. To turn them on, right-click anywhere on the toolbar and then select Customize from the pop-up menu. When the Customize dialog box appears, click the Options tab. Make sure a check mark appears next to Show ScreenTips. Click on Close to make the dialog box vanish.

If the ScreenTip isn't enough to jog your memory, just look at the Status Bar as you point at the mysterious toolbar button. Access 97 displays a longer explanation of the button's purpose down there.

Menus, Menus Everywhere (And Keystrokes That Work as Well)

Truth be told, there isn't a lot to say about the Access 97 menus. The main thing that you're sure to notice is that they change every time you do something new. Gone are the days of *one program, one menu*. Now we have *context-sensitive* menus that show different options depending on what you're doing at the moment.

Some things never change, though. Here's a brief rundown of generic menu truisms:

- ✔ If your mouse dies, you can get to the menu items from the keyboard. Just hold down the Alt key and press the underlined letter of the menu item you want. For instance, press Alt+F to open the File menu.

- ✔ Some menu items have a specific key assigned to them. The Copy command (Edit⊃Copy on the menu) also works without the menu by pressing Ctrl+C. If an item has a keyboard equivalent, Access lists that key combination right next to the item in the pull-down menu.

- ✔ If you can't remember what a menu item does, pull down the menu by clicking once on the menu name (File, Edit, and so on) and then move the mouse pointer to the menu item. Check the Status Bar for a brief synopsis of what the option does.

Playing with the Other Mouse Button

After surviving years of neglect and general indifference, the right mouse button comes into its own with Windows 95. Finally, there's something for it to do. Right mouse buttons of the world, rejoice!

In Access 97 (just like its other Windows 95 counterparts), the right mouse button pops up a list of things you can do with the current on-screen item. In Figure 2-8, I right-clicked on the Customers table. Access 97 is right there, offering a list of common things to do with tables. Instead of working through the main menu to copy the current table, for instance, I can right-click and select Copy from the pop-up menu. Talk about a time-saver!

Experiment with the right mouse button. Try right-clicking on everything in sight — see what happens. Don't worry about messing up your system because you can't do any lasting harm with the mouse. See what you can find!

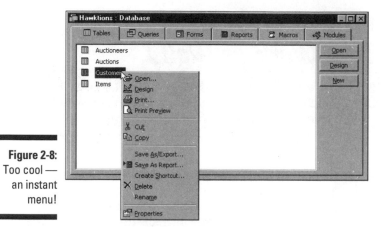

Figure 2-8:
Too cool —
an instant
menu!

Chapter 3

Calling the Online St. Bernard and Other Forms of Help

*G*etting in over your head is easy, sometimes. For example, mountains are *much* taller after you start climbing than they were when you looked up from the ground. Plus, your equipment *never* seems to fail when you're packing it. Instead, your trusty gear waits until you're in the middle of nowhere, dangling precariously from the crumbling edge of a craggy peak. Then — and only then — does your gear remember its mortal fear of heights and have heart failure.

That's what St. Bernards are for. When you're lost in the alpine wilderness — cold, wet, and alone — it's reassuring to know that a St. Bernard will be along soon. I'm a little unclear about precisely what the dog *does* when it finds you; but at that point, I'd probably settle for the companionship.

Access 97 has its own built-in St. Bernard, although on-screen it looks more like a few dialog boxes than a husky canine. This chapter explores several different ways to find answers to your Access 97 questions. Knowing where to look for information is as important as knowing the information itself, so browse through this chapter and discover your options.

When in Doubt, Press F1

No matter where you are in Access 97, help is available at the touch of a key. Just press F1, and the perky Office Assistant leaps into action (Figure 3-1). The Assistant is a new feature of Office 97, showing up in all the Office 97 applications. It replaces the old Answer Wizard and simplifies the help process even more. The Office Assistant even tosses in some entertaining animated moments at no extra charge.

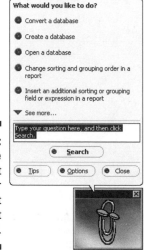

Figure 3-1:
The Office Assistant reports for duty (but don't ask it for coffee).

When you call up the Assistant, it tries to figure out what you're trying to accomplish in Access 97 and suggests three to five Help topics that it thinks are relevant. If one of these topics hits the spot (which, in my experience, happens most of the time), click on the button next to the topic and the Assistant presents the information to you.

Even though the Assistant is a good guesser, it doesn't always come up with the right topics. For moments like that, the Assistant includes a do-it-yourself question box along the bottom of the window. Here's a step-by-step layout of how to use this marvel of modern technology to ask the Assistant a detailed question:

1. **Click on the Office Assistant window or press F1.**

   The Assistant's dialog box pops up (looking quite perky, I might add).

2. **In the box at the bottom of the window, type your question in plain language, just as in Figure 3-2.**

Figure 3-2:
No
computerese,
no jargon —
just a simple
question.

You read it right — in *plain language.* Can you believe it? A program that actually *understands* you. Who knows where this dangerous trend may lead?

3. **Click on S̲earch or press Enter when you finish typing.**

The Assistant does its thing and displays a list of Help topics that it thinks will answer your question (see Figure 3-3). If none of the topics is quite what you had in mind, rephrase your question and give it another try.

Figure 3-3:
Click the
Help topic
most likely
to lead to
the answer
you need.

4. Click on the Help topic that sounds like the best match.

If, after reading through some Help topics, you still aren't satisfied, close the Help window and then start again with Step 1 to ask the Assistant another question.

The default Assistant is an animated paper clip named Clippit (no, I'm not making this up — someone actually *named* the cartoon paper clip). Access 97 ships with several different Office Assistants, so if ol' Clippit doesn't match your working style, feel free to give him the boot in favor of another choice. To change the Office Assistant, right-click on the Assistant window and then select Choose Assistant from the pop-up menu. Access 97 presents you with a gallery of options ranging from a mundane Office logo to an nicely rendered cartoon version of Albert Einstein. Click on the Next and Back buttons to cycle through the various Assistants. When you find *precisely* the right one for you, click on OK. You need to have the Office 97 CD or Access 97 disk set handy to install the new Assistant.

Sitting behind the Assistant are the Access 97 traditional Help files. After the Assistant points you to a particular Help topic, the normal Help system takes over. If you're more comfortable with the way Help worked in Access for Windows 95, have no fear — the Help system you knew and loved is still available in Access 97.

To open up the traditional Help system in Access 97, choose Help⇨Contents and Index from the menu bar. The classic Help window appears, looking much like Figure 3-4. The three tabs across the top of the window offer different ways to find answers. There's a method here for everyone, regardless of how you like to do research. The following sections explore each of the Help window tabs in order of usefulness: Contents, Index, and Find.

Figure 3-4:
The classic
Help system
is still ready
to serve.

Combing the Contents

The *Contents tab* is for casual browsers or people who enjoy digging around in a book's Table of Contents in search of something. Here's how to use it:

1. Click on the Contents tab.

The Help window lists the available master Help topics, complete with little book icons next to each one.

The book icon means that this entry leads to other Help topics or specific Help documents.

2. Find a Help topic that looks interesting and double-click on it.

The system opens the Help topic, changes the closed book icon to an open book (too cute!), and shows you either another list of topics or specific Help documents (see Figure 3-5).

Figure 3-5:
Here's the information I want.

The Help documents are marked with the question-mark-on-a-page icon (but you probably figured that out on your own).

If you choose the wrong topic, double-click on the topic name again to make it go away.

3. Repeat Step 2 until you find what you're looking for.

After you're done reading a Help document, click the Help Topics button to see the Contents page again.

Inspecting the Index

If you prefer diving into the index rather than rattling through the table of contents, click the *Index tab*. It works just like the index of a book, except that it's automated. Here's how to use it:

1. **Click on the Index tab.**

   The screen changes to show the Index page.

2. **Type the term you're looking for in the box at the top of the window.**

   As you type, the list at the bottom of the window highlights the best match it can find. Because this list is organized just like a book index, start with the most general part of what you're looking for, then look for specific topics when you get there (see Figure 3-6 for an example).

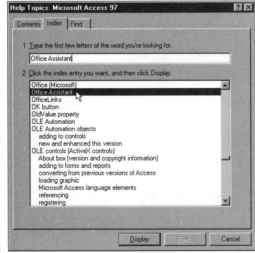

Figure 3-6:
You could
read about
the Office
Assistant
all day.

3. **When you find the topic you're looking for, double-click to see the Help document.**

   If a couple of items match your topic, the Help system displays a dialog box like Figure 3-7. If that happens, double-click on your choice to see it.

To get back to the Index page from a Help document, click on the Help Topics button at the top of the Help document screen.

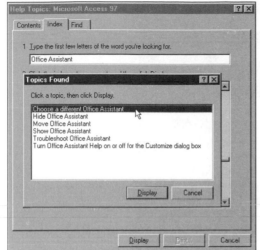

Figure 3-7:
Topics,
topics
everywhere!

Fiddling with Find

The last Help tab is the *Find tab*. Arguably, last is a good place for this tab. Compared to the other options (especially the Office Assistant), Find is absolutely archaic. But if your frustration quotient is a little low for the day and you want to raise it a notch or two, this ought to do the trick:

1. Click on the Find tab.

As you expect, the Find page appears on-screen.

If this is your first time using Find, the Help system tells you that it has to create a word list before you can do the search. Just patiently follow along with the prompts, and soon you're ready for Step 2. Didn't I warn you this would be frustrating?

2. In the box at the top of the window, type a couple of key words that describe what you're looking for.

As you type, the Find system searches for topics that match your entry and displays a list of possible matches in the big window at the bottom of the screen. Unfortunately, Find has no intelligence whatsoever, so proceed on to Step 3 to go answer-wading.

3. Scroll through the list at the bottom of the window until you find something that looks like your topic.

When (and if) you find a topic of interest (see Figure 3-8), double-click on the topic to see the Help document.

Figure 3-8:
I finally
found my
topic (and
I'm not sure
that Find
helped
at all).

Better yet, why not click on the Office Assistant or maybe the Index tab and look for your answer that way?

The Whatzis Menu Option

Whatzis isn't the technical term for this menu entry, but I think it should be (sometimes those programmers just aren't particularly clever about naming things). The item in question is the Help➪What's This menu option — the one with a mouse pointer and question mark on it. I call this the *Whatzis* item — it's your tool for quickly finding out what any button or menu item in Access 97 does.

Here's how the little bugger works:

1. Choose Help➪What's This?

The mouse pointer suddenly grows a large question mark on one side — Access 97 is telling you that you're now in Whatzis mode.

2. Select the menu item or click on the button you want to know more about.

Access 97 displays a Help screen with the name of the item and a brief description of what that item does.

3. **Click once more to make the helpful little Help screen go away.**

   Quick and easy answers for those brain-blank moments of life — it just doesn't get any better than this.

Your Modem Knows More Than You May Think

There's gold in them thar online services! If you have access (pardon the pun) to the Internet or an account on America Online, CompuServe, GEnie, or Prodigy, then a world of answers waits at your modem.

Microsoft maintains official support areas on the major online services, plus a very complete World Wide Web page for the Internet crowd. A host of informal question and answer areas cover Microsoft products as well. Table 3-1 explains how to find the support areas on each system.

Table 3-1	Microsoft Support Areas Available Online	
System	*Access Command*	*Notes*
America Online	keyword PCApplications	Look for *MS Access Q&A* in the message boards under Database Use and Development
CompuServe	go MSACCESS	This whole area is devoted to Access; lots of good stuff
GEnie	move to page 505	Includes the Microsoft Roundtable and knowledge base
Newsgroups	comp.databases. ms-access	Requires access to the Internet newsgroups
Prodigy	jump MICROSOFT	Offers support forums and the knowledge base
World Wide Web	http://www. microsoft.com/ Support/	Requires access to the Web

If you have an Internet e-mail address and enjoy having your mailbox full, you can sign up for the Access mailing list. See the nearby sidebar "Drinking at the never-empty well of a mailing list" for more details.

A slew of *...For Dummies* books are available to help you navigate the online world. Among them are *America Online For Dummies,* 3rd Edition (written by yours truly); *CompuServe For Dummies,* 3rd Edition (by Wallace Wang); and *The Internet For Dummies,* 3rd Edition (from John Levine, Carol Baroudi, and Margaret Levine Young). Of course, these fine books are brought to you by IDG Books Worldwide, Inc., the sponsor of today's program.

It's on the Tip of My Fax

Here's the easiest, most inexpensive way to get information about Access 97 (or any Microsoft product, for that matter). It's toll-free, quick, and relatively painless. What is it? (Drum roll please!) It's FastTips, the automated Microsoft information system.

FastTips offers recorded answers to common questions and documents from Microsoft's support library. To use the *answers to common questions* part of the system, you need a touch-tone phone. To receive documents, you also need a fax machine.

The FastTips system is available 24 hours a day, 7 days a week. It even works on weekends and holidays, just as real people like you sometimes do. That's why FastTips is such a great service to know about — it's available at those odd times of the day and night when you have a deadline looming and nowhere to turn for help.

Here's how to reach FastTips:

1. **Get some paper and a pencil and then take a few deep breaths to relax.**

   You're about to tangle with a menu-driven voice response system, so it's important to be in the proper frame of mind for the experience.

   Make sure that you have the fax number handy if you're requesting documents.

2. **Find a touch-tone phone and press 1-800-936-4100.**

   If you're planning to request faxed documents, you *don't* have to call from the fax machine; just know the fax number.

3. **Listen patiently to the first menu and then select the option for Access.**

   As of this writing, Access is option 4 on the main menu, but such things change with time. If they *did* change the menu item, write the new number into this book so that you have it the next time you call.

4. **Follow the menu prompts to find the information you want.**

Drinking at the never-empty well of a mailing list

If your company has Internet e-mail, consider signing up for the Access mailing list to join a never-ending discussion of Access at all levels, from novice to nerd. Aside from filling your mailbox with important-looking messages, the list gives you a way to get answers fast at any time.

To join the mailing list, send a message to LISTSERV@peach.ease.lsoft.com. You can write anything as the subject of your message (the computer on the other end doesn't care). In the body of the message, type **SUBSCRIBE ACCESS-L** followed by your real name, *not* your e-mail address. The mailing list computer automatically picks up your e-mail address from the message itself.

After you subscribe, your first message explains how the list works, how to send messages to it, and how to get off of the list when you decide you've had enough. Give it a try — mailing lists are great tools!

The first time you call FastTips, request a map and catalog. The menu has formal options to order these items. Navigating FastTips is just like driving to Cleveland, except without the car. The trip is easier if you know where you're going and what you're looking for. Before trying to do big things with FastTips, get a system map and catalog to review.

If you request a fax, don't worry if the fax doesn't arrive for 10 or 15 minutes. When the system is particularly busy, you may have to wait a little longer. Be patient — use the time for a stretch break.

Talking to a Human

Sometimes, you've had it up to *here* with computers and automation in general. At that point, you just want to talk to a human — any human — who can help solve your problem. Microsoft provides a variety of phone numbers for just such occasions.

✔ To reach Access 97 phone support, call 206-635-7050 from the United States. Live human beings are available from 6:00 a.m. to 6:00 p.m. Pacific time, Monday through Friday (except holidays). In Canada, the free support number is 905-568-3503. The Canadian line is staffed from 8:00 a.m. to 8:00 p.m. eastern time, Monday through Friday.

On these numbers, you pay for the phone call, but the first two answers are free. After two calls, the free ride is over — it's time to get out your credit card and use the *per incident* line described next.

✔ For fast answers to your Access 97 problems at any hour of the day or night, call 800-936-5500 (or 800-668-7975 in Canada). Unless your company purchased an annual support contract from Microsoft, solutions from this number cost a flat $55 *per incident.* So what's an incident? According to Microsoft, an *incident* is *all the calls related to the same problem* (or something close to that). The bottom line is that if you call several times trying to solve the same problem, you pay for only one call. Of course, the *really* nice thing about paying for support is that these numbers are staffed 24 hours a day. I guess you really *do* get what you pay for.

✔ If you have a light, fluffy question such as "What's the current version number of Microsoft Access?" (or "What's the weather like in Redmond, Washington?"), call the Microsoft sales department at 800-426-9400. These folks are at the phones, waiting for your call, from 6:30 a.m. to 5:30 p.m. Pacific time, Monday through Friday.

✔ If you are deaf or hearing-impaired and have a TDD or TT modem, call 206-635-4948 between 6:00 a.m. and 6:00 p.m. pacific time, Monday through Friday. This number works for all Microsoft products (Word, Excel, PowerPoint, and the others).

Part II
Truly Tempting
Tables

The 5th Wave By Rich Tennant

"NAAAH – HE'S NOT THAT SMART. HE WON'T BACK UP HIS HARD DISK, FORGETS TO CONSISTENTLY NAME HIS FILES, AND DROOLS ALL OVER THE KEYBOARD."

In this part . . .

With Access 97 well in hand, you begin a life of storing, managing, organizing, and reorganizing data. (By the way, welcome to your new life. I hope you enjoy your stay here.) Because data hangs out in tables, you need to know how to do the whole table thing if you have any hope of making your data do tricks.

This part eases you into the role of Commander of All Tables by covering the basics. You go from creating tables through using tables and on into maintaining and repairing tables. Heck, if you're not careful, you may find yourself attacking the dining room table by the end of Chapter 9.

Chapter 4

Designing and Building a Home for Your Data

. . . .

In This Chapter

▶ Fields, fields everywhere

▶ Sample fields to simplify your day

▶ Flat files and relational databases revealed

▶ Designing your tables

▶ Creating the database

▶ Building a table with the Table Wizard

▶ Assembling a table by hand

. . . .

*T*his may be the single most important chapter in this book. Why? Because really useful databases grow from carefully considered plans. The problem is that nobody ever explains stuff like how to successfully string a bunch of fields together and make a table out of them. For some unknown reason, *they* think you already know how to do it — that it's instinct, like the birds flying south for the winter or my wife finding the best sales in the mall.

If you didn't pop from the womb muttering, "phone numbers and postal codes are treated as text even though they're numbers," then this chapter is for you. The following pages divulge the secrets of fields, tables, and databases in Technicolor glory. The chapter covers the terms you need to know, tips for choosing fields and designing tables, and details on how to put together cool tables and great databases.

Sometimes, the stuff in here isn't pretty. This information takes you to the very edge of nerddom, so tread carefully (and shoot lots of pictures — the nerdlets are just *too* cute in their little taped-together glasses!).

Database Terms to Know and Tolerate

Wait! Don't skip this section just because it's about terminology. I promise to keep the techno-weenie content of this book to a minimum, but you simply *must* know a few magic nerd words before your foray into database development.

If you just felt faint because you didn't realize that you are developing a database, just put the book down for a moment, take a few deep breaths, and remember that it's *only* a computer, not something really important like kids, kites, or chocolate mousse.

The few terms you need to know are listed in the following sections. There's a brief explanation of each one, plus a translation guide for people migrating to Access 97 from the other major Windows databases: dBASE, Microsoft FoxPro, and Paradox. The terms are listed from smallest to largest, like a backwards version of that "flea on the wart on the frog on the bump on the log in the hole in the bottom of the sea" song that my kids sing incessantly some days. The definitions kinda build on each other, so it makes the most sense if you start with *data* and work your way down to *database*.

Data (your stuff)

Data is the stuff that Access stores, shuffles, and stacks for you. Every time some company calls and asks for Your Name (*last name first,* of course), you're providing data. In a database program's skewed approach to the world, *Your Name* may be one piece of data (your whole name, last name first), two pieces (first and last name), or even more pieces (title, first name, middle initial, last name, and suffix). The details depend on how the database's *fields* are organized — and that's what the next section explains.

> ✔ dBASE, FoxPro, and Paradox all agree that data should, in fact, be called *data.* Don't expect this degree of cooperation to continue much beyond the term *record,* because that's where it ends.

> ✔ Database programs view data differently than you and I do. If you see 16773, you know it's a number — it's an intuitive thing. Access 97 and the other database programs see 16773 as either a number or a group of characters, depending on what type of *field* it's stored in. There's more about this peculiar behavior in "Frolicking through the Fields" later in the chapter. For the sake of your sanity, please make sure you're comfortable with this little oddity because it can *really* throw you for a loop sometimes.

Fields (homes for your stuff)

Because nobody wants their data to wander around homeless, the technical wizards created *fields* — places for your data to live. One field holds one piece of data. If you're storing information about a baseball card collection, possible fields would include Player Name, Position, Year, Team, Manufacturer, Condition, and so on. Each of those items is a unique *field* in your database.

✔ As with the term *data,* dBASE, FoxPro, and Paradox all agree about what a *field* is.

✔ The programs begin to disagree when you talk about the specific types of fields available. Just because you *always used to do it this way in Paradox* doesn't mean the same method works in Access 97. For more details, flip ahead to "Frolicking through the Fields," just a couple pages away in this chapter.

Records (the homes on one block)

Having fields is a good start, but if you stopped there, how would you know which last name went with which first name? Something needs to keep those unruly fields in order — something like a *record.* All the fields for one baseball card, one accounting entry, or one of whatever it is you're tracking with Access 97 are collectively known as a *record.* If you have two baseball cards in your collection, then you have two records in your database, one for each card. (Of course, you *also* have a mighty small card collection, but that goes without saying.)

✔ In one final burst of similarity, dBASE, FoxPro, and Paradox concur on the term *record* (but the party ends here).

✔ Each record in a *table* has the exact same fields, but probably different data inside those fields. By the way, I snuck *table* into the last sentence because that's the next term you need to know (plus I like the challenge of writing sneaky prose).

Table (the blocks of a neighborhood)

A *table* is a collection of *records* that describe similar data. The key phrase to remember in that last sentence is *similar data.* All the records in a single table contain similar data. The information about that baseball card collection might fit into a single table. So would the accounting data. However, a single table would *not* handle both baseball cards *and* accounting entries. Combining the two is a novel concept (and may even make accounting fun), but it's not going to work in Access 97.

✔ Paradox and FoxPro agree with Access 97 about what a table is. Isn't that nice?

✔ dBASE has its own ideas about this *table* thing. It prefers the term *database file*.

✔ Did you notice that I said the baseball card collection *might* fit in one table? I'm not hedging my bet because I think that the table can't physically hold entries about all your cards. Instead, it's because you may use a few *related* tables to hold the data. That's all you need to know for now, but this is an important topic to understand. Be sure to peek at "Flat Files versus Relational Databases: Let the Contest Begin!" later in this chapter for the whole scoop.

Database (a community of neighborhoods)

An Access 97 *database* (or *database file* — the terms are interchangeable) is a collection of everything relating to a particular set of information. The database contains all the tables, queries, reports, forms, and other things that Access 97 helps you create to manage and work with your stuff. Instead of storing all those items *individually* on the disk drive, where they can become lost, misplaced, or accidentally erased, they're grouped into a single collective file.

✔ dBASE and FoxPro call this a *catalog.* Conceptually, catalogs are like databases, except that the catalog is a separate file that just lists files that you claim are related. In Access 97, a database file actually *contains* the tables, reports, and such, so it's doing much more than merely organizing them.

✔ Paradox doesn't have anything like an Access 97 database file. The closest you can come is a subdirectory that contains all the tables, queries, reports, and forms.

Frolicking through the Fields

A *field,* you remember, is the place where your data lives; one field holds one piece of data. If you're storing information about a book collection, your database file may use fields like Title, Author, Copyright Date, Publisher, Edition, Price, and so on. Each one of those items is a unique *field*.

Because there are so many different kinds of stuff in the world, Access 97 offers a variety of field types for *stuff storage.* In fact, Access 97 puts ten different field types at your disposal. At first blush, ten choices may not seem like much flexibility, but believe me — it is. Thanks to the field options, you can customize the fields to suit your needs precisely.

Each field offers a number of options to make it incredibly useful. You can ask for some information, test the entry to see whether it's what you're looking for, and then automatically format the field just the way you want. Everything you need to know about this cool stuff awaits your attention in Chapter 7.

All the field types appear in the following list. They're in the same order as they appear on-screen in Access 97. Don't worry if you can't figure out why *anyone* would want to use one type or another. Just focus on the ones you need, make a mental note about the others, and go on with your work.

- ✔ **Text:** This field stores text — letters, numbers, and any combination thereof — up to 255 characters. The thing you need to remember is that numbers in a text field *aren't* numbers anymore; they're just a bunch of digits hanging out together in a field. Be careful of this fact when you design the tables in your database.

  Text fields have one more setting you need to know about: size. When you create a text field, Access 97 wants to know how many characters the field holds. That's the field *size.* If you create a field called First Name and make its size 6, *Joseph* fits into the field, but not *Jennifer.* This could be a problem. A good rule of thumb is to make the field a little larger than you think you actually need. It's easy to make the field even larger if you need to, but it's very dangerous to make it smaller. By the way, performing surgery on fields is covered in Chapter 9.

- ✔ **Memo:** This is a really *big* text field. It's great for general notes, detailed descriptions, and anything else that requires a lot of space. Memo fields hold up to 64,000 characters of information — that's almost 18 pages of text.

- ✔ **Number:** As you probably guessed, this field holds real for-sure numbers. You can add, subtract, and calculate your way to fame and fortune with these fields. *Currency* fields are a specific kind of number field. If you're working with dollars and cents (or pounds and pence), use a currency field. For your other numeric needs, try a number field.

- ✔ **Date/Time:** Time waits for no one (and if you're too late, your dates won't, either). Use a Date/Time field to track the whens of life. These fields store time, date, or a combination of the two, depending on which format you use. Pretty versatile, eh?

- ✔ **Currency:** In an Access 97 database, the bucks stop here. For that matter, so do the lira, marks, and yen. Use this field to track money, prices, invoice amounts, and so on. If you're in the mood for some *other* kind of number, check out the *number* field.

- ✔ **AutoNumber:** If I have to name one thing that makes Access 97 a truly cool product, this is it. The AutoNumber field does just what it says: It fills itself with an automatically generated number every time you make a new record. Just think — when you add a customer to your table, Access 97 generates the customer number *automatically!* This field type is an absolute boon for people like you and me because making an automatically numbered field used to require a programming degree. With Access 97, it just takes a mouse click.

✔ **Yes/No:** When you need a simple *yes* or *no,* this is the field to use. Depending on the format you choose, this field type holds Yes/No, True/False, and On/Off.

✔ **OLE object:** You probably won't ever use this type of field. It falls under the heading of *technoweenie features in Access 97.* OLE (pronounced O-Lay) stands for Object Linking and Embedding, a very powerful, very nerdy technology. If you simply *must* learn more about the OLE object field, consult the Office Assistant or pick up a copy of the *Access for Windows 95 Bible,* 3rd Edition, by Cary Prague and Michael Irwin.

✔ **Hyperlink:** If you use Access 97 on your company's network or use the Internet extensively, then this field type is for you. Thanks to this field type (and a little bit of Net magic provided by Microsoft Internet Explorer 3.0), Access 97 now understands and stores the special link language that makes the Internet such a cool place. For more about this new field type, as well as other Access 97 Internet tricks, see Chapter 21.

✔ **Lookup Wizard:** One of a database program's most powerful features is the *lookup.* It makes data entry go faster (and with fewer errors, I might add) by letting you pick a field's correct value from a preset list. No typing, no worry, no problem — it's quite a helpful trick. In some database programs, adding a lookup to a table is really hard. Luckily, the Access 97 Lookup Wizard makes the process much less painful. Ask the Office Assistant for all of the details about the Lookup Wizard.

A Smattering of Fields to Get You Started

To give you a head start in the database race, Table 4-1 lists some common fields already starring in databases around the world. Some oldies-but-goodies are in here, plus some examples especially for the computer-oriented 1990s.

Table 4-1	A Field for Every Occasion		
Name	*Type*	*Size*	*Notes*
Title	Text	4	Mr., Ms., Mrs., Mme., Sir
First Name	Text	15	person's first name
Middle Initial	Text	4	person's middle initial; allows for two initials and punctuation
Last Name	Text	20	person's last name

Name	Type	Size	Notes
Job	Text	25	job title or position
Company	Text	25	company name
Address 1, Address 2	Text	30	include two fields for address because some corporate locations are pretty complicated these days
City	Text	20	city name
State, Province	Text	4	state or province; apply the name appropriately for the data you're storing
Zip Code, Postal Code	Text	10	zip or postal code; note that this is stored as text characters, not a number
Country	Text	15	not needed if you work within a single country
Office Phone	Text	12	voice telephone number; increase the size to 17 for an extension
Fax Number	Text	12	fax number
Home Phone	Text	12	home telephone number (only necessary for people with lives)
Cellular Phone	Text	12	cell phone or car phone
America Online	Text	10	screen name on America Online
CompuServe	Text	12	user ID on CompuServe; even though it's all numeric, treat the number as text for storage purposes
Prodigy	Text	8	Prodigy user ID
E-mail address	Text	30	Internet e-mail address
Telex	Text	12	standard Telex number; use size 22 to include answerback service
SSN	Text	11	U.S. Social Security Number, including dashes

All these samples are *text* fields, even the ones for phone numbers. That's because Access 97 sees most of the stuff you want to pack a database with as *text*. Remember that computers think that there's a difference between an actual *number* and a string of digits, such as the string of digits that makes up a phone number or government ID number.

Playing the (field) name game

Of all the Windows database programs out there, I think Access 97 has the simplest field-naming rules. Just remember three things, and your field names will be perfect every time.

✔ First, *start with a letter or number.* After the first character, you're free to use any letter or number. You can include spaces in field names, too!

✔ Second, *make the field name short and easy to understand.* You actually have up to 64 characters for a field name, but don't even

think about using all that space. But don't get stingy and create names like N1 or AZ773 unless they mean something particular to your company or organization.

✔ Finally, *just use letters, numbers, and an occasional space in your field names.* Although Access 97 lets you include all kinds of crazy punctuation marks in field names, don't do it. Keep it simple so that the solution you develop with Access 97 doesn't turn into a problem on its own.

These quick tips should keep you on the right path for creating good fields:

✔ Here's an easy test for when to put a number into a text field instead of a number field. Ask yourself, "Will I ever do *math* with this number?" If so, it goes in a number field. Otherwise, stuff it into a text field.

✔ The Table Wizard is packed with ready-made fields for your tables. Look ahead to "Creating Tables at the Wave of a Wand" later in this chapter for more information.

Flat Files versus Relational Databases: Let the Contest Begin!

Unlike ice cream, cars, and summer days, the tables in your database come in only two basic flavors: *flat* and *relational.* These two escapees from the *Nerd Term of the Month Club* explain how information is stored in the tables of your database. And *you* get to choose which one your new database uses!

In a *flat* system (also known as *flat file*), all the data is lumped together into a single table. The phone directory is a good example of a flat file. Names, addresses, and phone numbers (data) are crammed into a single place (the database). Some duplication does occur — if one person has three phone lines at home, her name and address are listed three times in the directory — but overall, things work just fine.

A *relational* system (or *relational database*) tries to use as little storage space as possible by cutting down on the redundant data. Using the phone book example, one table may contain customer name and address information, and another holds the actual phone numbers.

The key to this advanced technology is, in fact, called just that: the *key field* (or *linking field*). Both tables contain this field. The key field's data links together matching records from different tables, just like the claim stub you receive when you drop off film for processing. To join up with your film again, you present the claim number. That number connects (or *links*) you and your film.

A database is either flat file or relational — it can't be both. Each approach has its unique plusses and minuses:

- ✓ Flat systems are easy to build and maintain. They're great for simple things like mailing lists, phone directories, and video collections. Flat systems are simple solutions for simple problems.

- ✓ Relational systems really shine in *big* business problems such as invoicing, accounting, or inventory. If you have a small problem to solve (like a mailing list or membership database), a relational approach may be more solution than you need.

Anyone can create a very workable flat database system — and I *do* mean anyone. Developing a solid relational database takes skill and practice (and, in some countries, a nerd license).

Your company probably has a lot of information stored in relational database systems. Understanding how to *use* relational systems is important for you, so that's covered just about everywhere you turn in this book. Specifically, check out Chapter 5 to find out about dealing with the relationships between tables.

On the other hand, I don't recommend that you set off to *build* a relational database system by yourself. If you're *sure* you need one, enlist either the Database Wizard or a friendly guru to help you bring the database to life. There's a lot to understand about how fields work together to form relations (imagine a cross between Biology 101 and your first computer science class). Get some help the first time and then try it on your own later.

The following section explores the steps you use to design your database's tables, which is the next step toward creating your database. Here's one final note before I send you careening down the path toward your database: Even though Access 97 is a relational database program, it does flat systems quite nicely. Don't worry — whichever way you go, you bought the right program!

Great Tables Start with Great Designs

You're *almost* ready to start up the computer and run Access 97. Almost, but not quite. There's one more step: designing the tables for your database. I know this seems like a lot of paperwork, but it's absolutely necessary to build good databases. When I create systems for my clients, this is exactly how I do it.

1. **Get out a clean pad of paper and something to write with.**

   Despite the wonders of PCs and Windows 95, some things still work best on paper. Besides, if the database design work isn't going well, you can always doodle.

2. **Write brief descriptions of the reports, lists, and other things you want to come *out* of the system.**

   It seems kinda backward, but these reports and such are the *real* reason you're creating the database. If you can't get the information that you need out of the system, why have the system at all?

3. **On another sheet of paper, sketch some samples of the reports, lists, and other outputs you listed in Step 2.**

   You needn't create a detailed design at this point — that's not the goal. Right now, you're figuring out what information you need to build the stuff that ultimately comes out of your database (the reports, lists, mailing labels, and everything else). Just get a rough idea of what you want the most important reports to look like and write down the stuff that's on them. This list becomes the road map to your database's fields. (After all, you can't print something that doesn't exist one way or another in your database.) Now that you know the big picture of where you're going, it's time to fill in some details.

4. **For each field in your list, write a name, field type, and, for text fields, a specific size.**

   You need to do this step even if you're planning to use the Database Wizard or Table Wizard when you build the table. Although those wizards automatically size and name the fields you create, you can still customize the fields to your liking.

5. **Organize the fields into one or more tables.**

   Look for data that naturally goes together, like name, address, and phone number for a contact database, or product ID, description, distributor, cost, and selling price for an inventory system. If you have a lot of fields or if you run out of ideas for putting them together, get help from your friendly guru.

   The last step is the hardest one, but it gets easier with experience. (I've done this so many times that I can practically design databases in my sleep, although my wife finds it a little disconcerting when I start jabbering about field sizes in the middle of the night.) To build your experience, create some sample databases with the Database Wizard and look at how they fit together. Pick a topic you know about (accounting, event scheduling, or — if you're like me — compact disc collecting) and see how the pros at Microsoft did it.

It's Finally Time to Build the Database

After reading page after page of this book, writing reams of notes, and sucking down two or three cans of pop, the moment is finally here — it's time to build the database! Here's where you create the master holding file for your tables, reports, forms, and other stuff. Plus, if you use a Database Wizard, this step *also* creates all the tables, reports, and forms for you — it's one-stop shopping!

If you worked with some *other* database program in the past, then in your mind the term *database* may mean "where you store the data." Access 97 calls that a *table*. Tables live *inside* databases, along with all the other sundry stuff you create to get the job done. If the terms still aren't clear, flip back a few pages to "Database Terms to Know and Tolerate," earlier in this chapter.

Without further ado, here's how to create a database:

1. **If it's not already running, take a moment to start Access 97.**

   I know, I know — but I *have* to say it; it's an author thing.

2. **Choose File⇨New Database from the main menu (see Figure 4-1) or click on the New Database toolbar button.**

3. **When the New dialog box appears, click on the Databases tab.**

   The New database window appears on-screen, displaying a fine array of Database Wizards to assist you.

Figure 4-1:
It only takes
a quick click
to create a
database.

If you just started Access 97, your screen looks more like Figure 4-2. In that case, click on the <u>D</u>atabase Wizard radio button to enlist the wizard's help and then click on OK to bring up the New Database window.

Figure 4-2:
If you just started Access 97, making a new database is even easier.

To create a new database by hand, click on the <u>B</u>lank Database radio button and then click on OK. Continue with Step 4 below.

4. **Scroll through the list until you find a Database Wizard that sounds close to what you want to do, and then double-click on it.**

   To create a database by hand, double-click on the Blank Database icon in the upper-left corner of the window.

   Either way, the File New Database dialog box appears.

5. **Type a name for your database and then click on Create (see Figure 4-3).**

Figure 4-3:
One new database, coming right up!

To store the database somewhere other than the default location (usually the My Documents folder), choose a different folder by clicking on the down arrow next to Save in and working through the directory tree until you find the one you're looking for.

Are you getting a headache from all this talk of folders, directory trees, and such? *Windows 95 For Dummies,* by Andy Rathbone, is the perfect remedy. Read once before bedtime and throughout the day as needed.

If a dialog box pops up and asks whether you want to replace an existing file, Access 97 is saying that a database with the name you entered is already on the disk. If this is news to you, click on No and then come up with a different name for your new database. On the other hand, if you *intended* to replace that old database with a new one, click on Yes and proceed.

6. **Skim over the brief this-is-what-I'm-up-to window to see what what the wizard has to say and then click on Next to continue.**

   If you chose the Blank Database option, you see a blank database (see Figure 4-4). To create tables for your new database, skip ahead to the next section in this chapter.

Figure 4-4:
Yup — it's blank all right.

7. **If you want to add or remove standard fields from the database that the wizard is building for you, do so in the Fields dialog box (see Figure 4-5) and then click on Next.**

   Unless you're particularly moved to change something, leave this box alone and just click on Next.

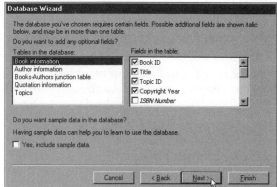

Figure 4-5:
The fields
look good
and fresh
to me.

One cool feature of this dialog box is the *sample data check box,* on the lower-left side of the window. To have Access 97 generate some sample data for your table, click on the check box. This option is really helpful when you're planning to quickly test some reports. You don't *have* to click this option, but doing so makes a lot of sense.

8. **Now that the hard part is done, the wizard wants your opinion on some aesthetic questions. First, the wizard wants you to choose a style for the database's on-screen displays. Single-click on the options to see what's available and then double-click on the one you like.**

Although my wife will accuse me of being bland again, I recommend sticking with the *Standard* option. The others are pretty, but most of them take more time to load. If you simply *must* add some diversity to your database, try the *Colorful, Pattern,* or *Stone* options — they don't slow you down.

9. **Pick the font and style for your report (at last) and click on <u>N</u>ext.**

As with the previous page, single-click on the options to see what's available. I have no cool recommendations for you here — just pick something you like and move on.

10. **Name your masterpiece and click on <u>N</u>ext.**

The wizard kindly offers his own name, but you're free to change it by simply typing something new in the box at the top of the window.

11. **If you're really into graphics, tell the Database Wizard to add a picture to your reports.**

To pick an image, click the *Yes I'd like to include a picture* check box and then click on the Picture button to choose the graphic you want to feature on the database's reports.

12. **Click on <u>F</u>inish to build the database.**

The wizard clunks and thunks for a while, giving you constant updates on how it's doing (see Figure 4-6).

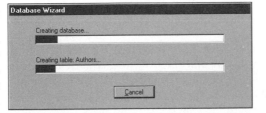

Figure 4-6:
The wizard
at work —
your
database is
moments
away.

The Database Wizard lets you create a friendly switchboard screen, something like the one I use to keep track of my book collection (see Figure 4-7).

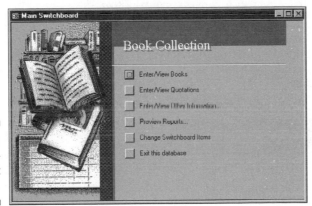

Figure 4-7:
Whoa —
instant
database.

Now that the database is ready, flip through Chapters 6 and 7 for information on entering data, customizing the tables, and getting comfy with your new addition.

Creating Tables at the Wave of a Wand

Adding a new table to an existing database is easy with the Access 97 Table Wizard. The Table Wizard offers a variety of ready-made fields to choose from, plus it does all the dirty work of table creation behind the scenes, so you can focus on important stuff (like wondering when you can go home for the day).

With the Table Wizard, you don't so much *build* a table as *assemble* it. The wizard brings lots of pieces and parts — you pick out what you want and go from there.

This approach is helpful when you're completely new at building tables. Instead of worrying about details like field types and sizes, you get to worry about bigger stuff, like field names and purposes. After building a few tables, though, you probably won't use the Table Wizard anymore. Instead of helping, he starts getting in the way because you already know what fields you want and how to make them.

As of this writing, the Table Wizard still has some rough edges. Hopefully, the Great Ones Who Write Software will smooth things out before Access 97 hits the shelves at your local retailer. Because I can't be sure that they really *will* fix the problems, though, the following steps include notes to protect your digital knees from scrapes and scratches on the trouble spots.

Without further ado, here's how to ask the wizard to help you build a table:

1. **Choose File⇨Open or click on the Open Database button on the Toolbar to open the database file that needs a new table.**

   The database pops into its on-screen window.

   If you see a fancy form instead of the database window in Figure 4-8, click on the Windows 95 Close button to close the form and then click on the Restore button (third from the right) on the database window that's hiding in the lower-left corner of the screen. *Now* your database window is ready and waiting.

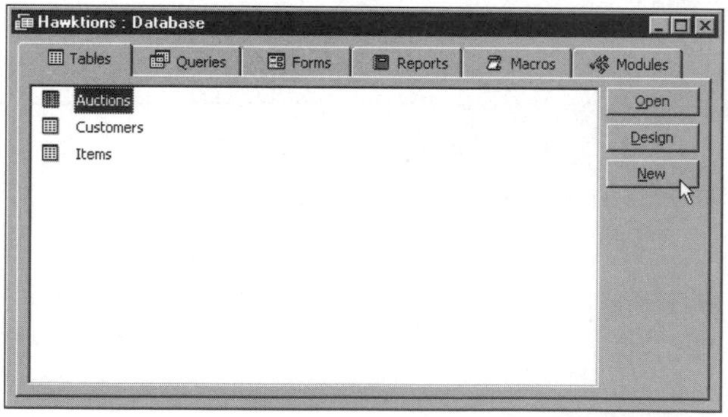

Figure 4-8:
Get rid
of the
switchboard
and then
view the
database.

2. **Click on the Tables tab and then click on New to start the creation process.**

   Access 97 is now aware that you want to add a table to the database. If you forget to click on the Tables tab first, Access 97 may think you want to make a new report, form, or goodness knows *what* else. In that case, just close whatever bizarre window appears and then do this step again.

3. In the New Table dialog box, double-click on the Table Wizard entry.

Your disk drive probably sounds like it's lost its mind right now, but that's just part of waking up the wizard and getting him ready for the show. Pretty soon (in less than a minute), the Table Wizard dialog box of Figure 4-9 pops into view.

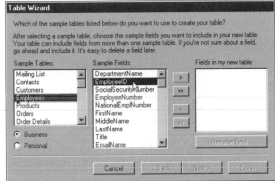

Figure 4-9.
All hail the mighty Table Wizard!

4. Click on a sample table to display the available fields.

Remember those "rough spots" I mentioned? The Sample Tables list is a big one — it's a *mess.* The tables are jumbled together on the list in no particular order, plus the list includes no descriptions of the fields and what they do. If you look up the term *user friendly* in the dictionary, this dialog box would *not* be listed as an example. To make your life with this dialog box a little easier, check out the upcoming "Highlights from the sample tables" sidebar. It contains some tips to guide you through this seething data morass.

The Table Wizard offers you all kinds of ready-made fields to assemble into a table.

5. Double-click on the fields you want for the table.

When you double-click, the field name hops into the Fields in my new table column. Select the fields in the order you want them to appear in the new table. Don't worry if you get one or two out of order — it's easy to fix that later (Chapter 9 tells you how).

If you like *all* the fields from a particular table, click on the >> button. That button copies the table's entire set of fields.

To remove a field you chose by accident, click on the field name and then click the < button. To remove *all* the fields and start over with a clean slate, click on the << button.

If you're not happy with the current name of a field in your new table, click on the field name and then click on Rename Field. Type the new field name into the dialog box and click on OK to make the change. Too easy, eh?

6. **Repeat Steps 4 and 5 until your table is populated with fields (see Figure 4-10).**

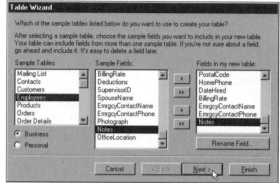

Figure 4-10:
After reworking the fields a bit, it's time to move on.

7. **When you're done picking fields, click on Next to continue.**

So far, so good — now you're down to the simple stuff. On-screen, the field information runs off to hide as the wizard needs to know some general stuff about the table.

8. **Type a name for the table and click on Next when you're done.**

The table name information vanishes, only to be replaced with the table relationship screen.

Leave the primary key settings alone for now. You can mess with those later (see Chapter 5).

9. **If this table is related to any of the other tables in the database, click on the Relationships button and explain how the tables are involved with each other and then click on Next.**

The Table Wizard is pretty intelligent about this relationship stuff. It checks for fields that may link this new table to the existing ones in your database. The wizard reports its findings in this dialog box.

If you *thought* there would be a relationship but the wizard couldn't find one, click on the related table's entry in the dialog box and then click on Relationships. Follow the on-screen prompts to explain how the link works.

Chapter 5 has more about table relationships. Look in that chapter if you're a little foggy about the how's and why's of linking tables together.

Highlights from the sample tables

In hopes of making the Table Wizard a little more useful, here are some brief descriptions of the sample tables. This list doesn't cover all the sample tables — just the ones that I think are most useful.

Many of these tables link together to form relational databases. For instance, Calls, Contacts, Contact Types, and "To Do's" work together as a single system. Don't bother trying to put the individual pieces together with the Table Wizard. Use the Database Wizard instead — it's a *lot* easier!

✔ **Attendees:** General mailing list information (name, address, and so on) geared toward seminar attendees

✔ **Calls:** Rudimentary customer contact database

✔ **Clients:** Customer mailing list information

✔ **Contacts:** Very full-featured customer information table; stores details about your customers

✔ **Customers:** You guessed it — a customer information list, complete with a field for e-mail address

✔ **Employees:** Solid employee information table; good example of the detail you can include in a single table

✔ **Events:** Great for meeting planners or trainers setting up their own room information

✔ **Orders:** Tracks customer order data

✔ **Order Details:** Covers the line items for each order

✔ **Products:** General product information for a catalog and sales system

✔ **Registration:** Fields for checking people in at seminars, training courses, or other events requiring pre-registration

✔ **Reservations:** Handles event reservations and pre-paid fees

✔ **Service Records:** Great example of a table that manages call information for a service business

✔ **"To Do's":** Tracks to-do items

You're *really* done — click on Finish to complete the task and build the new table.

---

10. **You're *really* done — click on F̲inish to complete the task and build the new table.**

The final window offers a couple of other interesting and time-saving options to consider before whacking that Finish button. To take the table design directly into Design mode after closing the wizard, click the Modify the table design radio button and then click Finish. To have the wizard whip up a quick data entry form, click the long-named *Enter data into the table using a form the wizard creates for me* radio button; then take a few breaths and click Finish.

Whew! You did it. The table proudly takes its place in your database (see Figure 4-11).

Figure 4-11:
Here's
the new
table —
this thing
really
worked!

Building Tables by Hand, Just as in the Old Days

Although automation is a generally great thing, at times it just plain gets in the way. For instance, I appreciate the fact that with the right automatic gizmo, I can clap my hands and turn off the television. This feat becomes a problem when I start keeping time with my favorite song and accidentally drive the TV insane.

Likewise, the Table Wizard makes life easy at first, but soon you know more about what you want than it does. Don't worry — when you're ready for independence, Access 97 is there with a straightforward way to build tables by hand.

Actually, you have *two* easy ways to build a table without the Table Wizard. The easiest is *Datasheet view,* where Access 97 displays a blank datasheet and you just start typing in data. After you're done entering everything, Access 97 looks at your entries and assigns field types based on the data it sees. The only problem is that Access 97 frequently misunderstands your data, leaving you to tweak the field types by hand. The bottom line: For anything more complicated than a *really* simple table, don't use Datasheet view. It's a nice thought, but it drives you nuts in the end. Instead, use Design view.

Design view is the formal, almost nerd-like way to build new databases. In this mode, you have full control over the new table's fields. Don't get all weirded out because the screen looks complicated — just go slow, follow the information in the steps, and everything will be fine. (Trust me on this one.)

To create a new table by hand, cruise through these steps:

1. **Choose File⇨Open from the main menu; then double-click on the database that needs a new table.**

The database file appears on-screen. If a cool-looking form appears in its place, click the Windows 95 Close button in the form's upper-right corner to make the form go away; then click the Restore button on the database window to bring the database front and center on the screen.

You can also click on the Open Database button on the toolbar, but that's old news by now.

2. Click on the Tables tab and then click on New.

The New Table dialog box appears, ready for action.

If Access 97 thinks you want to create a report, form, or other odd electronic accoutrement, click on Cancel and then click on the Table tab. Now click on the New button again.

3. Double-click on the Design View option.

Access 97 displays a blank table design form that looks a whole heckuva lot like Figure 4-12.

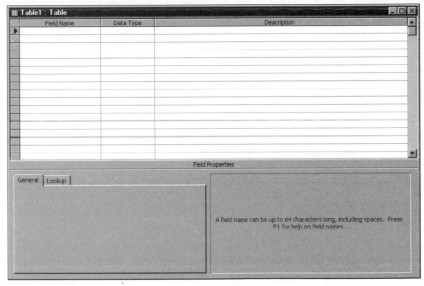

Figure 4-12:
A fresh, clean datasheet, anxiously awaiting your instruction.

Remember the note earlier about creating tables in Datasheet view? If you're heavily into pain, agony, and doing things the hard way, double-click on the Datasheet View option and use it to build the new table. Also, refer to Chapter 8 for lots of cool tips about working with a datasheet (believe me, you need all the help you can get).

4. **Type the field name and then press Tab to move on.**

   The cursor moves to the Data Type column. See — this manual stuff isn't so bad, is it?

5. **Click on the down-arrow to list all available field types, click on the field type you want (see Figure 4-13), and then press Tab to continue.**

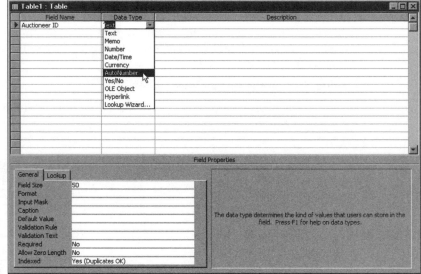

Figure 4-13:
You can
select from
all available
field (data)
types.

The cursor moves into the Description field.

If you create a Text field, you also need to adjust the field size (the default size is 50, which is too much field for almost anyone). Click in the Field Size box in the lower-left side of the screen *before* tabbing elsewhere; then type the correct field size.

6. **Type a clear, concise description of what this field contains and then press Tab once more to move the cursor back into the Field Name column.**

This step is *really* important! The Description information appears in the status line at the bottom of the screen — it's automatic help text. *Please* take the time to write a quick field description. It makes your tables so much easier to use that you won't believe it.

7. **Repeat Steps 4 through 6 until all the fields are in place (see Figure 4-14).**

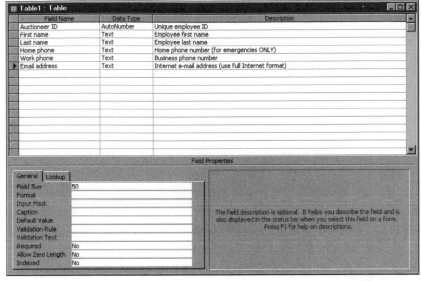

Field Name	Data Type	Description
Auctioneer ID	AutoNumber	Unique employee ID
First name	Text	Employee first name
Last name	Text	Employee last name
Home phone	Text	Home phone number (for emergencies ONLY)
Work phone	Text	Business phone number
Email address	Text	Internet e-mail address (use full Internet format)

Figure 4-14:
The fields
are in
place . . .
time to
give it the
stress test!

Field Properties

General	Lookup
Field Size	50
Format	
Input Mask	
Caption	
Default Value	
Validation Rule	
Validation Text	
Required	No
Allow Zero Length	No
Indexed	No

The field description is optional. It helps you describe the field and is also displayed in the status bar when you select this field on a form. Press F1 for help on descriptions.

What a feeling of achievement! Your new table is almost ready to work.

8. Select File⇨Save to write the new table to your disk drive or click on the Save button on the Toolbar.

9. In the dialog box, type the name you want to use for the table and press Enter.

Access 97 may send you a dialog box complaining that There is no primary key defined. This message means that your table won't automatically put itself into any kind of order. Click on Yes in the dialog box to create a key field and then check out Chapter 5 for more about the whole key field thing.

10. Enjoy your new table!

That's not bad for doing the work without automated intervention! Congratulations on a job well done.

Chapter 5

Indexes, Keys, and Relationships: Why You Care

....

....

*E*very year, it's the same things over and over. Do more with less. Work smarter not harder. They're not problems, they're *opportunities for achievement*. Why do I bring up such wonderful thoughts in a fun book like this? Because this chapter is at least a partial cure for these phrases that afflict you.

You need to get more done in less time, right? If that's you, then check out the index feature in Access 97. This feature makes your queries fly, your sorts sing, and your hair hold firm in its current position. Are you plagued with *opportunities* because of all the duplicate data infesting your tables? Ferret out the problems with a well-placed key field. A good key ensures that records appear once (and only once) in the table.

This chapter is your source for information about indexes and keys, plus explanations and tips about building good relationships between your tables (goodness knows you don't want dysfunctional tables!). Whether you're new to databases or are an old hand with them, valuable information awaits you here.

Indexing Your Way to Fame, Fortune, and Much Faster Queries

Psst — you with the book. Yeah, you. C'mere for a minute. Want some inside information about your software? I've got a hot tip on a feature that'll blow you away. It speeds up your queries, makes sorting a snap, and prevents duplicate records in your tables. Pretty cool, eh? Oh, you *are* interested. Okay, then — here's the scoop.

The cool, semi-secret feature in question is an *index*. An Access 97 table index works just like the index in a book. When you want to find something in the book, it's quick and easy to flip to the index, discover that the information is on page 731, and then turn immediately to the right page. That's a whole lot faster than flipping page after page in a hopeless search for the correct passage.

An Access 97 index works just like a book index, but instead of listing page numbers, it tracks *record* numbers. When you sort or query a table using an indexed field, most of the work is already done by the index. That's why indexes dramatically speed up queries and sorts — the index lets the query zero in on the information it's looking for without having to sift through the whole table to find it.

Here are a few random thoughts about indexes:

- ✔ Each field in a table can be indexed.

- ✔ Key fields are automatically indexed. (See the next section for more about keys.)

- ✔ Although indexes make queries, searches, and sorts a whole lot faster, building too many indexes in a table actually *slows down* some things. Adding records to a table with several indexes takes a little longer than adding records to an unindexed table. Access 97 spends the extra time updating all those indexes behind the scenes.

- ✔ Indexes either *allow* duplicate entries in your table or *prevent* them. The choice is yours. How do you choose the right one for your table? Most of the time, you want to *allow* duplicate records. The big exception is with key fields. Most of the time, key fields should be indexed as *No duplicates* — after all, you don't want two customers with the same Customer Number. The *No duplicates* setting tells Access 97 to make sure that no two records have the same values in the indexed field.

- ✔ To list the table's indexes, open the table in Design view and click on the Indexes button on the toolbar.

The programmers at Microsoft made creating an index a pretty straightforward operation. Here's how it works:

1. **With the table open in Design view, click on the name of the field you want to index.**

   The blinking toothpick cursor lands in the field name.

2. **Click on the Indexed box in the General tab of Field Properties.**

   The toothpick cursor, always eager to please, hops into the Indexed box. A down arrow appears on the right end of the box as well.

3. **Click on the down arrow at the end of the box to list your index options. Select the kind of index you want from the list (see Figure 5-1).**

   Most of the time, choose Yes (Duplicates OK). In special cases when you want every record to have a unique value in this field (like Customer Numbers in your Customer table), select Yes (No Duplicates).

4. **Click on the Save toolbar button or choose File⇨Save to make the change permanent.**

   Depending on the size of your table, it may take a few moments of effort to create the index. Don't be surprised if you have to wait a few moments before Access 97 is done.

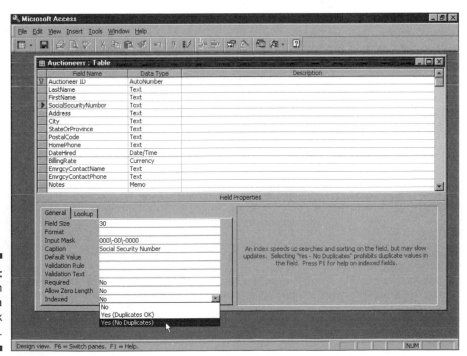

Figure 5-1: Building an index is a one-click operation.

To remove an index, follow the preceding steps. In Step 3, choose No on the pull-down menu. Access 97 wordlessly deletes the field's index.

Primarily Keying Up Your Table

A table's *primary key* is a special kind of indexed field. Just about every table you create *should* have a primary key. Why? Because it helps keep your data more organized (and because many nerds pitch a snit if you don't).

You need to know a few things about the primary key before running off to create one:

- First, a table can have only *one* primary key. A single table can have lots of indexes, but only *one* primary key.

- If you create a new table without a primary key, Access 97 automatically asks whether you want to add one. If you say yes, the program gleefully creates an AutoNumber field at the beginning of your table and sets it as the primary key. If the first field already happens to be an AutoNumber type, Access 97 annoints it as the primary key without adding anything else to the table.

- Most of the time, the primary key is a single field, but in special circumstances two or more fields can share the job. The technical term for this type of key is a *multifield key.* The big drawback of a multifield key is the simple fact that they're a pain to work with. If you ever have the urge to create a multifield key in one of your tables, stop for a moment and try very hard to talk yourself out of it. If you're *still* convinced that a multifield key is the answer to your problems, collar your local database guru and ask for her opinion. Hopefully, she can come up with a better solution for the table.

- Only certain field types can be keys. Text, number, date/time, and AutoNumber fields all qualify for primary key status. Yes/No, OLE, and memo fields can't be the primary key.

- Records are automatically sorted by the primary key. This feature is part of the organizational thing I mentioned before — it just keeps things neat and tidy in your table.

- By default, the values in the primary key field *must* be unique. If they aren't, how can you hope to find anything?

- Unlike many other database programs, Access 97 doesn't care where the primary key field is in the table design. The key can be the first field, the last field, or some field in the middle. The placement choice is all yours. For your sanity's sake, I recommend putting the key field first in a table. In fact, make it a habit (you can thank me later).

Picking the right field is a *key* issue

What makes a good key field? How do you find the right one? Good questions — in fact, they're the two most important questions to ask about a primary key.

The top criterion for a good key field is *uniqueness*. The values in a key field *must* be unique. Access 97 won't tolerate duplicate key values. Each and every entry in the key field must be the only one of its kind.

With the word *unique* firmly imprinted in your mind, it's time to look for a natural key field in your table. Do you have any fields that *always* contain unique data? Is there a Customer

Number, Stock Keeping Unit, Vehicle ID, or some other field that's different in every record?

If you have a natural key, that's great. Use it! If you don't, I recommend adding an AutoNumber field to your table. This field type automatically inserts a new, unique number into each record of your table. AutoNumber even keeps track of numbers that you delete so that Access won't try to use them again. You don't have to worry about programming or any special tricks to make the system work. The AutoNumber field takes care of everything.

To nominate a field for the job of primary key, follow these steps:

1. **Open the table in Design view.**

   If you're not familiar with this step, you probably *shouldn't* be messing with the primary key. I recommend spending a little time back in Chapters 1 and 4 before tackling the primary key thing.

2. **Right-click in the button next to the field you've picked for the primary key.**

   One of those cool pop-up menus appears. For some ideas on how to pick the *right* field for a primary key, see the nearby sidebar, "Picking the right field is a *key* issue."

3. **Select Primary Key from the menu (see Figure 5-2).**

   A little key symbol appears in the button. The primary key is set!

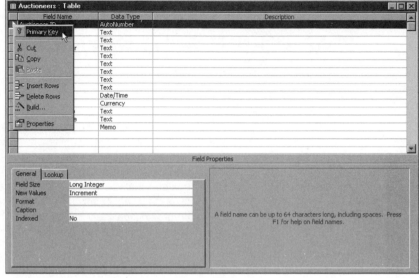

Divulging the Secrets of a Good Relationship

I introduce the relational thing back in Chapter 4. As a quick recap, databases come in two basic kinds. In a *flat file* system, all the data is lumped into one big file. It's called a flat file because, organizationally speaking, it's flat — like a company with only one job classification.

At the other end of the spectrum are *relational* databases. Here, data is split up among two or more tables. Access 97 uses a *linking field* to tie related tables together. For example, one table may contain customer names and addresses while another table tracks the customer's payment history. The credit information is tied to the customer's address with a linking field, which, in this example, is probably some kind of customer number.

- Usually, the linking field is one table's primary key, but just an average, mild-mannered field in the other table. For instance, the customer table in the example is probably arranged by customer number, while the credit data is likely organized by payment number.

- Tables don't magically begin relating to each other just because they're cooped up inside the same database file. You explain the relationships to Access 97 and it handles the details. Instructions for doing that very thing are in the next section.

> ✔ Linking fields should be *identical* — same name, same data type, same size, same everything. If you're in the mood for individuality, this is *not* the place to express it. Lock-step precision goes a whole lot further with linking fields in the weird world of databases.

When you link two tables together, they form one of four possible relationships. Although this information borders on the technical side, Access 97 is particularly fond of these terms, so please take a minute to check them out.

> ✔ *One-to-One* relationships are the simplest, but they don't happen often. Here, one record in the first table links to *exactly* one record in the second table. Back in the example, if one customer has one (and only one) store credit account, then the customer and credit tables have a one-to-one link.

> ✔ *One-to-Many* is a much more common relationship. In this relationship, one record in the first table links to *many* records in the second table. One sample customer may make many purchases at the store, so one customer record is linked to many sales records in the transaction table.

> ✔ *Many-to-One* relationships are simply the reverse of *one-to-many*. Look at the relationship from the sales record end this time instead of the customer record end. Many sales transactions are linked back to one customer (a customer that *we* want to keep happy).

> ✔ *Many-to-Many* relationships are very complicated (just like real life). Here, many records in one table link to many records in another. Each store sales clerk sells many products, and each product is sold by many sales clerks. To have any hope of figuring out what's going on, you need a table in the middle to play traffic cop. Sound confusing? Trust me, it is. Creating and using tables in a many-to-many relationship is strictly the realm of database professionals (and even *they* don't like it).

The first three relationships are very common, particularly if you're in a corporate environment. If you're a particularly nice individual, lead a good life, and follow the straight and narrow path, you hopefully won't ever come across a many-to-many relationship. If you *do* fall into one, stock up on junk food and put out the word that you're looking for a hungry technoid who knows Access 97.

Linking Your Tables with the Relationship Builder Thingie

The mechanics of linking tables together in Access 97 are quite visual. There's none of Paradox's informal sneaking around behind your data's back, nor is it a technical mating dance as in FoxPro. In Access 97, look at tables, draw lines, and get on with your business. I hate to say this, but it's actually kinda fun. Keep these three limitations in mind:

✔ You can only link tables that are in the same database. Sorry, but that's how life goes in the big city.

✔ Although you can also link queries to tables, that's a little outside the range of normalcy. For more about that, check out the *Access for Windows 95 Bible* (IDG Books Worldwide, Inc.).

✔ Unlike Paradox and FoxPro, you need to specifically tell Access 97 how your tables are related. And you can't tell this stuff to Access on-the-fly — this is a formal process (kinda like ballroom dancing).

When you're ready to arrange some formal relationships among your more impassioned tables, here's how to do it:

1. **From the database window, choose Tools⇨Relationships or click on the Relationships button on the toolbar.**

   The Relationships window appears, probably looking quite blank at the moment.

   If some tables are already listed in the window, someone (or some-Wizard) has already defined relationships for this database. If you're in a corporate environment, *please* stop at this point and seek assistance from your Information Systems folks before mucking around with this database.

2. **Choose Relationships⇨Show Table from the menu or click on the Show Table button on the toolbar.**

   The Show Table dialog box appears on-screen, listing the tables in the current database file.

3. **Click on the first table involved in this would-be relationship and then click on Add.**

   Repeat the process with the other tables you want to get involved. As you add tables to the layout, a little window appears for each table, listing the fields in that table. You can see these windows next to the Show Table dialog box in Figure 5-3.

4. **Click on Close when you're finished adding tables.**

   With the tables present in the window, you're ready to start the relationships! (Do you feel like a matchmaker yet?)

5. **Decide which two tables you want to link together. In each table's window, scroll through the field list until the linking fields are both visible on-screen.**

   In Access 97, you need to *see* the two linking fields on-screen before you can make a relationship.

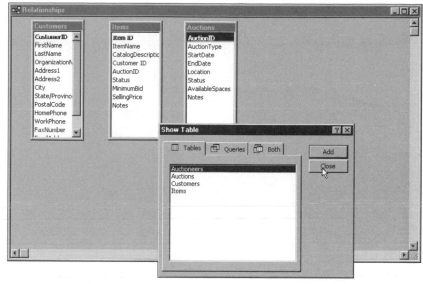

Figure 5-3:
Three of my
four tables,
reporting for
relationship
practice.
Ten, hut!

6. **Put the mouse pointer on one of the fields you want to link and hold the
left mouse button down.**

Did I mention that the same people who developed the old *Twister* game
also designed the relationship builder? No? Hmm... that must've slipped
my mind. Oh well, carry on — you'll discover that soon enough.

7. **While holding down the mouse button, slide the mouse from one
linking field to the other.**

The pointer becomes a rectangle. When the rectangle is next to the linking
field (see Figure 5-4), release the mouse button.

A dialog box detailing the soon-to-be relationship appears.

Access 97 is *very* picky about your aim on this step. You *must* put the tip of
the mouse pointer *right next* to the field you're linking to. In Figure 5-4, I
want to make a relationship between the AuctionID field in the Auctions
table and the field of the same name in Items. I already clicked on
AuctionID in the Auctions table. Then I hold down the mouse button and
put the boxy mouse pointer right next to the AuctionID field in Items. At
this point, all I need to do is let up on the mouse button and the relationship is made.

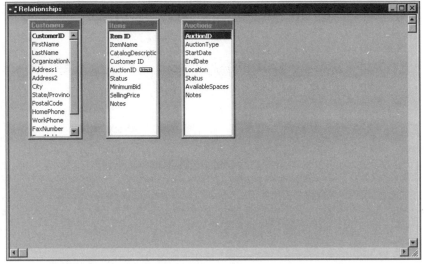

Figure 5-4:
With careful aim and a steady hand, a relationship using Auction ID begins.

8. **Make sure that the table and field names in the dialog box are correct. When you're confident that the entries are correct, click on Create (see Figure 5-5).**

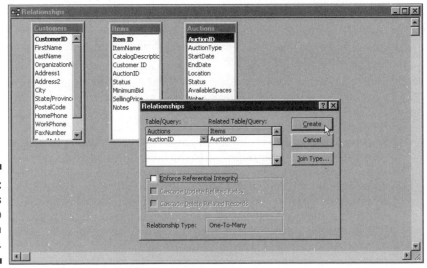

Figure 5-5:
This relationship is off to a good start.

A line appears to show you that the tables are linked, as you see in Figure 5-6.

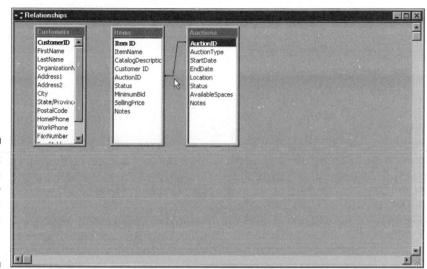

If the table names or field names listed in the dialog box are wrong, just click on Cancel and try Steps 5 through 7 again.

9. **To link another pair of tables, go back to Step 4 and begin again.**

When you're done, the Relationships window may look a little messy, as in Figure 5-7. To clean it up, put the mouse pointer on the title bar of a table window and then click and drag the table window to another part of the screen (see Figure 5-8). This process doesn't change the relationship — it just moves the window around. In no time at all, things start looking neat and tidy.

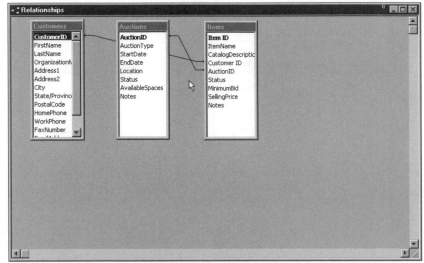

Figure 5-7:
With
relationships
like this, it
could be a
soap opera.

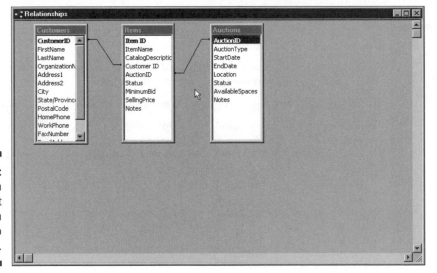

Figure 5-8:
That's much
neater, not
to mention
easier to
understand.

Chapter 6

New Data, Old Data, and Data in Need of Repair

In This Chapter

▶ Opening databases and tables

▶ Adding new records

▶ Changing an existing record

▶ Deleting the pointless ones

▶ What to do after saying, "oops!"

*T*he biggest cost surrounding *everything* in your life is maintenance. No matter what you're talking about — house, car, stereo, television, child, pet, significant other — keeping the thing in good working order *always* costs more than acquiring it in the first place.

Your data, however, is a lone exception to the rule. Thanks to the tools in Access 97, data maintenance is easy, relatively painless, and doesn't cost anything. In fact, keeping your data up to date is one of the program's main goals.

This chapter covers basic data upkeep: adding new records, deleting old ones, and fixing the ones that are broken. If you're looking for *table* maintenance hints (such as adding new columns, renaming fields, and so on), check out Chapter 9.

Dragging Your Table into the Digital Workshop

Because records cluster together in tables, you need to open a table before worrying about records. Tables prefer company, too. They hang out inside databases. Databases don't care a whit about anything other than themselves, so you may find them lounging in a folder, sulking on a diskette, or holding forth on a network drive.

That fancy buildup simply means that the first step on the road to record maintenance is *opening a database.* You have several different ways to open a database, but they all ultimately work the same way.

If you just opened Access 97, the program displays a massive dialog box (see Figure 6-1) that offers the opportunity to create a new database, reopen one you worked on recently, or wander off into another dialog box to open whatever database strikes your fancy right now.

Figure 6-1:
Is this too
handy or
what?

- ✔ To use one of the databases listed at the bottom of the dialog box, double-click on its name. Access 97 automatically opens the database.

- ✔ If the database you want isn't on the list, double-click on the More Files option to bring up the Open dialog box. This dialog box gives you access to all the table files in the current file folder.

- ✔ What? The database you want isn't there *either?* In that case, check out the nearby sidebar ("Bo Peep needed the Find File option") for some tips about the fortuitous file-finding features of the Open dialog box.

- ✔ If you're in the mood to create a new table, then you need to be in a different chapter. Flip to Chapter 4, where all the create-a-table stuff is.

These hints are all well and good if Access 97 just came roaring to life, but what if it's already running? In that case, you've got a whole different way to open up your database. Here's how it works:

1. **Choose File➪Open Database or click on the Open Database button on the toolbar.**

   The Open dialog box pops onto the screen (see Figure 6-2).

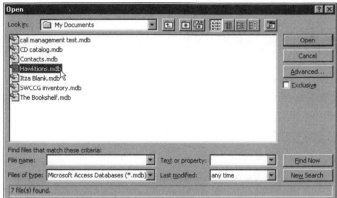

Figure 6-2:
Here's the database I was looking for.

2. **Scroll through the list until you find the database you're looking for.**

   If the database you want isn't on this list, it's probably in another folder, on another disk drive, or out on your network. To search for it, click on the Down arrow in the Look in box (along the top of the Open dialog box) to see a list of your local and network disk drives. Click on the drive you want to search. Access 97 displays a list of all databases and file folders in the current directory of that drive.

3. **When you find the database, open it by double-clicking on its name.**

   The database file opens with a flourish, as seen in Figure 6-3. This window shows how a normal, well-mannered database file acts in polite company. The rest of this chapter assumes that your database behaves this way.

Figure 6-3:
An average database file opens onto the screen.

An introductory screen of some kind (known as a *switchboard*) may appear instead of the tabbed dialog box. Access is telling you that your database either contains some custom programming or was created by the Database Wizard. You probably have some special forms that help you interact with the information in your database. Unfortunately, I can't tell you much more than that, because the possibilities are endless. The best suggestion I can offer is to look for instructions from your favorite local database nerd.

4. **If it's not already selected, click on the Tables tab.**

   The tables tab lists the tables in your database.

5. **Double-click on the table you want to edit.**

   The screen fills with your data, displayed eloquently in Datasheet view.

Adding a Little Something to the Mix

Few tasks are more frustrating than packing your car for vacation and then suddenly discovering the *one* thing you forgot to put in (and it's always something big). In the real world, this discovery is a repacking nightmare, but in the digital world of Access 97, adding one or one hundred extra items to your database is easy.

In fact, adding another record to a table takes only a couple steps. The following instructions assume that you already opened the database file and selected the table you want to work on. (If you haven't, then follow the instructions in the preceding section.) Here's how to add a new record to your table:

1. **Choose Insert⇨Record or click on the New Record button at the bottom of the datasheet window.**

   Access 97 responds by opening a blank record in your table and moving the toothpick cursor there (see Figure 6-4).

   The first field in many databases is an AutoNumber type field, because this field does such a good job assigning unique customer numbers, part numbers, or whatever kind of number you have in mind. At this point in the process, it's normal for an AutoNumber field to just sit there and stare at you. The AutoNumber field doesn't start working until the next step.

2. **Begin typing your information.**

   If the first field is an AutoNumber type, press Tab and begin typing in the second field. As soon as you start typing, the AutoNumber field generates a new number and displays it in the field.

Customers : Table							
Customer ID	**First Name**	**Last Name**	**Organization N**	**Address1**	**Address2**	**City**	**St**
24	Gretchen	Hankla	Daisyfield Shop	227 Daisyfield D		Noblesville	IN
25	Byron	Jiles		1122 Belden Dr.		Greenwood	IN
26	Clarence	Micy		385 Carlton Arr		Newton	IN
27	Mario	Schussler		1625 Euclid Ave		Fortville	IN
28	Harry	Nelson		19474 Vermeer		Carmel	IN
29	Callie	Logan	Eye 4 Antiques	227 Polk		Zionsville	IN
30	Judith	Reginald		338 Kealing Ave		Indianapolis	IN
31	Charles	Polliet		430 Rimwood Li		Indianapolis	IN
32	Jean	Quillican	The Sharper Qu	1235 Washingto		Woodfield	IN
33	BJ	Radel	Fitzgerald's Gal	4481 Delaware		Greensburg	IN
34	Race	McSwaggart		3287 E. 34th Av		Danville	IN
35	Daniel	Jameson		6811 Ruby Villa		Fishers	IN
36	Delisa	Frattington		127 Park Ct.		Greenwood	IN
37	Gerald	Hollingsly	Victorian Prope	2769 Roundtabl		Indianapolis	IN
38	Brenda	McWhirter		10 Braeburn Wa		Mooresville	IN
39	Anselmo	Riatelli		412 Hollow Broc		Fishers	IN
40	Barbara	Farrar	Gallerie BF	6320 Epperson		Broad Ripple	IN
(AutoNumber)							

Record: |◄ ◄| 41 ►|►|►* of 41

Figure 6-4:
A new record is born.

Don't panic if the AutoNumber field seems to skip a number when it creates an entry for your new record (see Figure 6-5). The field remembers the last number it assigned and automatically inserts the next sequential number. When an AutoNumber field skips a number, it means that you probably entered (or at least *started* to enter) a record and then deleted it.

Customers : Table							
Customer ID	**First Name**	**Last Name**	**Organization N**	**Address1**	**Address2**	**City**	**St**
22	Sam	Gregory	Whimseco	1620 Edmondsc		Plainfield	IN
23	Amanda	Tillery		6 E. Market	Suite 201	Indianapolis	IN
24	Gretchen	Hankla	Daisyfield Shop	227 Daisyfield D		Noblesville	IN
25	Byron	Jiles		1122 Belden Dr.		Greenwood	IN
26	Clarence	Micy		385 Carlton Arr		Newton	IN
27	Mario	Schussler		1625 Euclid Ave		Fortville	IN
28	Harry	Nelson		19474 Vermeer		Carmel	IN
29	Callie	Logan	Eye 4 Antiques	227 Polk		Zionsville	IN
30	Judith	Reginald		338 Kealing Ave		Indianapolis	IN
31	Charles	Polliet		430 Rimwood Li		Indianapolis	IN
32	Jean	Quillican	The Sharper Qu	1235 Washingto		Woodfield	IN
33	BJ	Radel	Fitzgerald's Gal	4481 Delaware		Greensburg	IN
34	Race	McSwaggart		3287 E. 34th Av		Danville	IN
35	Daniel	Jameson		6811 Ruby Villa		Fishers	IN
36	Delisa	Frattington		127 Park Ct.		Greenwood	IN
37	Gerald	Hollingsly	Victorian Prope	2769 Roundtabl		Indianapolis	IN
38	Brenda	McWhirter		10 Braeburn Wa		Mooresville	IN
39	Anselmo	Riatelli		412 Hollow Broc		Fishers	IN
40	Barbara	Farrar	Gallerie BF	6320 Epperson		Broad Ripple	IN
43	Gary	Soforic		2907 N. Hamiltc		Indianapolis	
(AutoNumber)							

Record: |◄ ◄| 41 ►|►|►* of 41

Figure 6-5:
The record takes shape, despite its odd numbering.

Bo Peep needed the Find File option

In terms of job responsibility, Bo Peep had it easy. All she needed to do was keep an eye on a few animals and make sure that they stayed in roughly the same geographic spot. Now fast forward to the 1990s, as Ms. Peep rides herd over databases scattered across a hard drive or network. Imagine the havoc!

The friendly folks who created Access 97 know that databases, like errant sheep, tend to run off and get lost from time to time. That's why they included the Find File options at the bottom of the Open dialog box. Of the several options available, File name search is the most useful.

If you know at least part of the database's filename, type it into the File name box. Access 97 lists all databases in the current folder that match your search text. To make Access 97 work a little harder (and help you a little more), tell it to search

the *subfolders* in the current folder, as well. To do that, click on the Commands and Settings button (the little button on the top-right side of the dialog box that looks like a menu with a check mark on top of it) and choose Search Subfolders from the menu that pops up. Access 97 immediately scours the current folder *and* all folders underneath it, seeking your misplaced database.

The real power of the Find File system comes when you tell Access 97 to search a disk drive. Click on the Down arrow in the Look in box (in the upper-left corner of the Open window) and choose a local or network disk drive from the pull-down menu. Almost immediately, your computer starts churning through the folders in the disk drive, looking here, there, and everywhere for files that match your specifications.

3. **When you're done, either press Tab to add another record or, if you just wanted to add one record, simply go on about your business.**

    Because Access 97 automatically saves the new record while you're typing it, you have nothing more to do. Pretty cool!

If you change your mind and want to kill the new addition, choose Edit⇨Undo Saved Record or press Ctrl+Z and then click on Yes when Access 97 asks about deleting the record. If the Undo Saved Record menu choice isn't available, click in the record you just added and then choose Edit⇨Delete Record. As before, click on Yes when asked whether you're sure about the deletion.

Changing What's Already There

Even though your stuff is safely tucked away inside a table, you can easily reach in and make changes. In fact, editing your data is *so* easy that I'm not sure whether this is a good feature or a bad one.

Whenever you're browsing through a table, *please* be careful! Access 97 doesn't warn you before saving changes to a record — even if the changes are accidental. (If I were one of those preachy authors, I'd probably make a big, guilt-laden point about how this "feature" of Access 97 makes doing regular backups all the more important. Luckily, I'm not that kind of guy, so I'm not even going to bring the subject up.)

To change something inside a record, scroll through the table until you find the record that needs some adjusting. Click in the field you want to change, and the blinking toothpick cursor pops into the field.

If you have Microsoft's new IntelliMouse, use the wheel button to quickly spin through the table. For such a small innovation, that wheel is a big time-saver! Check out Chapter 8 for more details about using the IntelliMouse.

What you do next depends on what kind of change you want to make to the field:

- ✔ To replace the *entire* field, press F2 to highlight the data and then type the new information. The new entry replaces the old one cleanly.

- ✔ To repair a portion of the data in a field, click in the field and then use the right- and left-arrow keys to position the toothpick cursor exactly where you want to make the change. Press Backspace to remove characters to the left of the cursor; press Delete to remove them to the right. Insert new characters by typing.

- ✔ If you're in a time/date field and want to insert the current date, press Ctrl+; (semicolon). To insert the current time, press Ctrl+: (colon).

When you're done with the record, press Enter to save your changes. If you change your mind and want to restore the original data, press Esc or Ctrl+Z to cancel your edits. If you're on a rotary-dial phone, please wait for operator assistance (hmm — perhaps I've been making too many phone calls lately).

Don't press Enter until you're *positively sure* about the changes you typed. After you save them, the old data is gone — you can't go back.

Kicking Out Unwanted Records

There's no sense mourning over unneeded records. When the time comes to bid them adieu, do it quickly and painlessly. Here's how:

1. **With the table open, right-click on the button to the left of the record you want to delete.**

    The standard *I-right-clicked-on-something* pop-up menu appears.

Be sure that you click on the correct record before going on to the next step! Discovering the mistake now is much less painful than finding it in just a moment.

2. Choose Delete Record from the pop-up menu.

Access 97 does a truly cool screen-effect and visually swallows the old record.

3. When Access 97 displays the dialog box in Figure 6-6, pause and reflect once more about deleting the record.

Figure 6-6:
Access 97
asks the
fateful
question:
Are you
sure?

If you're sure, click on Yes and banish the record to oblivion.

If you're the slightest bit unsure, click on No and do some more thinking before exercising the Delete Record command on anything else in your table.

Instead of the Are you sure dialog box, Access 97 may display the box in Figure 6-7. This message means you *can't* delete that record, no matter how much you may want to. In this case, you're working with a table that's related to another one. Access 97 won't let you remove the record because records in another table are linked to the one you want to kill. Sorry — you can't get out of this one. If you *still* want to delete the record, ask a data hit man (or your local computer jockey) to do the dirty work for you, because there's more to this problem than meets the eye.

Figure 6-7:
Oops — this
record is
going
nowhere.

Recovering from a Baaaad Edit

I have only two suggestions for picking up the pieces from a bad edit. Unfortunately, neither is a super-cool elixir that magically restores your lost data. I wish I had better news to close the chapter with, but I'm fresh out of headlines.

First, double-check any change you make before saving it. If the change is important, *triple-check* it. When you're sure that it's right, press Enter and commit the change to the table. If you're not sure about the data, *don't* save the changes. Instead, get your questions answered first and then feel free to edit the record.

Second, keep a good backup so that you can quickly recover missing data and get on with your work. Good backups have no substitute. If you make good backups, the chance of losing data is greatly reduced, your boss will promote you, your significant other will unswervingly devote his or her life to you, and you may even win the lottery. (Truth be told, backups do only *one* of those things, but it's the thought that counts.)

Chapter 7

Making Your Table Think with Formats, Masks, and Validations

In This Chapter

▶ Finding where the settings live

▶ Better formatting for prettier data

▶ Keeping bad data out with input masks

▶ Performing detailed testing through validations

*S*cientists have incredibly detailed, long-winded explanations of what it means to "think," but my definition is much simpler. If you see dragons in the clouds, marvel at a child's playtime adventures, or wonder what makes flowers grow, you're thinking.

Whether you use my definition or one from the experts, one thing is for sure: Access 97 tables *don't* think. If you have nightmarish visions of reading this chapter and then accidentally unleashing The Table That Ate Microsoft's Competitors, have no fear; it's not going to happen. (After all, if such a scenario *could* happen, don't you think Microsoft would've arranged it by now?)

This chapter explains how to enlist your table's help to spot and prevent bad data from getting into your table. The chapter focuses on three different tools: *formats, masks,* and *validation rules.* These three tools may sound kinda technical, but you can handle them (trust me).

Each tool has its own section, so if you're looking for specific information, feel free to jump ahead. (And pay no attention to those computers discussing philosophy in the corner.)

Finding the Place to Make a Change

The first bit of knowledge you need is *where* to make all these cool changes to your table. Luckily, all three options are in the same place: the General tab of the Table Design window.

Use the following steps to put your table into Design view, and then flip to the appropriate section of the chapter for the details on applying a format, input mask, or validation to a field in your table.

1. **With the database file open, click on the table you want to adjust and then click <u>D</u>esign (see Figure 7-1).**

Figure 7-1:
Prepare for
some
serious
design work.

The table flips into Design view, showing its nerdish underbelly to the world.

By the way, if the table you want is already on-screen in Datasheet view, just click on the Design button on the far left side of the toolbar to get into Design view.

2. **Click on the name of the field you want to work on.**

The General tab in the Field Properties section (the bottom half of the window) displays the details of the current field, as seen in Figure 7-2. You're ready to do your stuff!

3. **Click in the appropriate box in the Field Properties section (along the bottom of the window) and type in your changes.**

Format, Input Mask, and Validation Rule each have a box. (There's also a box for Validation Text, but you have to look in the validations section later in this chapter to find out more about it — it's a secret for now.)

4. **If you want to work on other fields, go back to Step 2 and repeat the process.**

You can add one, two, or all three pieces of intelligence to a field at once. Access 97 automatically saves your changes when you click another field.

5. **When you're through, close the table to save your changes.**

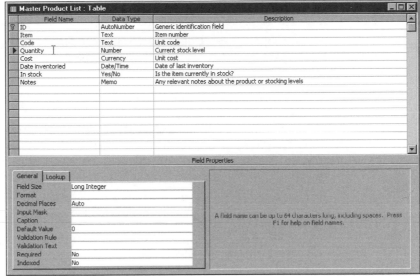

Figure 7-2:
Get ready
for some
work on the
Quantity
field.

Granted, using formats, masks, and validations involves many more details, but the steps to get started are the same no matter which tool you apply. The following sections tackle each tool individually, so continue on for full discussions of the tools' finer points.

To Format, Perchance to Better See

Formats only change the way you *see* your data on-screen, not how your data is actually stored in the table. Although formats don't directly catch errors, they *do* make your information look simply marvelous (and that's gotta be worth something these days).

Each field type has its own set of formats. Pay close attention to the type of field you're working with; applying the wrong format to a field is both pointless and frustrating (and goodness knows there are *enough* pointless and frustrating aspects of your computer without actively courting another one) because your data won't *ever* look right, regardless of how hard you try.

To prevent exactly that error, the following formatting information is organized by field type. Check the field type you're working with and then refer to the appropriate section for the available formatting options. By the way, if your format command doesn't work the first time — that happens to me, too — just double-check the field type and then review the format commands. In no time at all, you ferret out the problem.

Text and memo fields

You have four possibilities here. Unfortunately, no ready-made examples are built into the Format text box, unlike the other field types. I guess that means text and memo fields are tough and don't need the help.

Here are your four text and memo formatting options:

✔ The *greater than symbol* (>) makes all the text in that field appear in uppercase, regardless of how the text was entered. Although Access 97 stores the data *just as it was typed,* the data appears in uppercase only. To use this option, put a single greater than symbol in the Format text box.

✔ The *less than symbol* (<) does just the opposite of the greater than symbol. The less than symbol shows all that field's text in lowercase. If you entered the data in mixed case, it's still stored as lowercase. As with the greater than symbol, only the display is changed to protect the innocent. Apply this format by putting a single less than symbol in the Format text box.

✔ The *at sign* (@) forces Access 97 to display either a character or a space in the field. If the field data is smaller than the format, Access 97 adds extra spaces to fill up the format. For example, if a field uses @@@@@@ as its format but the field's data is only three characters long (such as *Tim* or *now*), Access 97 displays three spaces and *then* the data. If the field data is four characters long, the format pads the beginning of the entry with two spaces. See how the at sign works? (Kinda odd, isn't it?)

✔ The *ampersand* (&) is the default format. It means "display a character if there's one to display; otherwise don't do anything." Why create a special format for this option when it's what Access 97 does by default? I don't know . . . for now, it remains a mystery to me.

✔ By the way, you include one at sign or ampersand *for each character* in the field, unlike the greater than and less than symbols, which require only one symbol for the whole field.

Number and currency fields

The friendly folks at Microsoft did all the hard work for you on these two field types. They built the six most common formats into a pull-down menu right in the Format text box. To set a number or currency field format, click in the Format text box and then click on the down arrow that appears at the right side of the box. Figure 7-3 shows the pull-down menu, laden with your choices.

Hey Access, save my place!

This tip is a certified Nerd Trick, but it's so useful I *had* to take the chance and tell you about it. When entering data, sometimes you need to skip a text field because you don't have that particular information at hand. Wouldn't it be great if Access 97 automatically marked the field as blank as a reminder for you to come back and fill in the info later?

Access 97 can create such a custom text format for you, and you don't even have to be a master magician to pull off this trick. Here's how to do it:

Type **@;"Unknown"[Red]** into the field's Format text box.

This peculiar notation displays the word *Unknown* in red print if the field does not contain a value. You *must* type the command *exactly* like the example (quotation marks, square brackets, and all), or it doesn't work. Feel free to substitute your own word for *Unknown,* though — the command doesn't care what you put between the quotation marks.

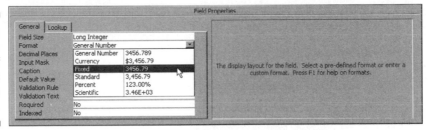

Figure 7-3: Choose the format of your dreams right from the menu.

Each format's given name is on the left side of the menu. The other side shows a sample of how the format works. Here's a quick rundown of the most common choices:

- **General Number:** This format is the Access 97 default. It merely displays whatever you put into the field without making any editorial adjustments to it.

- **Currency:** This format makes a standard number field look just like a currency field. It shows the data with two decimal places, substituting zeros if decimals aren't present to begin with. Currency format also adds the appropriate currency sign and punctuation, according to the Regional Settings in the Windows 95 Control Panel.

- **Fixed:** This format locks the field's data into a specific number of decimal places. By default, this format rounds to two decimal places. To specify a different number of decimal places, use the Decimal Places setting right below the Format setting.

✓ **Standard:** This format does the same thing as Fixed, but adds a thousands separator as well. Adjust the number of decimals by changing the Decimal Places setting.

✓ **Percent:** This format is especially for the percentages of life. It turns a simple decimal percentage such as .97 into the much prettier 97%. Remember to enter the data as a decimal (.97 instead of 97); otherwise Access 97 displays some truly awesome percentages! If your percentages display only as 0.00% or 1.00%, see the next paragraph for a solution.

If your entries automatically round to the nearest whole number and always display zeros in the decimal places, change the Field Size setting (right above Format) from Long Integer to Single. This tells Access 97 to remember the decimal part of the number. By default, Access 97 rounds the number to an integer as you enter it. (Stupid computers.)

Date/time fields

Like the Number and Currency format options, date/time fields have a ready-to-use set of formats available in a pull-down menu. Click in the Format text box and then click on the down arrow that appears on the box's right side, and the menu in Figure 7-4 dutifully pops down to serve you.

Figure 7-4:
A format for
every date,
and a date
for every
format.

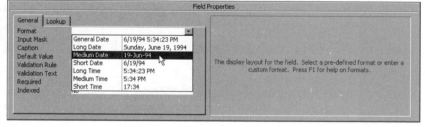

The choices are pretty self-explanatory, but I do have a couple of tips for you:

✓ When using one of the larger formats such as General Date or Long Date, make sure that the datasheet column is wide enough to display the whole date. Otherwise, the cool-looking date doesn't make sense because a major portion of it is missing.

✓ If the database is used by more than one person, choosing a format that provides *more* information rather than one that provides less is much better. My favorite is the Medium Date format, because it spells out the month and day. Otherwise, dates such as 3/7/95 may cause confusion, because people in different countries interpret that format differently.

Yes/No fields

You can only say so much about a field with three options. Your preset formatting choices are somewhat limited, as Figure 7-5 shows. By default, Yes/No fields are set to the Yes/No formatting (programmers are *so* clever, sometimes). Feel free to experiment with the other options, particularly if they make more sense in your table than Yes and No.

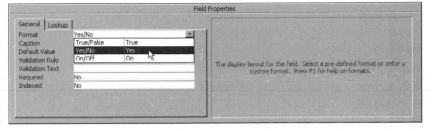

Figure 7-5:
The format
cupboard is
pretty bare.

To display your *own* choices instead of a boring Yes and No, you have to type a customized format. This procedure works very much like the custom text format earlier in this chapter. A good example format is something like this: `;"In stock"[Green];"REORDER"[Red]`. If an item is in stock, the text *In stock* appears in green. Otherwise, *REORDER* screams a warning in bright red. Substitute your own words for mine if you like, because Access 97 displays whatever you put between the quotes without making any editorial decisions about the content.

What Is That Masked Data?

Although they have a funny name, *input masks* are filters that allow you to enter only certain data into a field. When they're paired with validations (covered later in this chapter), the fields in your table are *very* well protected against bad information.

An input mask is just a series of characters that tells Access 97 what kind of data to expect in this field. If you want a field to contain all numbers and no letters, an input mask can do the job. It can also do the reverse (all letters and no numbers) and almost any combination in between. Input masks are stored in the Input Mask area of the field's General tab, along with everything else discussed in this chapter.

Each field in an Access 97 table (except a memo field) can have its own input mask. Before creating the mask, you have to know *exactly* what the field's data looks like. Creating a mask that allows only letters into a field doesn't do any good if your goal is to store street addresses. Know your data intimately *before* messing around with input masks.

Input masks work best with *short, highly consistent* data. Numbers and number/letter combinations that all look alike are excellent candidates. Part numbers, stock-keeping units, postal codes, phone numbers, and Social Security numbers beg for input masks to ensure that the right data gets into the field.

You create an input mask in one of two ways: You can either type in the mask manually or ask the Input Mask Wizard for some help. As luck would have it, the Input Mask Wizard isn't terribly bright — he only knows about text and date fields. And even then, he offers just a few options to make your life easier. To accomplish anything more means cracking your knuckles and doing it by hand.

Using the Input Mask Wizard

The Input Mask Wizard gleefully helps if you're making a mask for a phone number, Social Security number, United States zip code, or simple date and time field. Beyond those fields, he's clueless, so don't look for his help with anything other than text or time/date type fields.

To ask the wizard's help, go through these steps:

1. **With the database file open, click on the table you want to work with and then click on <u>D</u>esign.**

   The table flips into Design view.

2. **Click on the name of the field you want to adjust.**

   The General tab in the Field Properties section (the bottom half of the window) displays the details of the current field.

3. **Click on the Input Mask box.**

   The cursor hops into the Input Mask box. To the right of the box, a small button with three dots appears. That's the Build button, which comes into play in the next step.

 4. **Click on the Build button at the right side of the Input Mask text box.**

   The wizard appears, making a glorious entrance just like in Figure 7-6.

   You can use the wizard only with text and date fields. Don't tempt the wizard's wrath by rousing it to work with another kind of field.

   If Access 97 complains that the Wizard isn't installed, you didn't include the developer tools option while installing Access 97 (don't fret if you get this error message — I did, too). To fix the problem, get out your original Access 97 or Office 97 CD-ROM and put it in your CD-ROM drive. Close Access 97 and then choose Start⇔Settings⇔Control Panel. In the Control Panel window, double-click Add/Remove Programs. Follow the prompts to install the Access 97 developer tools. If you're in a corporate environment and don't have the original master CD-ROM, contact your computer support folks for help.

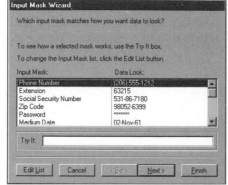

Figure 7-6:
The Input
Mask
Wizard
doesn't do
much, but it
tries hard.

5. **Scroll through the list of available input masks to find what you want. Click on your choice and then click on Next.**

   The dialog box displays the sordid code behind the mask, plus some other information (see Figure 7-7).

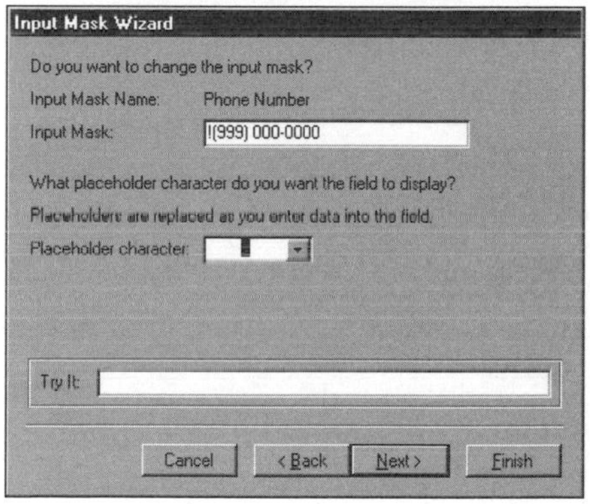

Figure 7-7:
Here's what
the wizard
says you
need.

   If you chose the Password option (refer to Figure 7-6), nothing is left for you to do, so click on Finish.

6. **If you want to play with the input mask and see whether it *really* does what you want, click in the Try It area at the bottom of the dialog box. When you're done, click on Finish to use the mask with your field.**

   The chosen mask appears in the Input Mask area on the table design screen. (You can click on Cancel to call off the sordid mask affair and make the wizard go away.)

If you click on <u>N</u>ext instead of <u>F</u>inish, the wizard offers you an arcane choice about storing characters along with your data. The wizard wants to know whether you want the dashes, slashes, and parentheses that the input mask displays to be stored in your table along with the data you typed. The default is No, which I recommend sticking with. Click on <u>F</u>inish to complete the process.

Making a mask by hand

Few projects are more gratifying than making something yourself. Building an input mask with your bare hands, raw nerve, and these instructions *may* give you that same feeling of accomplishment. (If so, please seek professional help soon — you're in danger of becoming a technoid.)

✔ The stuff that input masks *do* isn't terribly complicated, but a finished mask often *looks* complicated. Don't worry, though. After you get the hang of it, building powerful input masks is easy.

✔ My friends told me the same thing about water skiing, but during my first lesson, I suspected that they were *really* trying to drown me and make it look like an innocent water sports accident. You have my word that building input masks in Access 97 isn't anything like that. (Besides, how can you drown in front of a computer?)

With that confidence-building introduction behind you, get ready to roll up your sleeves and plunge your hands in the alphabetic goop of input masks. Designing and using an input mask takes just a few steps:

1. **On a piece of paper, write an example of the data that the mask is supposed to let into the table.**

   As I mention earlier in the chapter, knowing your data really *is* the first step in the input mask process.

   If the information you're storing has subtle variations (such as part numbers that end in either a letter/number or letter/letter combination), include examples of the various possibilities so that your input mask accepts them all.

2. **Write a simple description of the data, including which elements are required and which are optional.**

   If your sample is a part number that looks like 728816ABC7, write **six numbers, three letters, one number; all parts are required**. Remember to allow for the variations, if you have any. The difference between *one number* and *one letter or number* can be crucial.

Required information must be entered into the field (such as a phone number). *Optional* elements are just that — optional (such as an area code or extension number). Access 97 uses different codes for required and optional data, so you need to note the difference.

3. Using the codes in Table 7-1, create an input mask for your data.

Because you know what kind of data you're storing (numbers, letters, or either one), how many characters you need, and whether each one is required or optional, working through the table and creating the mask is easy.

To include a dash, slash, or parenthesis in your mask, put a backslash (\) in front of it. To include more than one character, put quote marks around them. For example, the mask for a phone number with an area code is !\(999") "000\-0000. This mask uses both the backslash and quote mark to put parentheses around the area code plus a space between the area code and phone number. (See the sidebar "The exclamation point: To know it is to love it" to find out why I included an exclamation point in this example.)

Here's a pop quiz, just to see whether you're paying attention. In the example, is the area code optional or required? What about the phone number itself? Why? Write a long, detailed answer on a very small piece of paper; then rip it to shreds and throw it like confetti into the air. Wasn't that fun?

4. If your field includes letters and you want them to always be uppercase, add a greater than symbol (>) to the beginning of your mask.

To make the letters lowercase, use a less than symbol (<) instead.

You're ready to tell Access 97 about your input mask.

5. Follow the steps at the beginning of the chapter ("Finding the Place to Make a Change"); when you get to Step 3, click in the Input Mask box.

The blinking toothpick cursor hops into the box, ready for action.

6. Carefully type your finished mask into the Input Mask area of Field Properties (see Figure 7-8).

Don't worry if the mask looks like a text version of the Frankenstein monster. Beauty is optional in the world of technology.

7. At the end of the mask, add ;;_ (two semi-colons and an underscore character).

These three characters tell Access 97 to display an underscore where you want each letter to appear. This step isn't required, but I think that input masks make more sense with this option. Your mileage may vary.

8. Click on the Table View button on the toolbar to check out your handiwork.

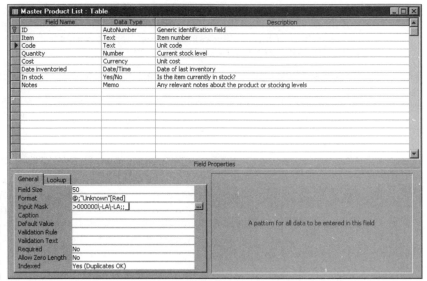

Figure 7-8:
Putting a
mask on the
Code field.

The exclamation point: To know it is to love it

Getting to know the exclamation point took me a while. After all, my input masks seemed very happy without it. Even the explanation in the Access 97 online Help file didn't change my mind. (I suppose that if the Help file's explanation had made *sense,* it may have had a better chance.)

While playing with the phone number example, I *finally* realized what the exclamation point does and why it's so useful. The exclamation point tells Access 97 to fill up the field from the *right* instead of the *left.* Although this notion may sound like the unintelligible ramblings of an over-caffeinated nerd, it really is an important point. Let me show you why.

In the phone number example, the area code is optional, but the number itself is required. If I leave the exclamation point *out* of the input mask, Access 97 lets me skip the area code and type a

phone number into the phone number spaces. Everything looks fine until I press Enter. Then my seven-digit phone number displays as (555) 121-2. Eww — not exactly what I had in mind. That's because Access 97 filled the mask from the *left,* starting with the optional numbers in the area code (the numbers I didn't enter).

By adding the exclamation point to the input mask, Access 97 takes my data and fills the mask *from the right.* This time, the phone number appears on-screen as ( ) 555-1212, which is what I wanted all along.

By the way, the exclamation point can go anywhere in the input mask, but try to get into the habit of putting it either at the beginning or the end. I suggest making the exclamation point the first character in the mask, simply because you won't overlook it in that position.

Try typing something into the now-masked field. The input mask should prevent you from entering something incorrectly. If it doesn't work, take the table back into Design view (click on the Design View button on the left side of the toolbar) and make some repairs.

If you're adding a mask to an existing table, the mask doesn't ferret out incorrect data that's *already* in the table. You have to click on each entry in the masked field (yes, that means clicking on this field in *every* record of the table) in order to check it. If something is wrong, Access 97 tells you, but not until you click.

Table 7-1	Codes for the Input Mask	
Kind of Characters	*Required Code*	*Optional Code*
Digits (0 to 9) only	0 (zero)	9
Digits and +/- signs	*(not available)*	# (U.S. pound sign)
Letters (A to Z) only	L	? (question mark)
Letters or digits only	A	a (must be lowercase)
Any character or space	& (ampersand)	C

Validations: The Digital Breathalyzer Test

Your third (and, arguably, most powerful) tool in the War Against Bad Data is the *validation*. With a validation, Access 97 actually tests the incoming data to make sure that it's what you want in the table. If the data isn't right, the validation displays an error message (you get to choose what it says!) and makes you try the entry again.

Like the other options in this chapter, validations are stored in the General tab of the Field Properties area. Two spaces relate to validations: Validation Rule and Validation Text. The rule is the actual validation itself. The text is the error message you want Access 97 to display when some data that violates the validation rule wanders in.

Validations work best with number, currency, and date fields. Creating a validation for a text field is possible, but the validations usually get *very* complicated *very* fast. In the name of protecting your sanity and hairline, Table 7-2 contains some ready-to-use validations that cover the most common needs. They're organized by field type, so finding the validation rule that suits your purpose is easy.

I include different kinds of examples to show off the power of the logical operators that validations use. Feel free to mix and match with the operators. Play around and see what you can come up with!

- ✓ When using AND, remember that both sides of the validation rule must be true before the rule is met.

- ✓ With OR, only one side of the rule needs to be true for the whole rule to be true.

- ✓ Be careful when combining >= and <= examples. Accidentally coming up with one that won't *ever* be true (such as <= 0 And >= 100) is too easy!

Table 7-2	Validations for Many Occasions	
Field Type	*Validation Rule*	*Definition*
Number	> 0	Must be greater than zero
Number	<> 0	Cannot be zero
Number	> 0 And < 100	Must be between 0 and 100 (noninclusive)
Number	>= 0 And <= 100	Must be between 0 and 100 (inclusive)
Number	<= 0 Or >= 100	Must be less than 0 or greater than 100 (inclusive)
Date	>= Date ()	Must be today's date or later
Date	>= Date () Or Is Null	Must be today's date, later, or blank
Date	< Date ()	Must be earlier than today's date
Date	>= #1/1/90# And <= Date ()	Must be between January 1, 1990, and today (inclusive)

Chapter 8
Making Your Datasheets Dance

• •

In This Chapter
▶ Wandering around your datasheet

▶ Adjusting column width, row height, and more

▶ Seeing the datasheet in a whole new font

▶ Changing the background

• •

*H*aving your new datasheet look and act just like every *other* datasheet is pretty boring. Where's the creativity in that? Where's the individuality? Where's the life, liberty, and pursuit of ultimate coolness?

Granted, Access 97 *is* a database program, and databases aren't generally known for being the life of the party. But that doesn't mean you're trapped into a monotonous world of look-alike datasheets. This chapter explores the tools at your disposal to turn even the most dreary datasheet into a slick-looking, easy-to-navigate presentation of your data.

The following pages focus on datasheet tricks — things to do when you're working with information in a datasheet. These tricks work with datasheets from both tables and dynasets, so use them to amble through and spruce up every datasheet in sight.

If you haven't heard about dynasets yet, don't worry. They're covered in Part III.

Wandering Here, There, and Everywhere

When a table appears in Datasheet view, Access 97 presents you with a window to your data. That window displays a certain number of rows and columns, but (unless you have a really small table) what's shown certainly isn't the whole enchilada. To see more, you need to move through the table — which means moving your window around to see what else is out there.

Access 97 offers several ways to hike through a datasheet. Which method you choose depends on how far you want to go:

- **To move from field to field:** Use the right- and left-arrow keys ($\rightarrow \leftarrow$). Clicking in the arrows on either end of the horizontal scroll bar does the same thing using the mouse.

- **To move between records:** Try the up- and down-arrow keys ($\uparrow\downarrow$). If you're a mouse-oriented person, click in the arrows at the ends of the vertical scroll bar.

- **To display a new page of data:** The PgUp and PgDn keys come in handy (depending on your keyboard, these may be called Page Up and Page Down, instead). PgUp and PgDn scroll vertically through the datasheet; Ctrl+PgUp and Ctrl+PgDn scroll horizontally. Clicking in either scroll bar does the same thing.

Table 8-1 looks at the process from a keystroke-by-keystroke point of view. Between the preceding movement tips and the following table, you now know just about every possible way to move through an Access 97 datasheet.

Table 8-1	Moving through a Table
Keystroke or Control	*What It Does*
Ctrl+End	Jumps to the last field in the last record of the table
Ctrl+Home	Jumps to the first field in the first record of the table
Ctrl+PgDn	Scrolls one screen to the right
Ctrl+PgUp	Scrolls one screen to the left
$\downarrow$	Moves down one record in the table
End	Goes to the last field in the current record
Home	Goes to the first field in the current record
Horizontal scroll bar	Scrolls right or left one window at a time through the table
$\leftarrow$	Moves one field to the left in the current record
IntelliMouse wheel	Turn the wheel to scroll up or down three records at a time through the table (only available with IntelliPoint mouse and driver software)
IntelliMouse wheel button	Press the wheel like a button and it becomes a super-arrow key; scroll one row or column at a time through the table (only available with IntelliPoint mouse and driver software)
PgDn	Scrolls one screen down

Keystroke or Control	What It Does
PgUp	Scrolls one screen up
→	Moves one field to the right in the current record
↑	Moves up one record in the table
Vertical scroll bar	Scrolls up or down one window at a time through the table

Seeing More (Or Less) of Your Data

First on the datasheet tune-up list is fiddling with the look of your datasheet. You have plenty to fiddle with, too. At first blush, your datasheet looks pretty mundane, much like Figure 8-1. To perk it up a bit, you can change the column width, row height, and column order, and you can lock a column in place while the others scroll around it. Heck, you can even make columns temporarily disappear.

Each of the following sections explores one technique for changing the way your data looks. You can use one option (such as changing the column width) or a number of options — you make the call. Each adjustment is independent of the others. Plus, these changes don't affect your actual data at all — they just make the data appear differently on-screen.

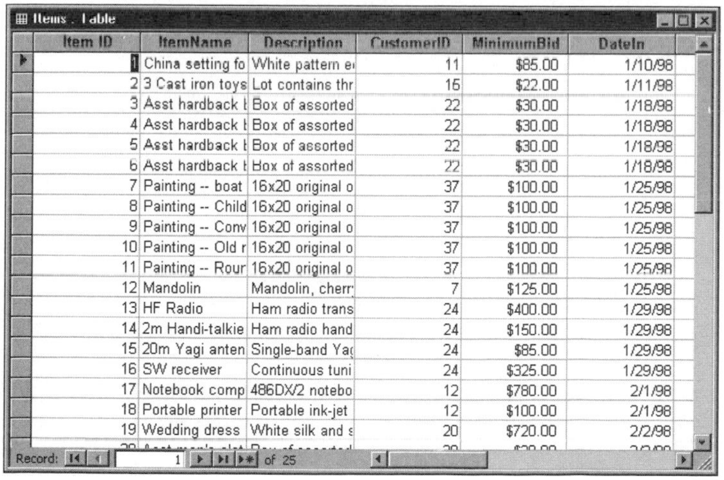

Figure 8-1:
Both the
ItemName
and
Description
columns are
brutally
clipped.

Item ID	ItemName	Description	CustomerID	MinimumBid	DateIn
1	China setting fo	White pattern e	11	$85.00	1/10/98
2	3 Cast iron toys	Lot contains thr	15	$22.00	1/11/98
3	Asst hardback b	Box of assorted	22	$30.00	1/18/98
4	Asst hardback b	Box of assorted	22	$30.00	1/18/98
5	Asst hardback b	Box of assorted	22	$30.00	1/18/98
6	Asst hardback b	Box of assorted	22	$30.00	1/18/98
7	Painting -- boat	16x20 original o	37	$100.00	1/25/98
8	Painting -- Child	16x20 original o	37	$100.00	1/25/98
9	Painting -- Conv	16x20 original o	37	$100.00	1/25/98
10	Painting -- Old r	16x20 original o	37	$100.00	1/25/98
11	Painting -- Rour	16x20 original o	37	$100.00	1/25/98
12	Mandolin	Mandolin, cherr	7	$125.00	1/25/98
13	HF Radio	Ham radio trans	24	$400.00	1/29/98
14	2m Handi-talkie	Ham radio hand	24	$150.00	1/29/98
15	20m Yagi anten	Single-band Yag	24	$85.00	1/29/98
16	SW receiver	Continuous tuni	24	$325.00	1/29/98
17	Notebook comp	486DX/2 notebo	12	$780.00	2/1/98
18	Portable printer	Portable ink-jet	12	$100.00	2/1/98
19	Wedding dress	White silk and s	20	$720.00	2/2/98

Record: 1 of 25

IntelliMouse: a new way to get around

If you're blessed with a new Microsoft IntelliMouse and its special IntelliPoint driver software, you have an extra tool for moving through your Access 97 datasheets. Between the two regular mouse buttons, the IntelliMouse sports a wheel that acts as a third button.

✔ Rolling the wheel scrolls up and down through your datasheet three lines at a time.

✔ Clicking and dragging with the wheel button moves the window around the datasheet in whichever direction you move the mouse.

(This maneuver works just like a normal click and drag, except that you're using the wheel button instead of the left mouse button.)

If you spend a great deal of time with Access 97 or jumping among the Office 97 applications, I suggest you take the new mouse for a test drive. Each program applies the wheel button a little differently, but *all* the programs (and even Windows 95 itself) use it to make your life a little easier.

Most of the commands work from the mouse, but some of them send you back to the menu bar. If a command is in both places, it works the same either way.

After making any of these adjustments to your table, be sure to tell Access 97 to save the table's formatting changes, or all your hard work is lost forever. To notify Access 97, either select File⇨Save from the menu bar or simply close the window. If any unsaved changes are in the table when you try to close the window, Access 97 automatically prompts you to save the new formatting.

Changing the column width

Even though Access 97 is pretty smart, it has trouble figuring out how wide to make a column. In fact, it usually just gives up and sets all the column widths identically, leaving some far too wide and others way too narrow. Pretty wimpy solution for a powerful program, if you ask me.

Setting a new column width is a quick operation. Here's what to do:

1. **With your table in Datasheet view, put the mouse pointer on the vertical bar to the right of the field name (see Figure 8-2).**

   The mouse pointer changes into a bar with arrows sticking out of each side.

2. **Click and hold the left mouse button while moving the mouse appropriately.**

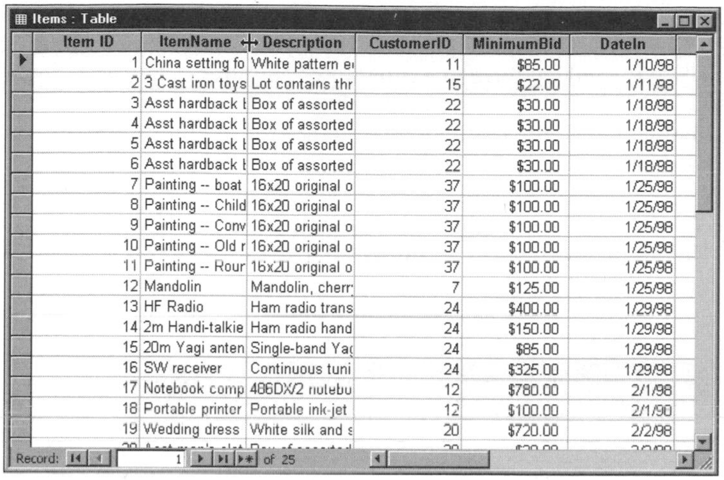

Figure 8-2:
Ready to
widen the
column.

To make the column wider, move the mouse to the right. To make it smaller, move the mouse left.

3. When the width is just right, let up on the mouse button.

The column is locked into its new size, as Figure 8-3 shows.

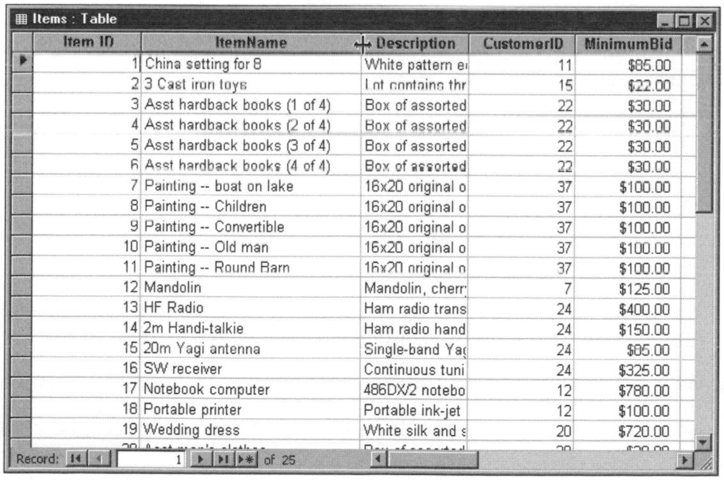

Figure 8-3:
That looks a
whole lot
better.

Changing the row height

Access 97 does a little better in the row height department than it does with column widths. It automatically leaves enough room to separate the rows while displaying plenty of information on-screen. Access 97 still has room for improvement, though, because you can't see all the data in your table's longest fields. Changing the row height fixes this problem by showing more data in each field while displaying the same number of columns on-screen.

Like changing column width, adjusting the row height takes only a couple of mouse clicks:

1. **While viewing your table in Datasheet view, put the mouse pointer in the far left side of the window on the line between any two rows in your spreadsheet (see Figure 8-4).**

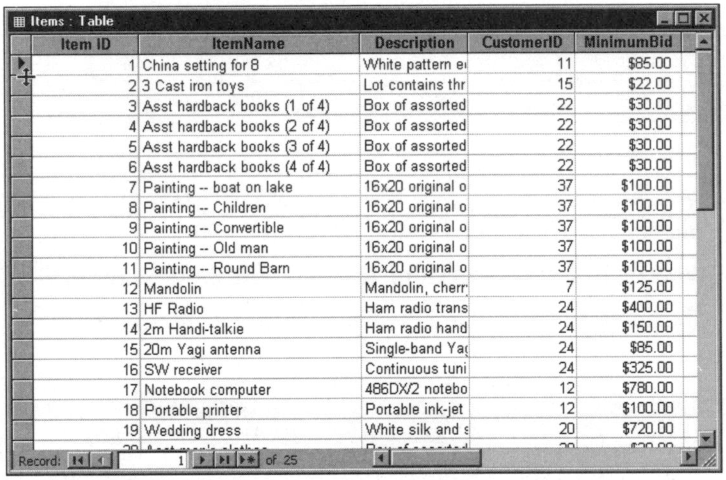

Item ID	ItemName	Description	CustomerID	MinimumBid
1	China setting for 8	White pattern ei	11	$85.00
2	3 Cast iron toys	Lot contains thr	15	$22.00
3	Asst hardback books (1 of 4)	Box of assorted	22	$30.00
4	Asst hardback books (2 of 4)	Box of assorted	22	$30.00
5	Asst hardback books (3 of 4)	Box of assorted	22	$30.00
6	Asst hardback books (4 of 4)	Box of assorted	22	$30.00
7	Painting -- boat on lake	16x20 original o	37	$100.00
8	Painting -- Children	16x20 original o	37	$100.00
9	Painting -- Convertible	16x20 original o	37	$100.00
10	Painting -- Old man	16x20 original o	37	$100.00
11	Painting -- Round Barn	16x20 original o	37	$100.00
12	Mandolin	Mandolin, cherr	7	$125.00
13	HF Radio	Ham radio trans	24	$400.00
14	2m Handi-talkie	Ham radio hand	24	$150.00
15	20m Yagi antenna	Single-band Ya	24	$85.00
16	SW receiver	Continuous tuni	24	$325.00
17	Notebook computer	486DX/2 notebo	12	$780.00
18	Portable printer	Portable ink-jet	12	$100.00
19	Wedding dress	White silk and s	20	$720.00

Figure 8-4:
One taller row, coming right up (or is that down?).

The mouse pointer changes into a horizontal bar with arrows sticking out vertically.

2. **Click and hold the left mouse button; then move the mouse to change the row height.**

Move the mouse down to make the row higher. Move it up to squash the row and put the squeeze on your data.

3. **When the row height is where you want it, release the mouse button.**

Access 97 redisplays the table with its new row height (see Figure 8-5).

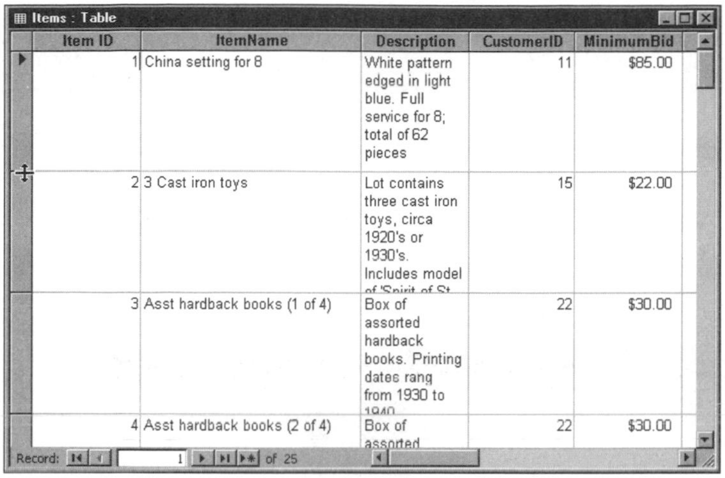

Figure 8-5:
The data
automatically
fills the new
field space.

Reorganizing the columns

When you laid out the table, you put quite a bit of thought into which field came
after which other field. Most of the time, your data looks just the way you want
it on-screen, but occasionally you need to stir things up a bit.

To move a field to a different place on the datasheet, use these steps:

1. **Click on the field name of the column you want to move; then click and
hold the left mouse button.**

   The whole column darkens, with a smaller box at the bottom of the
   column, and the mouse pointer changes to an arrow (see Figure 8-6).

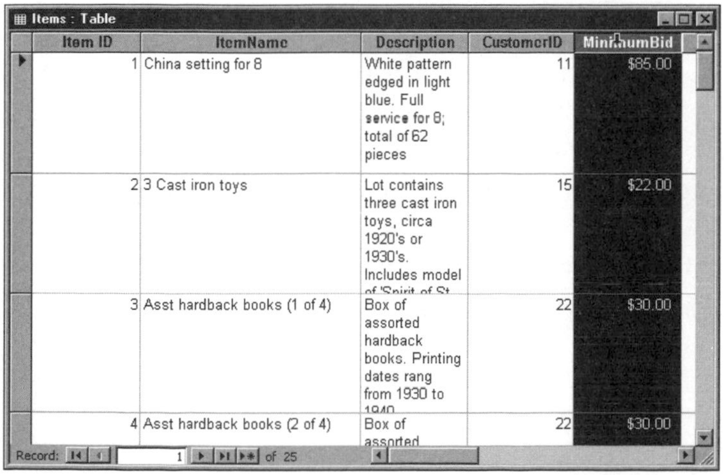

Figure 8-6:
You're ready
to move that
column.

2. **Drag the column to its new destination.**

   As you move the mouse, a dark bar moves between the columns, showing you where the column will land when you release the mouse button. If you accidentally let go of the button before the dark bar appears, Access 97 doesn't move the column. In that case, start again with Step 1 (and keep a tight grip on that mouse).

3. **When the column is in place, let up on the mouse button.**

   The column, data and all, moves to the new spot (see Figure 8-7).

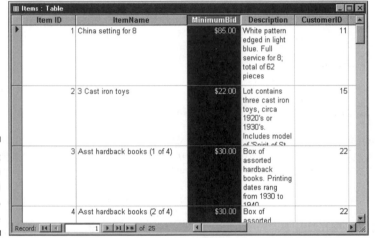

Figure 8-7:
Bringing the column in for a nice, soft landing.

Hiding a column

Hiding a column is one of those features that seem totally unimportant until the moment you need them, and then they're worth their weight in gold. If you want to temporarily not display a particular column, just hide the little fellow. The data is still in the table, but it doesn't appear on-screen. Too cool, eh?

To hide a column, follow these steps:

1. **With your table in Datasheet view, right-click on the name of the column to hide.**

   The whole column goes dark, and a pop-up menu appears.

2. **Choose Hide Columns from the menu (see Figure 8-8).**

   {Poof!} The column vanishes.

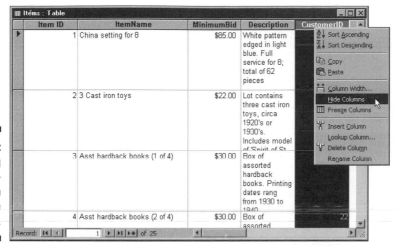

Figure 8-8:
Playing
hide-and-
seek with
the
columns.

To hide more than one column at a time, click and drag across the names of the columns you want to squirrel away and then choose Format➪Hide Columns.

When you're ready to bring back the temporarily indisposed column, do this:

1. **Choose Format➪Unhide Columns.**

   Up pops a small dialog box listing all the fields in the current table. The fields with a check mark in the box next to them are already displayed.

2. **Click in the check box next to each field you want to see on-screen again and then click on Close (see Figure 8-9).**

   Depending on the number of fields in the list, you may have to scroll around to find all the fields.

Figure 8-9:
Aha — I
found its
hiding
place!

Making design changes in Datasheet view — danger, Will Robinson!

So far, everything in this chapter changes the look of the datasheet without doing anything to the table underneath it. Moving or hiding columns, changing column widths, adjusting row heights — all these are innocuous settings that simply make your digital world a prettier place.

The story changes with the *Rename Column, Insert Column, Insert Lookup Column,* and *Delete Column* options that appear on the right-click pop-up menu. These choices actually *change* the structure of your table, so go slow and treat them carefully!

Rename Column changes the field name. Insert Column adds a new column on the datasheet, which translates into a new field in the table. Insert Lookup Column starts the Lookup Wizard and helps you insert a column for data pulled in from another table. Delete Column is pretty self-explanatory (remember that Access 97 undoes only the *last* action you took, so don't delete anything until you're sure that it's the right thing to kill).

You alter the table's structure with these options. Have a look through Chapter 9 for more about these options and how to use them safely. (It's *that* important.)

Freezing a column

If you have many fields in a table, they don't all fit in the window. As you scroll from one side of the table to the other, fields are constantly appearing on one side of the window and disappearing from the other. What if you want to keep looking at a column way over on one side of the table *while* looking at fields on the other side?

The secret is to freeze the column in place. This action locks a column into the left side of the window so that it just sits there while you scroll merrily back and forth through the table. Of course, an *unfreeze* step goes along with it — you don't want your tables catching cold, do you?

Here are the steps to freezing a column:

1. **Right-click on the name of the column you want to freeze.**

   The column turns dark, and the ever-anticipated pop-up menu appears.

2. **Select Freeze Columns from the pop-up menu.**

   The column is now locked in place. You can now scroll back and forth through your table with impunity (and you don't have any restrictions, either).

If you want to freeze more than one column, select the columns by holding down the Control key and clicking on the column names. When all the columns you want to freeze are highlighted, choose Format⇨Freeze Columns from the menu bar. All highlighted columns are immediately frozen in place.

When you want to thaw out the columns, choose Format⇨Unfreeze All Columns.

Fonting Around with Your Table

Being your basic, business-oriented program, Access 97 displays your table in a basic, business-oriented font. You're not stuck with that font choice forever, though (a good thing, too, because that font is boring). You have control over the font, style, and even the *color* that your data appears in. The decision is up to you, so why not live on the edge and try a new look on your table?

These settings apply to the *entire table*, not just a particular row or column.

To change the font, style, or color of your table, follow these steps:

1. **With the table in Datasheet view, choose Format⇨Font.**

   The font dialog box elbows its way onto the screen.

2. **Click on your choice from the Font list on the left side of the box (see Figure 8-10).**

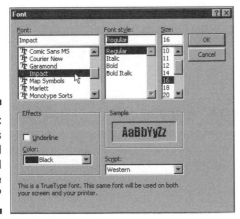

Figure 8-10:
This font is cool, but will it look good on the table?

Access 97 previews the font in the Sample box on the right side of the dialog box.

Picking a TrueType font instead of the other options is best. TrueType fonts have the little double-T symbol next to them in the list.

3. Click on the preferred style in the Font style list.

Some fonts may not have all the common style options (normal, bold, italic, and bold italic). Exactly which options you have depends on how the fonts were loaded onto your system. For more about fonts and font files, check out *Windows 95 For Dummies,* by Andy Rathbone (IDG Books Worldwide, Inc.).

4. To select a different size, click on a number in the Size list.

As with style, not every font is available in all sizes.

- If you chose a TrueType font back in Step 2, sizing isn't a problem because TrueType fonts are scaleable (Windows simply makes them whatever size it needs).

- If you clicked on a printer font in Step 2 (the ones with a picture of a printer next to them), then you may be limited to just a few size options.

The moral of the story is to use TrueType fonts as much as possible.

5. If you want a new color, click on the arrow next to the Color box and pick your favorite from the drop-down menu.

You're almost done — now's a good time to look at the Sample box and see whether your choices look good together. If they don't, click Cancel and start over with Step 1.

6. Click on OK to apply your font selections.

The datasheet now displays your table in its new finery (see Figure 8-11).

Giving Your Data the 3-D Look

This final change is purely cosmetic, but even tables like to feel good about how they look. Access 97 gives you a couple of cool looking, three-dimensional options for your datasheet. If a solution to the problem of boring-looking datasheets exists, 3-D must be it (because 3-D options serve no other purpose).

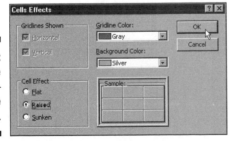

Figure 8-11:
Ewww . . .
back to the
font drawing
board.

Item ID	ItemName	MinimumE	Descripti	Customer	DateIn
1	China setting for 8	$85.00	White pattern edged in light blue.	11	1/10/98
2	3 Cast iron toys	$22.00	Lot contains three cast iron	15	1/11/98
3	Asst hardback books (1 of 4)	$30.00	Box of assorted hardback books.	22	1/18/98
4	Asst hardback books (2 of 4)	$30.00	Box of assorted hardback	22	1/18/98

To turn your datasheet into a cool work of art, follow these steps:

1. **Choose Format➪Cells from the menu bar.**

   The Cells Effects dialog box pops onto the screen.

2. **For a cool 3-D look, click on either the Raised or Sunken radio buttons in the Cell Effect area (see Figure 8-12).**

Figure 8-12:
The choice
is made —
let's see
how I did.

The Sample box previews your selection. (I think that Raised looks cool and is easy to work with, but that's personal preference.)

If you don't want the *gridlines* (the lines separating the rows and columns) cluttering up your datasheet, leave Cell Effect set to Flat and click in the Gridlines Shown check boxes so that they're blank.

3. **Click on OK when you're done.**

The datasheet changes according to your selections, just like Figure 8-13.

Item ID	ItemName	MinimumBid	Description	CustomerID	DateIn
1	China setting for 8	$85.00	White pattern edged in light blue. Full service for 8; total of 62 pieces	11	1/10/98
2	3 Cast iron toys	$22.00	Lot contains three cast iron toys, circa 1920's or 1930's. Includes model of 'Spirit of St	15	1/11/98
3	Asst hardback books (1 of 4)	$30.00	Box of assorted hardback books. Printing dates rang from 1930 to 1940	22	1/18/98
4	Asst hardback books (2 of 4)	$30.00	Box of assorted hardback books. Printing dates rang from 1940 to	22	1/18/98

Record: 1 of 25

Figure 8-13: That works for me!

Unless you're really good with color combinations, leave the color settings alone. Because I regularly attempt to wear stripes and plaid together, I let Access 97 handle this option on its own.

Chapter 9

Table Remodeling Tips for the Do-It-Yourselfer

· ·

· ·

*R*emodeling is a part of life — at least it is if you're a home owner. A touch of paint here, a new wall there, and pretty soon your entire house is a mess, because the jobs never *quite* get finished. For example, I think that my wife has given up hope that I'll finish updating the electrical outlets. I've been working on the job for three years now, and I still have eight outlets to go. I fix about one outlet per quarter, usually spurred to action because I need to plug in something that doesn't work in the old outlet.

My databases, on the other hand, are completely organized and up-to-date. When I start changing a table, I finish the job right then and there. My wife says the difference has to do with my aversion to physical labor, but the real reason is the tools that Access 97 provides to get the job done.

Whether you're adding a new field, removing an old one, or making some subtle changes to your table, this chapter guides you through the process. Be sure to read the chapter's first section before attempting any serious surgery on your tables. Some grim pitfalls await you out there, and I want you to miss them cleanly.

Even though you can do some of the tasks in this chapter (specifically, add and delete columns) through Datasheet view, I don't generally recommend that approach. Making a mistake and wreaking havoc in your table is too easy when you attempt some of these steps in Datasheet view. Instead, make your changes through Design view, where you're in full control of the process. The steps in this chapter walk you through making such changes in Design view.

This Chapter Can Be Hazardous to Your Table's Design

I'm all for starting on a pleasant note, but *now* isn't the time.

To properly set this chapter's mood, I wanted to begin with pictures of items that have a natural *don't touch* sign on them — such as snapping alligators, roaring lions, and the *please audit me* box on your income tax form. My editor suggested that I use a warning icon instead. In the name of compromise (and because finding good editors is so hard these days), I agreed.

Tread lightly in this chapter. You're tinkering with the infrastructure of your entire database system. A mistake (particularly of the *delete* kind) can cause massive hair loss, intense frustration, and large-scale data corruption. Put simply, it would be bad.

Putting a New Field Next to the Piano

No matter how well you plan, sometimes you just forget to include a field in your table design. Or, after using the table for a while, you discover some unforeseen data that needs a home. Regardless of the circumstances, Access 97 doesn't make a big deal out of adding a new field.

Is it a column or a field?

The answer to this lyrical question — is it a column or a field — is *yes.* In Access 97 lingo, *columns* and *fields* are really the same critter. When you insert a column into a table in Datasheet view, you actually add a new field to every record. If you build a field in Design view, you create a new column for the datasheet. Either way you say (or do) it, you get the same result.

So when is a field *different* from a column? It's different when you edit the data in a particular record. If you change one person's postal code in an address table, you aren't changing the whole column. Rather, you're changing the value of that record's field.

Here's a tip to help you keep the two terms straight. When Access 97 talks about *columns,* it means *this field in every record of the table.* When the program refers to a *field,* it usually means one entry in a particular record.

Dropping a new field into your table takes just a moment. Before starting this project, make sure that you know the following bits of information:

✔ Typical examples of the data the field will hold

✔ The field type (text, number, yes/no, and so on)

✔ The size the field needs to be to hold the data, if applicable

✔ What you plan to call the field

✔ Where the field fits in the table design

With that information in hand, you're ready to make a new field. To add the field in Design view, follow these steps:

1. **With the database file open, click on the table you want to work with and then click on Design.**

   The table structure appears in Design view.

2. **Highlight the row *below* where you want to insert your new field by clicking on the row button at the far left.**

   These instructions make more sense when you look at Figure 9-1.

   This action highlights the entire row. Pretty cool, eh?

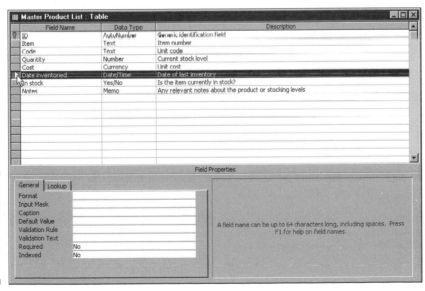

Figure 9-1:
Click on the
button on
the left to
highlight an
entire row.

3. **Choose Insert⇨Row.**

   A blank row appears *above* the row you clicked in Step 1.

4. **Click in the Field Name area of the new row and then type the name of your new field.**

   The field name flows smoothly into the text area.

5. **Press Tab to move into the Data Type area.**

6. **Click on the down arrow and pick the data type from the pull-down list (see Figure 9-2).**

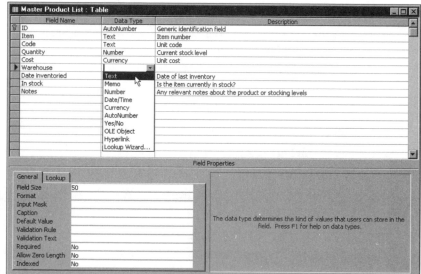

Figure 9-2:
Pick a data
type from
the list.

If you're uncertain which data type is for you, refer back to "Frolicking through the Fields," in Chapter 4.

7. **Press Tab to hop into the Description area and then type a short description of the data in this field.**

   Although this step is optional, I *highly* recommend adding a description.

8. **Save your changes by choosing File⇨Save or by clicking on the Save button on the toolbar.**

   Congratulations — I knew you could do it.

Saying Good-bye to a Field (And All Its Data)

Times change, and so do your data storage needs. When one of your fields is past its prime, send it to that Great Table in the Sky by deleting it from your design. Getting rid of the field *also* throws out all the data *in* the field. You probably know that already, but the point is important enough that I want to make sure.

✔ Killing a field *erases all data* in the field. Proceed with caution!

✔ If the data in a table is important to you, make a back-up copy before deleting any of the table's fields.

✔ If the data in a field *isn't* important, why bother with it at all? Why not do something fun instead?

Here's how to delete a field from your table:

1. **Open the database file, click on the table you plan to change, and then click on Design.**

   The Design window pops onto the screen.

2. **Click on the gray button on the left side of the row you want to delete.**

   This step highlights the doomed field so that all the other fields know what's about to happen and who the victim is.

3. **Choose Edit⇨Delete Row.**

   The Dialog Box of Doom appears, asking whether you really want to do the deed (see Figure 9-3).

Figure 9-3:
Don't click
that button
unless
you're
positively
sure!

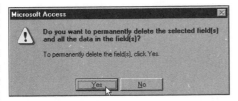

4. **Click on Yes to delete the field; click on No if you're having second thoughts.**

TIP

If you delete the field and immediately wish you hadn't, press Ctrl+Z or choose Edit⇨Undo Delete (see Figure 9-4). Your field instantly comes back from beyond.

Figure 9-4:
Change your
mind? Click
here to
restore the
field.

 5. Make the deletion permanent by choosing File⇨Save or by clicking on the Save button on the toolbar.

The key word in this step is *permanent,* as in *never to be seen nor heard from again.* You can't undo this step — when it's gone, it's gone.

A Field by Any Other Name Still Holds the Same Stuff

Access 97 really doesn't care what you name the fields in a table. Granted, it has some technical rules for what a legal field name looks like, but editorially speaking, it doesn't care. Field names are really a human element (silly humans, we're always running around naming stuff).

If you want to change a field name, you have two options:

✔ Use Design view (the *official* way)
✔ Do some right-clicking in Datasheet view (the fun, visual, and intuitive way)

This section explains both methods. Go with whichever method makes the most sense to you.

Changing a field name in Design view

Here's how to change a field name in Design view:

1. Open the database file, click on the table of the day, and then click on Design.

The table appears, laid out in Design view. (Granted, every step sequence in the chapter opens with this step, but you have to start somewhere.)

2. **Click on the field you plan to rename and then press F2 to highlight it (see Figure 9-5).**

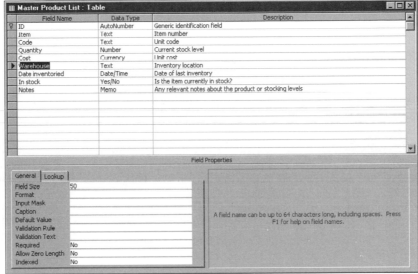

Figure 9-5:
The field name is highlighted and ready for the change.

You're ready to replace the field name.

3. **Type the field's new name.**

The new name overwrites the old one, just like in Figure 9-6.

4. **To save the change, choose File➪Save or click on the Save button on the toolbar.**

The process is complete!

Changing a field name in Datasheet view

Renaming a field in Datasheet view takes about the same number of steps, but some people think that this method is easier. In the name of diversity, here's how to change a field name in Datasheet view:

1. **Open the database file and double-click on the table name.**

Surprise — the first step is different! After surviving the shock of a new set of instructions, notice that the table is on-screen in Datasheet view.

2. **Right-click on the name of the field you want to change.**

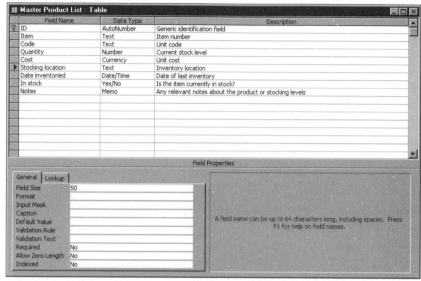

Figure 9-6:
The new
name
gracefully
takes its
place in the
table.

The column dons a snappy highlight, and a pop-up menu appears.

3. Choose Rename Column from the menu (see Figure 9-7).

Figure 9-7:
Ask and you
shall
receive, but
right-click to
rename.

The name of the column is highlighted, braced for the change.

4. Type the new name and then press Enter.

Even though you made the change in Datasheet view, Access 97 actually changed the table's design.

5. To make the change permanent, click on Save on the toolbar or choose File⇨Save.

You're done!

Part III
Finding the Ultimate Answer to Everything (Well, Not Everything)

The 5th Wave   By Rich Tennant

I DON'T KNOW - MY SPREADSHEET TELLS ME WE SHOULD BASE OUR OVERHEAD BUDGET ON SALES FIGURES RATHER THAN FIXED, MY PLOT CHART INDICATES WE SHOULD ESCALATE OUR MARKETING THRUST, AND MY PSYCHOANALYSIS PROGRAM TELLS ME I DEPEND TOO MUCH ON OUTSIDE INPUT AND SHOULD TRUST MY INSTINCTS MORE.

In this part . . .

Electronically collecting the data together in one place is nice, but if you're just stacking it on the hard disk instead of piling it around your office, what did you gain (apart from a less cluttered office)?

At the risk of sounding like a marketing brochure, the capability to interact with your data is one of the truly cool features of Access 97. Because this is a computer product, you can't just say that you're interacting with or questioning the data. No — that would be too easy. In database lingo, you're *querying* the tables.

Even though saying that you're going to query something sounds a lot cooler than saying that you're going to ask a quick question, the basic concept is the same. This part digs into the whole query concept, starting out with simple questions and leading you into progressively more complex prognostications. This is juicy stuff, so work up a good appetite before digging in.

Chapter 10

Quick Searches: Find, Filter, and Sort

In This Chapter

▶ Using the Find command

▶ Sorting your database

▶ Filter by selection

▶ Filter by form

$\mathcal{D}$atabases help you store information, but heck, so do 3 x 5 index cards (and I bet you never spent $600 upgrading your index-card box). To justify all the time, trauma, and accelerated hair loss associated with them, database programs have to do something that a simple stack of paper products just can't match — something like sifting through your table to find one specific piece of data in the blink of an eye.

Thanks to the magic of the Find, Sort, and Filter commands, Access 97 can track down and reorganize stuff in a table faster than ever. When you need a quick answer to a simple question, these three commands are ready to help. This chapter covers the commands in order, starting with the speedy Find, moving along to the flexible Filter, and ending with the organizational Sort.

Answering big, hairy questions still takes a full-fledged Access 97 query, but don't let that threat worry you — the next chapter explains the whole query procedure.

Finding Stuff in Your Tables

When you want to track down a particular record *right now,* creating a whole query for the job is overkill. Fortunately, Access 97 has a quick-and-dirty way to find one specific piece of data within your project's tables and forms — the Find command.

Find is available both on the Toolbar and through the main menu (choose Edit⇨Find). Access 97 doesn't care which way you fire up the Find command — it works the same from either avenue.

Although the Find command is pretty easy to use, you need to know some tricks to make the Find command do its best work. The next section explains how to do a simple Find within one field of your table. The following section explains how to tweak the Find settings for more detailed search missions.

Finding first things first (and next things after that)

Using the Find command is a pretty straightforward task. Here's how it works:

1. **Open the table or form you want to search. To search in one particular field, click in that field.**

   The Find command automatically searches the current field in all the records of the table, so picking the right field before beginning the Find process is important.

 2. **Start the Find command by either clicking on the Find toolbar button or choosing Edit⇨Find.**

   The Find dialog box pops into action.

3. **Type the text you're looking for into the Find What box, as shown in Figure 10-1.**

   Take a moment to check your spelling. Access 97 isn't bright enough to figure out that you actually mean *hero* when you type *zero*.

Figure 10-1:
The Find dialog box gets ready for a musical search.

Type what you are looking for here.

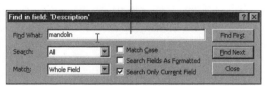

4. **Click on Find First to begin your search.**

   Before you can count to one by eighths, the Find command tracks down the record you want, moves the cursor there, and highlights the matching text.

On the other hand, if Find doesn't locate anything, it laments its failure in a small dialog box. In that case, click on OK to make the dialog box go away, and then make sure that you clicked in the correct field and spelled everything correctly in the Find What box. You may also want to check the special Find options covered in the next section to see whether one of them is messing up your search.

What if the first record that Access finds isn't exactly the one you're looking for? Suppose that you wanted the second or the fourteenth John Smith in the table? No problem — that's why the Find dialog box has a Find Next button. Keep clicking Find Next until Access 97 either works its way down to the record you want or tells you that it's giving up the search.

Tuning a search for speed and accuracy

Sometimes, just providing the information in the Find What box isn't enough. Either you find too many records or the ones that you match aren't really the ones that you want. The best way to reduce the number of wrong matches is to add more details to your search. As a bonus, precise adjustment makes the pursuit faster, too.

Access 97 offers several different tools for fine-tuning a Find. Here's a quick list of the various options and how to use them. All these descriptions assume that you have already opened the Find dialog by either clicking on the Find toolbar button (the one with the binoculars on it) or choosing Edit⇨Find.

✓ **Search Only Current Field:** By default, Access 97 looks for matches only in the *current* field — whichever field you clicked in before starting the Find command. To have Access 97 search the entire table instead, clear this check box by clicking in it and making the check mark go away, like in Figure 10-2.

Figure 10-2:
For a quick look through the whole table, turn off this option.

✔ **Search:** If you're finding too many matches, try limiting your search to one particular portion of the table with the Search option. Search tells the Find command to look at All the records in the table (the default setting) or to merely search Up or Down from the current record. Clicking on a record halfway through the table and then telling Access 97 to search Down from there confines your search to the bottom part of the table. Set this option by clicking on the down-arrow next to the Search box and picking the appropriate choice from the drop-down menu.

✔ **Match:** Access 97 makes a few silly assumptions, and this option is a good example. By default, Match is set to Whole Field, which assumes that you want to find only fields that *completely match* your search text. The Whole Field setting means that searching for Sam would *not* find a field containing Samuel. Not too bright for such an expensive program, is it? Change this behavior by setting the Match option. to Any Part of Field, which allows a match anywhere in a field (finding both Samuel and new sample product), or to Start of Field, which recognizes only a match that starts from the beginning of the field. To change this setting, click the down-arrow next to the option, and then pick your choice from the drop-down menu, as shown in Figure 10-3.

Figure 10-3:
Find a match
anywhere in
the field by
changing
the Match
option.

✔ **Match Case:** This setting is for the true power-mongers in the audience. Of all the options, Match Case is by far the most restrictive. Not only does the value in question have to meet the criteria in the preceding options, but it also has to *identically* match the search text's case as well. With this option turned on, a search for McNally would *not* match Mcnally or MCNALLY. To turn this setting on, click in the check box next to it to place a check mark there.

✔ **Search Fields as Formatted:** Most of the time, this option doesn't make much difference in your life. In fact, the only time you probably care about this Find option is when (or if) you search many highly formatted fields. Search Fields as Formatted instructs Access 97 to look at the formatted version of the field *instead* of the actual data you typed. Limiting the search in this way is handy when searching dates, stock-keeping unit IDs, or any other field with quite a bit of specialized formatting. Turn this setting on by clicking in the check box next to it to place a check mark there.

If your Find command isn't working the way you think that it should, check the options in the preceding list. Odds are that one or more of these options isn't set quite right!

Sorting Out Life on the Planet

Very few databases are already organized into nice, convenient alphabetical lists. So what do you do when your boss wants the world neatly sorted and on her desk within the hour?

The solution, of course, is the Sort command, which is *really* easy to use! The Sort command is on the Records menu, plus two buttons on the Toolbar (Sort Ascending and Sort Descending) do the job as well.

✔ Sort Ascending sorts your records alphabetically from top to bottom, so records that begin with A are at the beginning, and records that begin with Z are at the end.

✔ Sort Descending does just the opposite; records that begin with Z are at the top, and A is at the bottom of the list.

The Sort command handles dates and numbers with equal ease. Sort Ascending organizes numbers from smallest to largest and dates from oldest to most recent. Sort Descending puts the largest numbers or most recent dates at the start of the list.

To use the Sort command, click on the field that you want to sort by and then click on either the Sort Ascending or the Sort Descending button. Your records change their order to organize the field you have selected in alphabetical or numeric order. Figure 10-4 shows the auction customer list, sorted by Last Name.

Sometimes, the Sort function doesn't work so well. If you want to sort by a field that has numbers mixed in with spaces and letters (such as street addresses), Access 97 sorts the numbers by *position* rather than *value*. Unfortunately, this sort pattern means that Access 97 puts "10608 W. Vermont" before "119 Spring Mill." (The 0 in the second position comes before the 1 in the second position.) Oh well, I suppose that you can only expect so much from a program.

Customers : Table							
Customer ID	First Name	Last Name	Organization N	Address1	Address2	City	Sta
15	Edward	Anderson		431 Brentwood		Oaklandon	IN
6	Oslo	Bergenman		4278 Eden Ct.		Indianapolis	IN
11	Travis	Cooksey		5807 Layman A		Noblesville	IN
16	King	Daniels	Baystorm, Inc.	9 Graceland Pl.		Muncie	IN
12	Kevin	Davis		5646 Candelite		Greenfield	IN
40	Barbara	Farrar	Gallerie BF	6320 Epperson		Broad Ripple	IN
36	Delisa	Frattington		127 Park Ct.		Greenwood	IN
10	Kathryn	Grant	Universal Transp	3872 Port of Wa		Chicago	IL
22	Sam	Gregory	Whimseco	1620 Edmonds(		Plainfield	IN
24	Gretchen	Hankla	Daisyfield Shop	227 Daisyfield [		Noblesville	IN
4	Gary	Holko		2557 Fisher Driv		Anderson	IN
37	Gerald	Hollingsly	Victorian Propei	2769 Roundtabl		Indianapolis	IN
35	Daniel	Jameson		6811 Ruby Villa		Fishers	IN
25	Byron	Jiles		1122 Belden Dr.		Greenwood	IN
1	Alan	Kermit		17757 S. Lyons		Fairland	IN
7	Anistasia	Kimmerly		6774 Wildernes	Apt. 11A	Greenwood	IN
5	Christopher	Klayton	Tanbara, Inc.	4662 Jefferson F		St. Louis	MC
13	Jack	Laux		25 Lower Bay L		Highland	IN
29	Callie	Logan	Eye 4 Antiques	227 Polk		Zionsville	IN
34	Race	McSwaggart		3287 E. 34th Av		Danville	IN
38	Brenda	McWhirter		10 Braeburn Wa		Mooresville	IN
26	Clarence	Micy		385 Carlton Arm		Newton	IN
2	Rex	Morris		3627 Glenarm [	Apt. A	Beech Grove	IN

Record: 1 of 41

Figure 10-4: If you want to organize your data by a certain category, click on that category before you start.

Filtering Records with Something in Common

Sometimes, you need to see a group of records that share a common value in one field — they all list a particular city, a certain job title, or the same genre of books. Access 97 has a special tool for this purpose — the Filter command.

A filter takes the criteria that you want to look for and pulls out all the records that match the criteria, creating a sort of mini-table of those matching records. You can find the Filter commands on the Records menu and the toolbar.

Three kinds of Filter commands are available: Filter by Selection, Filter by Form, and Advanced Filter/Sort. Each command performs the same basic function, but in a different way and with different bells and whistles attached. The following sections cover the first two options; to find the details of Advanced Filter/Sort, flip to Chapter 11.

Filters work in tables, forms, and queries. Although you *can* apply a filter to a report, doing so is really a different kind of beast. Each section below focuses on applying filters to tables, but the same concepts apply when you're working with queries and forms.

Filter by Selection

The Filter by Selection command is the easiest of the three filter commands to use. It assumes that you have already found one record that matches your criteria. Using Filter by Selection is much like grabbing someone in a crowd and shouting: "Okay, everybody who's like him, line up over there."

To use Filter by Selection, click in the field that has the information you want to match. For example, suppose that you're looking at the items for sale at the auction and decide that you need to look only at those items that have a minimum bid of $30.00 (no more, no less). When you find one item that meets that criteria, click in the item's MinimumBid field and then click the Filter by Selection toolbar button (if you'd rather, you can choose the Records⇨Filter⇨ Filter by Selection command from the main menu). Access 97 immediately displays a table containing only the items with a minimum bid of exactly $30.00 (see Figure 10-5).

Figure 10-5:
Filter by Selection finds the records that match highlighted criteria.

Item ID	ItemName	MinimumBid	Description	CustomerID	DateIn
3	Asst hardback books (1 of 4)	$30.00	Box of assorted hardback books. Printing dates rang from 1930 to 1940	22	1/18/98
4	Asst hardback books (2 of 4)	$30.00	Box of assorted hardback books. Printing dates rang from 1940 to 1950	22	1/18/98
5	Asst hardback books (3 of 4)	$30.00	Box of assorted hardback books. Printing dates rang from 1950 to 1960	22	1/18/98
6	Asst hardback books (4 of 4)	$30.00	Box of assorted hardback books. Printing dates rang from 1960 to	22	1/18/98

Record: 1 of 4 (Filtered)

When you are done with the filter, click on the Filter by Selection toolbar button again to return your table or form to its regular display.

At this stage of the game, you may want to save a list of everything that matches your filter. Unfortunately, you can't. If you want a permanently saved record of your filtered search, you need to create a query (see Chapter 11).

Filter by Form

You can tighten a search by using additional filters to weed out undesirable matches, but doing so takes a ton of extra effort. For an easier way to isolate a group of records based on the values in more than one field, turn to the Filter by Form feature (try saying that three times fast!).

Filter by Form uses more than one criteria to sift through records. Say, for example, that you need a list of all the customers at your auction who came from Illinois or Indiana. Well, you can do two Filter by Selection searches and write down the results of each to get your list, or you can do just *one* search with Filter by Form and see all the records in a single step.

 To use Filter by Form, either choose Records⇨Filter⇨Filter by Form or click on the Filter by Form toolbar button. An empty replica of your table fills the screen, just like the one shown in Figure 10-6.

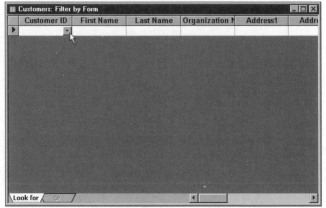

Figure 10-6:
The Filter by Form table lets you give detailed instructions on what to look for in your data.

Notice in Figure 10-6 that an arrow button is in the CustomerID field of the table. That arrow button is there because that field was active when the Filter by Form command was selected. The arrow is useful if you want to filter by customer ID number, but you're going to look at states of residence. Scroll right and click in the State/Province column — the little arrow obligingly jumps to that column. You can then click on the arrow to open a list box showing all the entries for that field in your open database, as displayed in Figure 10-7.

In the lower-right corner of the table is a tab labeled Look For. When that tab is highlighted, you can click on an entry to designate that entry as your primary search criteria. So you click on the abbreviation IL in the drop-down list of the State/Province list box, and IL moves into the State/Province column.

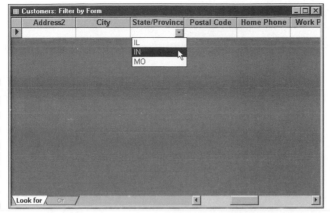

Figure 10-7:
The little arrow opens a list box showing all the entries for that field.

But wait! What about the records that have the state entered as "Illinois"? Don't worry — that's what Filter by Form is all about. Look back at the lower-left corner of the table. Do you see the little tab labeled Or (next to the Look For tab)? Click on Or and then open your list box again. You can click on any other entry and Access 97 searches for that entry, as well as for "Illinois."

Repeat this process as many times as you need and in any field you need. Every time you click on the Or tab, another Or tab comes into existence to let you add another criteria to your search. Figure 10-8 shows how the Filter by Form table looks with an extra Or tab in place.

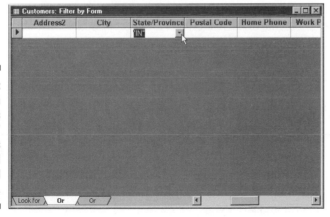

Figure 10-8:
You can use as many "Or" statements as you need to define all the criteria.

When you have entered all the criteria you want for the filter, click on the Apply Filter button, and Access 97 does the rest. Figure 10-9 shows the results.

Organization N	Address1	Address2	City	State/Province	Post
	17757 S. Lyons		Fairland	IN	44879
	3627 Glenarm C	Apt. A	Beech Grove	IN	47827
Stevenson Antic	28 W. Washing	Suite 203	Indianapolis	IN	46204
	2557 Fisher Dri		Anderson	IN	49877
	4278 Eden Ct.		Indianapolis	IN	46205
	6774 Wildernes	Apt. 11A	Greenwood	IN	46733
Yosemite Conci	8379 RR 1	Box 38	Hope	IN	40288
BHMS, Inc.	1010 Skyeway		Fishers	IN	46038
Universal Transp	3872 Port of Wa		Chicago	IL	49022
	5807 Layman A		Noblesville	IN	46039
	5646 Candelite		Greenfield	IN	44763
	25 Lower Bay L		Highland	IN	48572
Cardinal Antique	6917 N. Meridia		Indianapolis	IN	46206
	431 Brentwood		Oaklandon	IN	45884
Baystorm, Inc.	9 Graceland Pl.		Muncie	IN	48443
	102 Windsor Dr	Apt. F	Brownsburg	IN	45777

Record: 1 of 40 (Filtered)

Figure 10-9:
Access 97 successfully filtered your table just like the form asked.

Sometimes, you may want to create a group of records based upon the information in more than one field. Such a search is one of Filter by Form's best tricks. Just type the information to match into each field you want to use for the filter. When you apply the filter, Access 97 displays only records that match *all* the field examples.

Although you can get fancy and combine And searches and Or searches to your heart's content, keeping track of your creation gets pretty tough in no time at all. Before creating *The Filter That Identified Incredibly Detailed Sub-Sets of Manhattan,* remind yourself that Queries work better than Filters do when you're asking complicated questions. Flip to Chapter 11 for the low-down on Queries.

When you're done playing, click on the Filter by Form toolbar button again and watch it toggle off. At that point, your table returns to normal (or at least as normal as data tables ever get).

What to do when good criteria go bad

What do you do when you enter criteria by mistake? Or when you decide that you really don't want to include Ohio in your filter right after you click on OH? No problem — the Clear Grid button to the rescue!

When you click on the Clear Grid button, Access 97 dumps all the entries in the Filter by Form grid and gives you a nice, clean place to start over again.

If you want to get rid of just a single Or tab instead of clearing the whole grid, click on that tab and then choose Edit⇨Delete Tab.

Chapter 11

Make a Simple Query, Get 10,000 Answers

● ●

In This Chapter

▶ Using Advanced Filter/Sort

▶ Sorting your data on more than one field

▶ Establishing criteria and operators

▶ Cleaning up your queries

▶ Saving your queries

▶ Using Select queries

▶ Understanding Top Values

▶ Applying the Simple Query Wizard

● ●

*Q*ueries are the true heroes of Access 97. You use queries to make sense of all the data that you slavishly typed in for all those many hours or days. When you use queries, you start getting a return on all your labor.

So what is a query? Simply put, a *query* is a question about the data in your tables. Queries make lists from one or more tables, count records, and even do calculations based on what they find lurking in your database. They discover things like how much purple thread is in each Paris warehouse, which customers bought the most organic cactus face cream (I think they're all from California), and how the time of the year affects car sales. In short, queries are the real power behind the Access 97 throne.

Because queries are such robust and flexible tools, you need quite a bit of information about them to use them effectively. To get you started, this chapter explores Advanced Filter/Sort, the most powerful of the filters (or, to look at it another way, the simplest of queries). From there, the chapter delves into performing queries on a single table. The other chapters in Part III probe deeper into the mysteries of query logic and specialized queries.

On Your Way with Advanced Filter/Sort

As its name implies, Advanced Filter/Sort is more powerful than a run-of-the-mill filter. It's *so* powerful, in fact, that you can think of it as a mini-query (that's why it's here at the beginning of the chapter on queries). The steps for making an Advanced Filter/Sort are almost the same as those for making a query — and the results look quite a bit alike, too.

But even though it looks, acts, and behaves like a query, Advanced Filter/Sort is still a filter at heart. For example, Advanced Filter/Sort only works with one table or form in your database at a time, so you can't use it on a bunch of linked tables. In addition, you can only ask certain types of questions with Advanced Filter/Sort (you find more information about that limitation later in this chapter). Real, honest-to-goodness queries don't suffer such limitations.

Although this section only talks about applying filters to tables and forms, you can also filter a query. Precisely *why* you'd filter a query is a little beyond me, so just let the nerds worry about this feature — it definitely falls under the heading *Features for People with Too Much Time on Their Hands.*

You open the Advanced Filter/Sort from an open table or form by choosing Records⇨Filter⇨Advanced Filter/Sort. This command brings up the Design view of the Advanced Filter/Sort, as shown in Figure 11-1.

Figure 11-1:
Advanced
Filter/Sort is
a cross
between a
powerful
filter and a
simple
query.

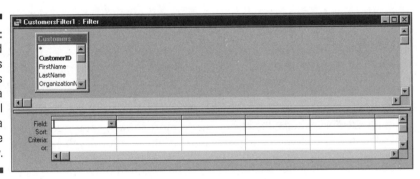

Notice in Figure 11-1 that the window is split. In the upper half is a small box labeled Customers. That's the *Field List,* which displays all the fields in the current table or form. The lower half of the screen contains a blank query grid where the filter information goes. (Even though you're building a *filter,* the area at the bottom of the screen is still a *query* grid. You can see almost the exact same grid later in the chapter, where I discuss building real queries.)

You use the Field List in two ways:

✔ Double-click on a field's entry in the Field List and a matching entry for the field appear in the query grid in the lower half of the Advanced Filter/Sort window.

✔ Click on the field you want to insert and then drag the field down to the query grid yourself.

Whichever method you use to move a field onto the query grid, the field automatically takes its correct place in the table, as shown in Figure 11-2.

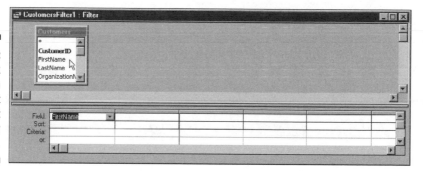

Figure 11-2:
Double-click
on a field in
the Field List
to include it
in the query
table.

When a field moves into the query grid, a downward-pointing arrow appears in the table next to the field name. If you accidentally pick the wrong field (I hate it when that happens), click that downward-pointing arrow and pick the *correct* field from the list; then continue with your work.

To add all the fields in the query grid for your filter, double-click on the heading for the Field List to highlight all the fields, and then drag the whole list down to the query grid. Doing so places one field in each column of the table, enabling you to use your entire database while establishing separate criteria for each field. As an added plus, you can also arrange the fields in any order you want (more about this stuff later in this section).

Sorting things out

After inserting all the fields you need for your query, you determine by which field you want to sort the data and click on the Sort row for that column in the query grid. The arrow indicating a list box appears, and you choose between ascending and descending sorts. Figure 11-3 shows a query grid for a mailing list. Thanks to the Ascending setting under Postal Code, Access 97 sorts the results by zip code.

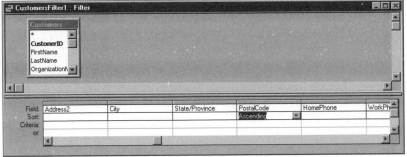

Figure 11-3:
You can tell Access 97 to sort by whatever field best suits your needs.

You can instruct Access 97 to sort by more than one field, but the sorting process always *starts* with the field that's furthest to the left in the query grid. When Access finds records with the same information in that field, it starts sorting by the other fields you specified, working from left to right through the list in the grid.

Adding selection criteria

The third row of the query grid is labeled Criteria. In this row, you describe what you want to find.

Luckily, entering criteria is a snap. You click in the Criteria area under the field name you want to search and then type in the search text. For example, to make a mailing list for customers in Indiana, you click in the Criteria area of the State column, type **IN**, and press Enter. Access 97 accepts your entry and puts quotation marks around it (isn't that nice?).

If Access 97 complains that `The expression you entered contains invalid syntax`, it's saying that the program is a little confused about your entry. Putting quotation marks around the entry usually fixes the problem.

What if you also want to include Illinois in your mailing list? Unlike the simple-minded Filter by Selection tool discussed in Chapter 10, Advanced Filter/Sort lets you include more than one criteria in the same filter. Simply move down to the Or row of the same column and type **"IL"**. Access 97 includes the Land of Lincoln in its search.

This flexibility has limits, though. Access 97 only accepts a maximum of nine criteria in the same column. (Okay, so it's not *that* much of a limitation.) Figure 11-4 shows what the table looks like now that you've entered all the information needed for the search.

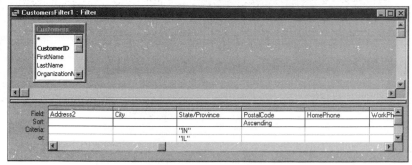

Figure 11-4:
You're almost ready to create a mailing list of customers in Illinois and Indiana.

Access 97 does one trick when you are entering criteria that can be very confusing. If you enter a bunch of criteria in the Or lines, your first entries seem to disappear. Don't worry — you didn't mess up anything. Access 97 just scrolled the table up a bit to make room for the new criteria. Click on the up arrow on the scroll bar to see your original entries again.

When you use more than one column or row within the table, you are actually combining criteria. You combine criteria by arranging them so that Access either tries to match both rules (AND) or either of the rules (OR). Working with the many rows and columns of the query grid is the topic of Chapter 13.

Rubbing your lucky Boolean operator

Contrary to popular belief, a *Boolean operator* is not someone who runs a big, industrial boolean machine during the night shift. Instead, Boolean operators are special symbols that help build the criteria in filters and queries. They stand for concepts such as *greater than, less than or equal to,* and the ever popular *not equal to* (known in the vernacular as *just plain different*). Table 11-1 offers a quick introduction to these valuable additions to your Access 97 knowledge. The table also provides examples of how to put the little fellows to work in your filters. (By the way, even though the examples in the Table are mostly numeric, all the filters work equally well with both numbers and text.)

Table 11-1		**Comparison Operators**
Symbol	*Name*	*What Does It Mean?*
Is	Is	This operator is what you get when you simply type something into a Criteria row. The information you enter must match the information in the field exactly.

(continued)

Table 11-1 *(continued)*

Symbol	Name	What Does It Mean?
Like	Like	You can put the word Like before text in a field to ask Access to search through the contents of that field to see whether it can find the text *anywhere* within the field. If it can, then that counts as a match. **Example:** The criteria Like "The" matches "The Wizard," "Home on the Range," and "Many Meanings of The."
<	Less Than	This operator lists all values that are *Less Than* your criteria. **Example:** <30 in the MinimumBid field finds all bids from $0 to $29.99.
>	Greater Than	Greater Than lists all values in the field that are *Greater Than* the criteria. **Example:** >30 in the MinimumBid field finds all bids that are more than $30 (starting with $30.01).
>=	Greater Than or Equal To	This works just like Greater Than, except that it also includes all entries that exactly match the criteria. **Example:** >=30 finds all values from 30 to infinity.
<=	Less Than or Equal To	If you add the = sign to Less Than, your query includes all records that have values below and equal to the criteria value. **Example:** <=30 includes not only those records with values less than 30 but also those with a value of 30.
<>	Not Equal (Less Than or Greater Than)	This operator finds all entries that do not match the criteria. **Example:** If you want a list of all records except ones with a value of 30, enter <>30.
=	Equals	This operator finds only those records that exactly match the criteria. **Example:** =30 only finds values of 30.

Access 97 uses Boolean operators a great deal, but don't worry if you still have a few questions. There's plenty more to find out about Boolean operators in Chapter 13.

Applying the filter

When all the criteria are in place, take that bold step and have Access 97 apply the filter to your data. To turn on the filter, choose Filter➪Apply Filter/Sort from the menu bar or click on the Apply Filter button on the Toolbar. After a moment of thinking (or whatever Access 97 does when it's figuring out something), your table view changes and only the records that match your filter are left on display (see Figure 11-5). Pretty cool, eh?

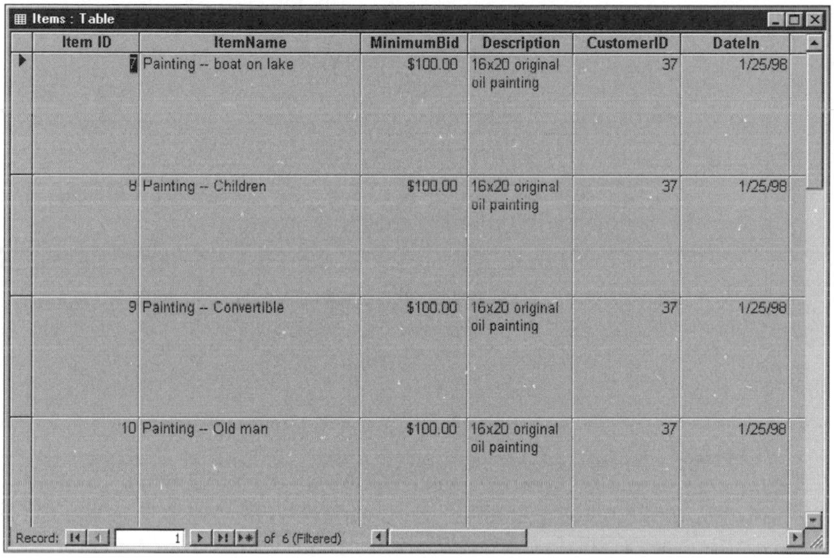

Item ID	ItemName	MinimumBid	Description	CustomerID	DateIn
7	Painting -- boat on lake	$100.00	16x20 original oil painting	37	1/25/98
8	Painting -- Children	$100.00	16x20 original oil painting	37	1/25/98
9	Painting -- Convertible	$100.00	16x20 original oil painting	37	1/25/98
10	Painting -- Old man	$100.00	16x20 original oil painting	37	1/25/98

Record: 1 of 6 (Filtered)

Figure 11-5:
Ta dah! You've just completed your first query!

When you're ready to see all the data again, turn off the filter by clicking on the Apply Filter button one more time. The filtered records join their unfiltered brethren in a touching moment of digital homecoming. (Sorry — it's the romantic in me.)

Sweeping up the debris: Clearing and deleting

In the Advanced Filter/Sort, you can also find a couple of nifty tools associated with all queries. On the bottom of the Edit menu, you see two commands: Delete Column and Clear Grid.

✔ You use the Delete Column command to remove a field from your query — *not* from the table itself. Simply click in the column that you want to remove, choose Edit➪Delete Column, and that field goes away.

✔ The Clear Grid command is more comprehensive. In fact, it's sort of like a swarm of killer bees. When you choose Edit➪Clear Grid, *all* your fields in the query grid are removed, and you can create your query again from scratch without having to start a new one.

What if you decide that you want to change the order of your fields in a query? Well, you *could* start over, but I don't like hearing that kind of language from my readers. You can rearrange the columns of your queries and tables quickly, easily, and without all that nasty language:

1. **Click on the column header to select the whole column, point to the column head again, and drag with the mouse.**

    You see a little box below your cursor, which tells you that your mouse is carrying something heavy.

2. **When your cursor is where you want the column to be repositioned, release the mouse, and that column pops into place.**

This procedure also works in Design view and Datasheet view.

Save me, Toto!

If you create a really useful filter, you may want to use it again later. All you need to do is save the filter as a query. To do that, click on the Filter by Form toolbar button again to see your illustrious filter on-screen again and then click on the funky-looking Save as Query toolbar button or choose File➪Save As Query from the main menu. The dialog box in Figure 11-6 pops onto screen. Type a name for the new query and then click OK.

Figure 11-6:
You can
save your
Advanced
Filter/Sort as
a query.

To use the query again, look for it on your database's Query tab. When you find it, double-click on it. Access 97 automatically loads and executes the query and then displays the results for you to enjoy.

Finding Elusive Answers with a Well-Placed Query

To work with Queries and the Query Wizard, go to the main database window (the one with the tabs for Table, Query, Form, and so on) and click on the Query tab. Under the Query tab you see a window that most likely is empty (unless you saved an Advanced Filter/Sort). On the right side are three buttons: Open, Design, and New. To create a new query, click on New (but you probably figured that out already).

You see the New Query dialog box, shown in Figure 11-7, which gives you a choice of how you want to set up your query.

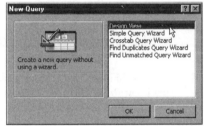

Figure 11-7: The New Query dialog box.

If you select the Design View option and click on OK, you see the Show Table dialog box in Figure 11-8.

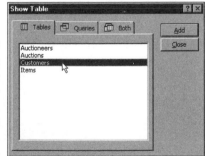

Figure 11-8: Select what tables or forms you need to look through.

You can select a table and/or a query from the Show Table dialog box and click on the Add button to include your selection in your search. You can select more than one table for your query, but that's a topic for Chapter 14.

After you select the table for the query and click on the <u>A</u>dd button, click on Close to make the Show Table dialog box go away. Now you're looking at the query in Design view (see Figure 11-9). If you used the Advanced Filter/Sort window before, most of the query grid should look familiar to you — all except for the new parts, that is.

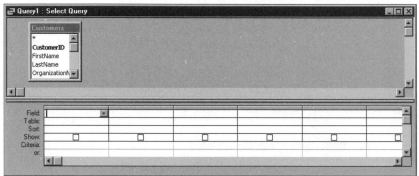

Figure 11-9:
Hey —
you're back
in Design
view!

The Select Query works a lot like the Advanced Filter/Sort. You move fields from your source table onto the query grid, establish sort order, and define the criteria the same way as you do for the Advanced Filter/Sort. The Select Query adds some more features, like the Table and Show rows.

Using Top Values: Who IS the top lion in the forest?

A new and *very* helpful addition to the toolbar, one that helps you create powerful queries with Access 97, is the *Top Values* box, displayed in Figure 11-10. The Top Values function lets you show only the top or only the bottom values in the field you designate.

Figure 11-10:
The Top
Values box
summarizes
your queries
in one step.

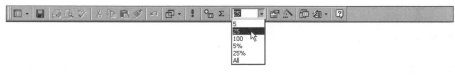

Say, for example, that you want to know what the five least expensive items on sale at the auction are. You click on the MinimumBid field in your query grid and designate an ascending sort (so that the lowest-priced items are at the start of the list). Next, click on the Top Values list box. You can either type the number 5 or select it from the drop-down list. When you tell Access 97 to run your query, it presents you with a list of the five items with the lowest minimum bids in the auction.

If you would rather have a list of the items that have the four highest prices at the auction, change the sort order for the field to Descending, change the number in the Top Values list box to 4, and run the query again.

Run, query, run!

How do you tell Access 97 to start working?

 You can use the Run button on the toolbar to get the query going, or you can use the menu and choose Query⇨Run to crack the whip.

 Alternately, you can use the Design View button on the toolbar. This button lets you to switch between Query Design view (where you set up your query), SQL view (which is used for working with databases on other computers — stay far away from this), and Datasheet view (which shows you the results of your query). You can find these same commands on the View menu.

If you click on the arrow to the right of the Design View button, you see a command list showing the three views available. Or you can just click on the button, and your screen switches to the Datasheet view (if you are currently in the Design view) or the Design view (if you are in the Datasheet view). Notice how even Access 97 tries to avoid the SQL view. The advantage of this button is that it enables you to easily switch between views, make changes to your design, and see how your changes affect the results.

 With a regular Select Query, whether you use the Run button or the Datasheet view button doesn't matter. With an action query like the ones discussed in Chapter 16, the difference can be quite important. For now, use the Datasheet view button to look at the results of your query. Leave the Run button alone until you have a chance to wander through Chapter 16.

 Sometimes, you need Access 97 to use certain fields in a query but display others in the Datasheet view. Fortunately, you have a really easy way to do so. In the Design view of every query is a row labeled Show. Each column in this row has a box. Because Access 97 wants to show *all* the columns in the Datasheet by default, each box has a check mark inside. To remove a column from Datasheet view, click in the check box for that field to remove the check mark. If you change your mind and want to put a column back into the Datasheet view, just click in the column's Show check box one more time to restore the check mark. When you open the Datasheet view, Access 97 displays only the fields you told it to.

Toto, Can the Wizard Help?

After you know how to work with the New Query function, you can understand how the Simple Query Wizard operates and can use it to your best advantage. Like all the other wizards in the land of Access 97, the Simple Query Wizard takes care of the behind-the-scenes work for you, but you have to enter the sorting and criteria information on your own. (Such is life in the 90s — maybe that feature will be in Access 2000!)

The next time you click on the <u>N</u>ew command from the Query tab, choose the Simple Query Wizard instead of New Query. When you do, the wizard appears in a flash of flame and thunder. You can see this wizardly manifestation in Figure 11-11.

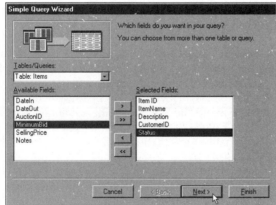

Figure 11-11:
The Simple
Query
Wizard of
Access
arranges the
data you
want into a
single query.

The wizard asks you to provide three bits of information:

> ✔ The first, <u>T</u>ables/Queries, enables you to select which tables you want to use in this query. Click on the arrow to see the drop-down list and choose from the available choices. Don't worry; the wizard is wise and includes all the queries and tables in the current database.

✔ After selecting the tables to use, the Available Fields box shows the table's available fields. Move these fields to the Selected Fields box by highlighting the fields that you want to use and clicking on the > button. Or, if you know that you want to use all the fields in the database, click on the >> button to see everything transfer over.

✔ If you decide that you don't want a field that you've already transferred, highlight that field in the Selected Fields box and click on the < button. If you want to remove all the selected fields, click on the << button.

When you're done telling the wizard which fields you want to use, go ahead and click on the Next button to see another face of the wizard, as revealed in Figure 11-12.

Figure 11-12:
This side of the wizard lets you put a label on your query and ask for help.

In the Select Query Wizard screen, you can type in a label for your query at the top. You can also determine whether you need to add sorting and criteria information to the query. If you do, click on the button marked Modify the query design to go to the Design view when you click on Finish. If you are satisfied with your options at this point, select the Open the query to view information button to see the Datasheet view.

The last check box on this screen (Display Help on working with the query?) automatically opens a Help file that explains how you can customize your query. After you make your selections, you're ready to click on the Finish button to see your handiwork.

That's it! You have all the information you need to work with single table queries. I'm sure that if Dorothy gets this information, she won't lose track of the Yellow Brick Road again.

Looking Ahead

Queries are a big topic, so I'm not throwing everything at you in one chapter. Chapter 12 covers the great joy of creating a query by using multiple tables (both with and without the Simple Query Wizard). Chapter 13 shows you how to combine criteria in a query, and Chapter 14 focuses on how to use crosstabs and create totals. Chapter 15 gives you tips on how to make mathematical computations and invoke Boolean logic on your behalf. Finally, Chapter 16 tells you how to make big changes in your queries by using a few simple commands.

Chapter 12

Searching a Slew of Tables

- -

In This Chapter

▶ Setting up queries with more than one table

▶ Enlisting the Query Wizard's help

▶ Building multiple table queries in Design view

- -

*Y*ou can use Access for much more than creating simple queries that use only one table. This chapter explains how to work with multiple tables in the same query and touches on some of the more complex types of queries that you can create. Ready? Get set. Go!

Some General Thoughts about Multiple-Table Queries

You may need to look at information from a variety of tables to get full use from your data. (In fact, if you're in the corporate world, it's almost a foregone conclusion that you'll need to blend data from multiple tables.) Fortunately, Access is specifically called a *relational database* because it enables you to establish *relationships* among the different tables you work with. This feature means that Access queries can look at two or more tables and recognize information that goes together.

In most cases, a multiple-table query works the same as a single-table query. You merely need to let Access 97 know that you are drawing on information from different sources, and the software does the rest. The primary difference between a multiple-table query and a single-table query is that, with queries that use more than one table, Access creates a link between the tables so that you can explore the relationship between the tables. In your Query Design view, Access represents this link (which it calls a *join*) by drawing a line between two or more field lists, as shown in Figure 12-1.

Figure 12-1:
In a multiple-
table query,
the tables
are linked to
share their
data.

Linking the tables when you first design them is always better than waiting until later (check out Chapters 4 and 5 for more about linking tables). Even if you didn't link the tables initially, you can still merge their information in a single query. If two or more tables have a field with exactly the same name and the same type of data, Access invokes its *Auto-Join* feature and automatically links these fields together. If the fields have even *slightly* different names, you have to link them on your own.

Your first step toward creating a good query is determining what problem you are trying to solve. With the problem well in hand, you can build a query that fills your need.

Imagine that you're running an auction house. You need a list of the people who have contributed items, what those items are, and how much the items are selling for. The database has one table listing Customer information and another with the items that are for sale. You *can* print both lists and spend an afternoon flipping between the pages, but that kinda defeats the purpose of using Access 97.

Instead, why not have Access 97 match the customers with their items? Given the preceding example, you need the SellerID, ItemName, and MinimumBid fields. The fields for SellerID are in the Customer table, while ItemName and MinimumBid are comfortably located in the Items table. Not a problem.

Calling on the Query Wizard

The Query Wizard wouldn't be much of a wizard if all it could do were create single table queries, but you can use it for multiple-table queries as well. Figure 12-2 shows the first screen of the Simple Query Wizard. (To get to this screen, start a new query and then double-click on the Simple Query Wizard option in the New Query dialog box.)

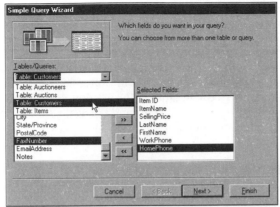

Figure 12-2:
You can use
the Simple
Query
Wizard to
create
queries
using more
than one
table.

To create a multiple-table query, follow these steps:

1. **In the database window, click on the Queries tab.**

   The window lists all of the queries currently living in the database.

2. **Click on the New button on the right side of the database window.**

   The New Query dialog box hops into action.

3. **Double-click on the entry for Simple Query Wizard.**

   The Simple Query Wizard window appears. Don't be surprised if the window looks familiar — it's the same one you use to make single table queries. With a twist of the wrist (and a click of the mouse), it *also* builds multiple-table queries!

4. **Click in the down-arrow next to the Tables/Queries box, and then click on the name of the first table to include in this query.**

   The Available Fields list displays, well, the fields available in the table (but you probably guessed that).

5. **Double-click on each field you want to include in the query.**

   If you click on the wrong field, just double-click on it in the Selected Fields list. The field promptly jumps back to the Available Fields side of the window.

6. **When you finish adding fields from this table, repeat Steps 4 and 5 for the next table you want use in the query.**

   When you've listed all the fields you want in Selected Fields, go to the next step.

7. **Click on Next to continue building the query.**

   A screen amazingly similar to Figure 12-3 *may* hop into action, but don't panic if it doesn't. If Access 97 wants you to name the query instead, skip ahead to Step 9.

If you included fields from two tables that aren't related, the Access 97 Office Assistant leaps into action when you click on Next. Office Assistant reminds you that the tables must related and suggests that you fix the problem before continuing. Actually, *suggests* isn't quite correct — it politely *demands* that you fix the relationship before trying to create the query. If this error appears, click on the OK button in the Office Assistant's message to go directly to the Relationships window. Repair the relationship, and then restart the Query Wizard and try again. Check out Chapters 4 and 5 for more about relationships.

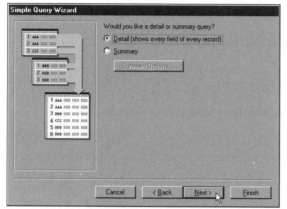

Figure 12-3:
The wizard needs more information from you when it's creating a multiple-table query.

8. If the wizard asks you to choose between a Detail and a Summary query, click on the radio button next to your choice and then click on Next.

Detail creates a datasheet that lists all the records that match the query. As the name implies, you get all the details.

Summary tells the wizard that you aren't interested in seeing every single record; you want to see a summary of the information, instead. If you want to make any special adjustments to the summary, click on Summary Options to display the Summary Options dialog box shown in Figure 12-4. Select your summary options from the list and then click on OK.

9. Type a title for your query into the text box and then click on Finish.

The query does its thing and Access 97 displays the results on-screen, as shown in Figure 12-5. Congratulations!

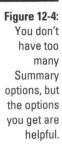

Figure 12-4:
You don't
have too
many
Summary
options, but
the options
you get are
helpful.

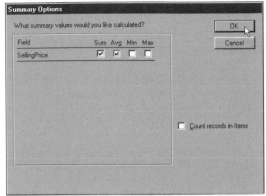

Figure 12-5:
The
Datasheet
view of the
multiple-
table
summarized
query.

A gaggle of geese, a waggle of wizards

Is there a collective noun for a group of wizards? If not, there should be, because Access 97 is loaded down with a whole plethora of wizardly assistants. Chapter 11 introduces the Simple Query Wizard, the most useful wizard for your general Access 97 query needs.

But the wizard corps doesn't stop there. Access 97 includes four other Query wizards that await your call: the Crosstab Query Wizard, Find Duplicates Query Wizard, Find Unmatched Query Wizard, and Archive Query Wizard.

Unfortunately, not all of the wizards are as straightforward as the Simple Query Wizard. Of the remaining four, the Crosstab Wizard is the only one that normal humans are likely to use. For more about the Crosstab Wizard, check out Chapter 14. The remaining three wizards (Find Duplicates Query Wizard, Find Unmatched Query Wizard, and Archive Query Wizard) are so weird that you don't need to worry about them.

Rolling Up Your Sleeves and Building the Query by Hand

Using a wizard to build your queries isn't always the best solution. Maybe the query is too complex or requires some special summaries (or perhaps you just don't feel up to tangling with the Query Wizard at the moment). For those times when creating a query by hand is the best choice, use Design view instead.

Although it sometimes looks a bit complicated, Design view is nothing to be afraid of. After you get the hang of it, you may discover that you *prefer* building queries this way. (What a scary thought!)

Here are a couple of quick starting thoughts to brighten your day before getting into the details of Design view:

- ✔ It's a *very* good idea to build the relationships between your tables *before* creating multiple-table queries. Although you can build temporary relationships within the query design, that's not the best approach. (After all, who really *wants* a temporary relationship?) For the scoop about relating tables together, see Chapter 5.

- ✔ If you know how to build single-table queries, you're already well on your way to creating multiple-table queries, because the process is almost exactly the same.

To build a multiple-table query by hand in Design view (the way Grandma used to make 'em, by golly), follow these steps:

1. **Click on the Queries tab in the database window, and then click on New.**

   The New Query dialog box appears, ready for action.

   Before starting a new multiple-table query, make sure that the tables are related! If you aren't sure about the table relationships, get back to the database window and click the Relationships button on the toolbar. For more about table relationships, see Chapter 5.

2. **Double-click on Design View in the New Query dialog box.**

   After a moment, the Show Table dialog box appears. Behind it, you see the blank query window where your query will soon take shape.

3. **Double-click on the name of the first table you want to include in the query.**

   A small window for the table appears in the query window (see Figure 12-6).

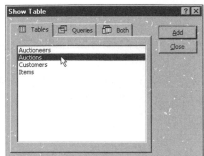

Figure 12-6:
The first
table takes
its place in
the query.

4. **Repeat Step 3 for each table you want to add to the query. When you're done, click on Close to make the Show Table dialog box go away.**

Don't worry if lines appear between your tables in the query window (see Figure 12-7). That's actually a good thing — it shows that Access 97 knows how to link the two tables.

 If you're done adding tables to the query but there aren't any lines between the tables, Access is telling you that it doesn't have a clue how to link the tables together. Your best bet at this point is to cancel the query by closing the query window, and then use the Relationships button to build some relationships.

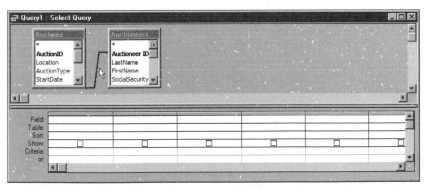

Figure 12-7:
Access 97
knows how
to link the
Auctions
table to
Auctioneers.

5. **Add fields to the query grid by double-clicking on them in the table dialog boxes (as shown in Figure 12-8). Repeat this step for all of the fields you want to include in the query.**

Pick your fields in the order you want them to appear in the query results. Feel free to include fields from any or all of the tables at the top of the query window. After all, that's why you included the tables in the query to begin with.

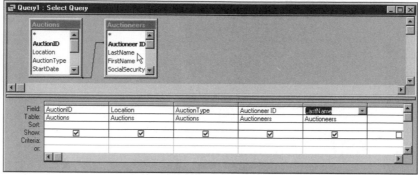

If you accidentally choose the wrong field, you can easily fix your mistake. Click on the field name's entry in the query grid and then select the oddly named Edit⇨Delete Columns option from the menu bar. The incorrect field's entry (its column) is gone.

6. **With your fields in place, take a minute to set the sort order, if you want one. To sort by a particular field, click in the Sort box under the field name and then click on the down arrow that appears at the edge of the Sort box. Click on either Ascending or Descending (see Figure 12-9).**

Repeat this step if you want to sort by more than one field.

7. **In the Criteria box for each field, set up the selection information for the query.**

Even though this is a multiple-table query, you build criteria in the same way you did for single table queries. Refer to Chapter 11 for help.

8. **If you want to include a field in the query but you don't want that field to appear in the final results, uncheck the Show entry for that field.**

   Odds are you won't ever need this step, but the nerd in me demands that I mention it.

9. **Review your work one more time. When you're sure it looks good, save the query by choosing File⇨Save.**

10. **In the Save As dialog box, type a name for the query and then click on OK.**

    You don't want to lose all that hard work by not saving your query!

11. **Cross your fingers and then choose Query⇨Run (or click on the Run button) to run your query.**

    How did it work? Did you get the answer you hoped for? If not, take your query back into Design view for some more work.

12. **Choose View⇨Design View (or click on the Design button).**

    Keep at it until you get your query just right. Remember to save your changes with File⇨Save!

Chapter 13

Lions AND Bears OR Tigers? Oh, My!

· ·

In This Chapter

▶ The difference between AND and OR

▶ Using the AND function

▶ Using the OR function

▶ Using AND and OR in the same query

· ·

*I*t's a fact of life: The longer you work with Access 97, the more complex are the questions that you ask of your data. Sorting your stuff up, down, right, and left, and filtering it through and through is not enough — now you want it to march in formation while doing animal impressions. (Well, you always did set high goals.)

Access 97 queries are good at making your data do tricks, but even queries need some help to complete the most advanced prestidigitation. That's where Dr. Boole and his magic operators enter the picture. By enlisting the unique capabilities of Boolean operators, your queries can scale new heights, perform amazing acrobatics, and generally amuse and astound both you and your coworkers. They may even surprise your boss!

This chapter looks at AND and OR, the two main operators in the world of Access 97. I explain what the operators do, how they do it, and (most importantly) why you should care. Get ready for a wild ride through the world of logic — make sure that your data is strapped in tight!

Comparing AND to OR

AND and OR are the stars of the Boolean sky. In spoken and written language, AND sticks phrases together into a complex whole, while OR describes a bunch of options from which to choose. In the world of databases, these terms perform much the same duty.

For example, if the woods are full of *lions AND tigers,* you can expect to find both types of animals anticipating your arrival. On the other hand, if the woods are full of *lions OR tigers,* then you know that *one or the other* is out there, but you don't expect to see both. In database terminology, AND means *both,* whereas OR means *either* (egad — this sounds like a grammar class).

Here are two easy rules that make this stuff really easy to remember:

- ✔ AND narrows your query, making it more restrictive.
- ✔ OR opens up your query, so more records match.

If you start looking for an individual with blue eyes AND red hair AND over six feet tall AND male, you have a relatively small group of candidates (and I'm not among them). On the other hand, if you look for people with blue eyes OR red hair OR under six feet tall OR male, the matching group is much, much bigger. In fact, almost everyone who worked on the book — including my Spitz puppy — meets the criteria.

Finding Things between Kansas AND Oz

One of the most common ways to combine expressions is to try to restrict the list to entries that are between two values. For example, you may want to find all the records that were entered after January 1, 1998, and before January 1, 1999. To ask this type of question, you need to use an AND criteria.

You simply put your two conditions together on the same line, separated with an AND. Figure 13-1 shows the query screen restricting DateIn in the Items table of the Auction database to sometime during the year 1997. Pay particular attention to the formula used to write this criteria.

Figure 13-1:
The AND function finds all dates between January 1, 1997, and January 1, 1998.

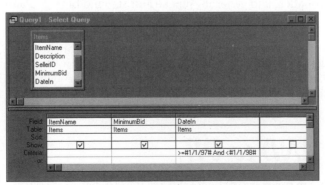

Access 97 figures out this query by checking through the records and asking the first question, "Was the record entered *on or after* January 1, 1997?" If the record wasn't entered then, Access 97 ignores the record and goes on to the next one. If the record was entered after January 1, 1997, Access 97 asks the second question, "Was the record entered before January 1, 1998?" If yes, Access 97 includes the record in the results. If not, the record gets rejected and Access 97 moves on to the next one. Notice that the comparison uses greater than or equal for the first date (January 1, 1997), because you want to include records written on the first day of the year as well.

You can create this type of "between" instruction for any type of data. You can list numeric values that fall between two other numbers or work with names that fall within a range of letters.

Use the AND criteria to ask a more specific question or reduce the number of matches that you find.

Multiple ANDs: AND Then What Happened?

Access doesn't restrict your use of the AND operator to within the same column. Rather, you can combine a number of criteria in different columns, restricting a group by using additional rules. In that case, each rule that you are combining must fall within the same row. Access 97 checks each record to make sure that it matches each of the expressions before allowing it to appear in the result table. Figure 13-2 shows an example of a query that uses three fields, with a rule in each, joined together on a single row (combining the rules with an AND statement).

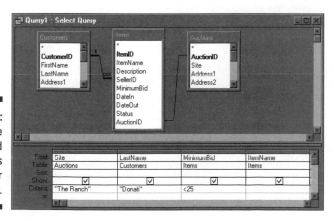

Figure 13-2: Finding the one record that meets all your requirements.

The first part of the rule restricts the list to those items that are for sale at the auction at The Ranch. That criteria gives a total of 21 records. The second part of the rule looks at those 21 records and finds the items that were submitted for sale by the Donati family. That restriction brings the list down to only two records. The final part of the criteria asks for only those items with a minimum bid of less than $25. That gives a list of only one item — a bunch of men's clothing.

When you have a very large database and are trying to restrict your results down to a very few records, you find that combining AND expressions is the most useful way to go.

Access 97 now enables you to create a Datasheet view of a table by using a query and then further restrict that table by using the filter and sort techniques discussed in Chapter 10.

Are You a Good Witch OR a Bad Witch?

Often, you may want to find a group of records that fall into a variety of possibilities, as I explain in the Advanced Filter/Sort for a mailing list in Chapter 11, where records are searched for people in Illinois OR Indiana. To use an OR in your criteria, you simply use a new line for each comparison.

To work with OR, simply list each criteria on its own line. The instructions can be listed in the same field as the same criteria. So, for example, with the Dorothy database, you can look in the Animals field for Lions on one row, Bears on another, or Tigers on a third row, as shown in Figure 13-3.

Figure 13-3:
The OR command lets you find all the scary beasties in the forest.

Field:	Animals	Where?	What they eat	
Table:	Animals in OZ	Animals in OZ	Animals in OZ	
Sort:				
Show:	☑	☑	☑	☐
Criteria:	"Lions"			
or:	"Tigers"			
	Bears			

Alternatively, you can list the criteria in different columns. For example, Figure 13-4 shows the Items table of the Auction database with a request for items that were entered by the Donati family OR which have a MinimumBid of $30 or less.

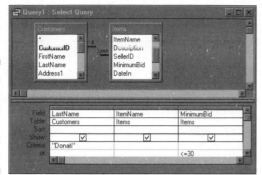

Figure 13-4:
You can
create OR
criteria from
different
fields.

Notice that each of the criteria is on a separate line. If the criteria were listed on the same line, you would be doing an AND operation, and only those records that matched both rules would appear.

Figure 13-5 shows the results of the query with labels indicating why each record is included. Notice that you have some records that match each of the rules and a few records that actually match both. Had you set this query up as an AND query, you would have gotten only the records that matched both.

Figure 13-5:
Breaking
down the
results of
the query.

¬This record is $30.

These records match
only the 'Donati' criteria.

These records match both criteria.

These records are $30 or less.

AND and OR? AND or OR?

Sometimes, using the AND and OR operators by themselves isn't enough. You need to ask a question about several different groups. Part of the question involves restricting the groups (with an AND), and other parts require including records based on a different criteria (with an OR).

Be careful with these queries. They get *really* fancy *really* fast. If a query grows to the point that you're losing track of which AND the last OR affected, then you're in over your head. Either start over or seek help from a qualified database nerd.

The most important point to remember is that each OR line (each line within the criteria) is evaluated separately. If you want to combine several different criteria, you need to make sure that each OR line represents one aspect of what you are doing.

For example, in the Auctions database, knowing which items will sell for less than $30 or more than $100 at auction site one may be useful. Well, finding the items in those price ranges requires the use of an OR condition. (If you were trying to find those items with a MinimumBid *between* $30 and $100, you would use an AND criteria here). Using an OR condition means that the entries go on separate lines.

However, that restriction isn't sufficient. You only want the items that are for sale at site one (The Ranch). For this query to work, you need to repeat the site information on each line. In order to set this query up, you need to ask for those items that are less than $30 AND at site one OR over $100 AND at site one. Notice that the OR separates two complete thoughts — the two price points — and neatly splits which criteria are put on separate lines. Figure 13-6 shows how to combine these two ANDs with an OR.

Figure 13-6:
Any criteria on the same line are AND functions and restrict the search. Criteria on different lines are OR functions and expand the search.

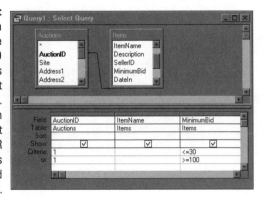

When reviewing your criteria, look at each line separately to make sure that line represents a group that you want included in the final answer. Then check to see that the individual lines work together to distill the answer you're seeking.

The AND criteria all go on the same line and are evaluated together. OR criteria go on separate lines, and each line is evaluated separately. If you have criteria that you want to use in each of the ORs, they must be repeated on each of the separate lines.

As with other types of queries, you don't have to use the same fields on each OR row. In fact, each row can be entirely separate. For example, Figure 13-7 shows a criteria asking for those items that are being sold by the Donati family at site one OR items that are being sold for less than $100 at site two. Notice that both rows use the site location, but that the items that are combined with them are separate.

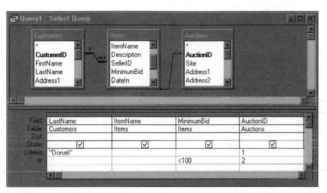

Figure 13-7:
Your OR rows can be represented in different fields.

The two groups that you get are those items sold by the Donati family at site one and any records that match the second row — items sold for over $100 at site two.

To add an additional OR row, simply fill in another row. As soon as you press enter, you can use the scroll bars on the right side of the screen to see additional query rows. The additional rows, even though they are not labeled, all function as separate OR rows.

Chapter 14
Teaching Queries to Count

● ●

In This Chapter

▶ Using the Totals row

▶ Grouping entries together

▶ Understanding the Count and Sum functions

▶ Asking crosstab queries

▶ Applying more functions

● ●

*G*etting quick answers to simple questions about the stuff in your database is nice, but there's more to life than finding out precisely how many folks from Montreal or Bombay bought pastel-colored back scratchers between January and May of the previous year. What if you needed to know the total amount of money they spent on back scratchers? Or the number of orders they placed?

In what's rapidly becoming a recurring theme of the book, it's Access 97 to the rescue. Well, technically speaking, it's Access 97 *query calculations* to the rescue.

Queries do simple math, count matching entries, and can perform several other tricks, provided you know how to ask for their help. This chapter explains the inner workings of these helpful functions. Read on and put those queries to work!

Totaling Everything in Sight

In addition to just answering questions, the standard query can also perform simple calculations on the information it finds. For example, if you tell the system to list all the customers from Germany, it can count them at no extra charge. What a deal!

The first step in adding a total to your query is making the Total row appear. With your query on-screen, choose View⇨Totals or click on the Totals button. Figure 14-1 shows the Select Query screen with the Total row added.

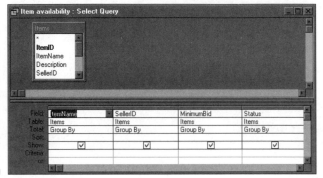

Figure 14-1:
The Total row is added between the Table row and the Sort row.

 The symbol on the face of the Totals button is the Greek letter *sigma,* meaning *to add everything up.* Mathematicians, engineers, and others with interpersonal communication difficulties use this symbol when they mean *sum it up.*

Grouping the Suspects

To use the Total row, start by picking the fields that you want to use in the query. You pick the fields the same way you do for a Select query. Simply drag the field name from the list at the top to one of the columns in the grid. As you add the fields to the grid, the Total row fills in with the Group By entry, indicating that Access is trying to use that field to organize your information.

You use Group By to have Access organize the information that you are displaying into groups based on that particular field. This arrangement can be useful for getting a list of all the different entries that appear in a single field. For example, Figure 14-2 shows a query with the Group By instruction in the DateIn category (from the Items database).

Figure 14-2:
Group By lets you display records by one set of criteria.

By doing Group By with the DateIn field, you can generate a list of all the dates on which new items were added to the auction. When you use this query, you get the results shown in Figure 14-3.

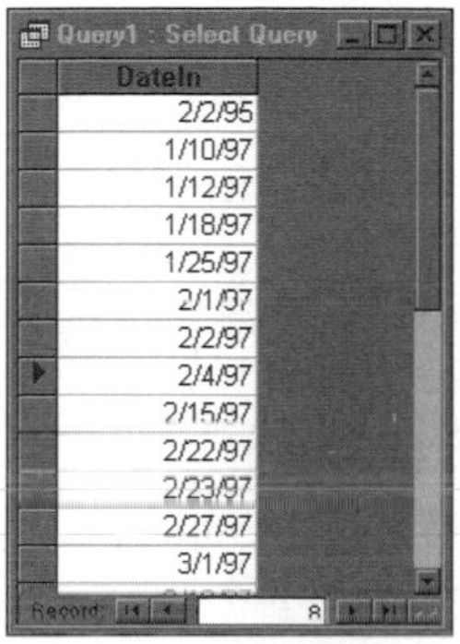
Query1 : Select Query
DateIn
2/2/95
1/10/97
1/12/97
1/18/97
1/25/97
2/1/97
2/2/97
2/4/97
2/15/97
2/22/97
2/23/97
2/27/97
3/1/97
Record:
8

Figure 14-3: The Group By instruction lists each entry in the field only once.

Each date is listed only once, even though on some dates, several items may have been brought to the auction (which means that several records with that date exist in the database). Without the Group By instruction, the list would repeat a date each time it appears in the database.

The Group By entry needs to stay in each field that Access uses to organize your data. In other words, if you're going to use a criteria for your field, you need to put Group By in the Total rows.

If you have more than one field showing with the Group By instruction, you see each unique combination of the two fields only once. Figure 14-4 lists the results of having the DateIn and Item Name fields listed from the Items table of the Auction database.

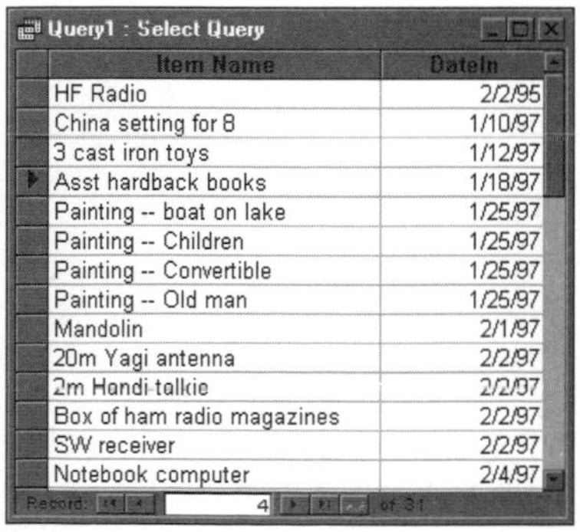
Query1 : Select Query
Item Name
DateIn
HF Radio 2/2/95
China setting for 8 1/10/97
3 cast iron toys 1/12/97
Asst hardback books 1/18/97
Painting -- boat on lake 1/25/97
Painting -- Children 1/25/97
Painting -- Convertible 1/25/97
Painting -- Old man 1/25/97
Mandolin 2/1/97
20m Yagi antenna 2/2/97
2m Handi-talkie 2/2/97
Box of ham radio magazines 2/2/97
SW receiver 2/2/97
Notebook computer 2/4/97
Record:
4
of 31

Figure 14-4: Here, all items with the same Item Name and DateIn are listed as a single record.

In Figure 14-4, each date shows every different type of item that was added on that date. Notice that for dates such as February 2, several different items are listed as having come into the auction. On the other hand, when the same type of item was brought in (such as the four boxes of books that came in on January 18), the item type is only listed once.

Counting the Good Count

Although getting a list of the different entries within a field can be useful, the Total line can also be used to give you information about the contents of a field. If you want to work with the contents of the field, you must use an instruction other than Group By. One of the easiest types of instructions to work with is Count, which tells you how many records are in each group. (You create groups from the entries in the field by using the Group By entry.)

To find out how many records are in each group, you simply need to use the Count function on one of your other fields (columns) in addition to the Group By instruction. Your query uses two fields — the one you are using to create the groups (Group By) and the one you are counting (Count).

The most difficult part of the whole operation is deciding which field to use for counting. If you want to make sure to count each record that matches, you must be certain that the field you use has a unique entry for each and every record. For example, Figure 14-5 shows the Query that Dorothy uses to count the number of members in each of the guilds.

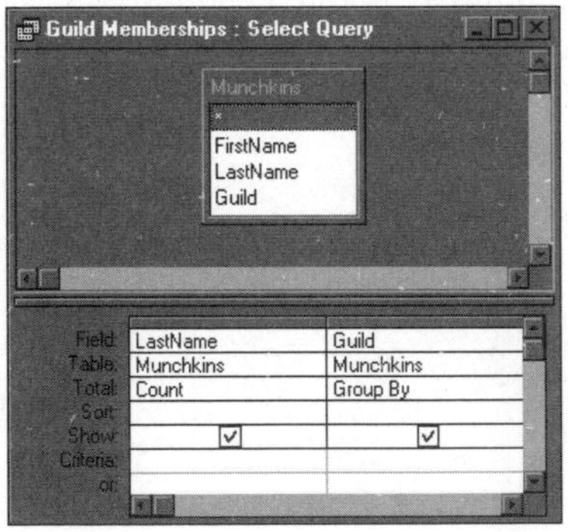

Figure 14-5:
Access
calculates
the number
of members
in each
guild.

Select the Count function by clicking on the cell in the Total row for the field that you want counted. When you click, a down-arrow button appears. Click on the down arrow to see a drop-down list of functions, one of which is Count.

In the Guild field's Total row, Dorothy uses the Group By instruction. For her other field in this query, she uses LastName. To do the arithmetic, she includes a Count instruction in the LastName field's Total row. Group By tells Access to group the records by the entry in the Guild field, and Count tells Access to count the records in each group (guild), increasing the count by one for each record with a last name. Because all Munchkins have last names, this instruction means that Access counts the number of Munchkins in each guild. Figure 14-6 shows the results of Dorothy's search.

Figure 14-6:
The Great
Guild
Membership
Count is
complete.

Select 'em and Then Count 'em

With Dorothy's problem solved, you can check back at the auction and see how Access 97 is helping there. The managers of the auction are considering whether to require a minimum bid of $50 for all items. Before they change the minimum bid, however, the managers want to find out how many items would be affected. To do this, they need to create a query that selects the items affected and then counts them. The only problem is that a different field must be counted than the one being used for the criteria. Figure 14-7 shows a query that can do this.

Figure 14-7:
The results
of this query
lists the
number of
records for
each
minimum bid
amount less
than $50.

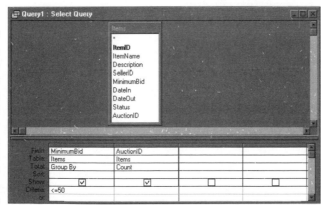

When you're working with the Total row, remember that *each field* you include must have an instruction on the Total row, even if it's only Group By (which Access 97 sticks in there as the default, anyway).

You can use a criteria in any field — even one you're not including in the final results — to narrow the query. To do this, put a Where instruction (which you can choose from the drop-down list that appears when you click in the field's Total cell) on the field's Total row. When you put the Where instruction in a field, Access uses in the query any criteria you create in the field but does not display the field itself in the results of the query.

You can also use a Where instruction in a field that you want to have treated as one group. If the managers use a Where instruction rather than a Group By instruction, the results are a single row — the total count of records in the database with minimum bids of less than $50.

Counting with Crosstab

Some types of information naturally lend themselves to being grouped by two categories. For example, polls often use gender (which is traditionally a two-option category) to break down their results. You can do the same kind of breakdown in Access with a crosstab (or *cross tabulation*) query.

Figure 14-8 is an example of what crosstab results look like. It shows a breakdown of the auction information organized by the home states of the customers and the location where their items were sold. Each row represents a different state, and each column represents one of the sites. Each box within the table contains the number of customers from that state who sold items at that site. Four states and two sites make eight values in the table.

Figure 14-8:
The
Datasheet
view of a
crosstab
query.

State/Province	Exposition Hall	The Ranch
IL	3	3
IN	7	15
OH	3	2
WV	2	1

Record: 1 of 4

A crosstab query grid includes both the Total and the Crosstab row (as shown in Figure 14-9). Crosstab queries always involve three fields. *Row Heading* is used for the row categories. *Column Heading* tells Access 97 where to find the column category. The third field explains where the values for the crosstab come from.

Figure 14-9:
In a crosstab
query, one
field
becomes
the Row
Heading,
one the
Column
Heading,
and one the
value.

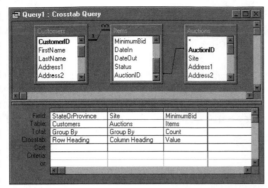

Both of the fields used as headings have a Group By instruction on the Total row. The field used for value has the function (usually Count, Sum, or Avg) that is used for calculating the values for the table.

You can also use one or many criteria to limit which records are included in the summary. As with other queries in this chapter, you do so by adding a criteria to one of the fields already being used. The easiest way to do this is by adding another field to the query, using the Where instruction (so that the field doesn't show up in the results), and then adding the criteria to that field.

Of course, you don't have to do all this stuff by hand. The Crosstab Query Wizard can guide you through each of the steps for a basic crosstab query. Take advantage of it; otherwise, the wizard begins to feel lonely.

Does It All Add Up?

You can use other functions on the Total row instead of Count, Where, or Group By. One of the most useful is the Sum function, which simply gives you a total. For example, you can use just the MinimumBid field from the Items table of the Auction database with the Sum function and no other field. By running that query, you get the total amount of all minimum bids, as shown in Figure 14-10.

Figure 14-10:
Total all the
values in a
field by using
the Sum
function.

To create a query that sums a total, add the MinimumBid field to your query grid and use the Sum instruction on the Total row. The rest of the grid is left blank. The records are put into one large group and then values in the MinimumBid field are added together to create the sum.

As with the Count function, you can combine the Sum function with other instructions on the Total row (or even with criteria). For example, you may want to find out what the total is for each Seller ID number. To do so, you simply add the SellerID field to your query with a Group By instruction, as shown in Figure 14-11.

Figure 14-11:
When you use the Total row, each field must have an entry. Here, I calculate the minimum bids total for each seller.

When you run that query, you see the results shown in Figure 14-12. Each Seller ID is listed individually with the total for that seller.

Figure 14-12:
If you combine SellerID with Group By, you get the total value of the minimum bids for each seller.

Seller ID	SumOfMinimumBid
3	120
5	45
6	100
9	750
11	85
12	2375
14	125
15	22
20	1350
21	225
22	120
37	400
41	2245
49	1030

If you want to have the seller's name rather than the ID number, all you need to do is set up a multiple table query that links to the Customer table by the ID number. To complete the process (for this example), you use the LastName field for your Group By rather than SellerID, as shown in Figure 14-13. When you run the query, the information is organized by last name with the total minimum bid for each individual instead of simply listing the seller number.

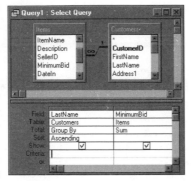

Figure 14-13:
Using the
Customer
table, you
can organize
your query
by seller
name rather
than by ID
number.

Here's a tidbit from the Since You're Already Here School of Access 97: You can also activate the Sort function and have the list organized in descending order (largest to smallest) by any field in your query. To do that, put the *Descending* instruction on the Sort line under the field you want to sort with. Figure 14-14 shows the Auction query set up with a descending sort on the MinimumBid field.

Figure 14-14:
Having
Access 97
sort the
minimum
bids in
descending
order is
easy.

The query's results are shown in Figure 14-15.

Figure 14-15:
The results
are in —
and in order
from largest
to smallest.

LastName	SumOfMinimumBid
Backmeyer	2375
Peters	2245
Donati	1350
Ingle	1030
Williams	750
Merk	400
Abercrombie	225
Vaubel	125
Hashimoto	120
Allen-Brown	120
Coffie	100
Cae	85
Haseman	45
Rosen-Sheid	22

You can find more about the Sort line in Chapter 11. If you're curious about sorting in general, flip to Chapter 10.

There's More to Life Than Sum and Count

Don't get the idea that the world of queries begins and ends with Sum and Count. Access 97 includes many other functions to organize, evaluate, and generally figure out what your data is saying. Some of the more popular and useful functions are listed in Table 14-1.

Each entry in the table includes the name of the function and a brief description of what it does. Each function can be selected from the drop-down list on the Total line.

Table 14-1	Access Functions and What They Do
Function	*Purpose*
Group By	Organizes the query results in this field
Sum	Adds up all the values from this field in the query results
Avg	Calculates the average of the values in this field
Min	Tells you the lowest value the query finds
Max	Gives you the highest value the query finds
Count	Tells you the number of records that match the query criteria
First	Returns the first record that Access 97 stumbles across that meets the query criteria
Last	Same as First, except that it returns the last matching record Access 97 finds
Expression	Tells Access that you want a calculated field (see Chapter 15 for more information)
Where	Tells Access to use this field as part of the query criteria

Chapter 15
Automated Editing for Big Changes

- -

- -

*O*ne of the first rules you learn about creating a database is to enter only the fields that you need and to not bother with data that Access can calculate based on information already in the database. Well, this chapter shows you how to get Access to do those calculations. The secret to this wizardly magic is the calculated field.

A *calculated field* takes information from another field in the database and performs some arithmetic on it to come up with new information. In fact, a calculated field can take data from *more* than one field and combine it to create an entirely new field, if that's what you want.

Although the examples in this chapter deal with calculated fields within queries, you use the same techniques to add calculated fields to a report. You can find more information about adding calculated fields to reports in Chapter 20.

A Simple Calculation

When you want to create a calculated field within a query, first make sure that all the tables containing fields that you want to use in the calculation are included at the top of the query screen. For example, suppose that you want to calculate an expected price for items in an auction. This calculation requires only that the Items table be added to the query. Because you're calculating with the item's price, the query also needs the MinimumBid field. Finally, so that you know which items are which, add the ItemName field to the query grid (see Figure 15-1).

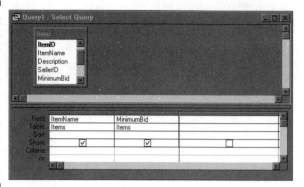

Figure 15-1:
To calculate the expected price for an item, you just need the Item Name and MinimumBid fields.

To start building your calculated field, simply click in the field name box of the column where you want the results to appear. Instead of selecting an existing field, you simply type into the box the calculation that you want Access 97 to perform.

Say that you've done your research and know that, in most auctions, an item sells for 47 percent more than the minimum bid price. So, to calculate the expected price, you simply need to add 47 percent to the MinimumBid. One formula to do this is

```
[MinimumBid] + ([MinimumBid] * .47)
```

Enter the calculation in the first empty field — in this case, the field next to MinimumBid. In order for Access 97 to recognize what you are typing as a field, you need to enclose MinimumBid in square brackets, as shown in the preceding sample formula and in Figure 15-2.

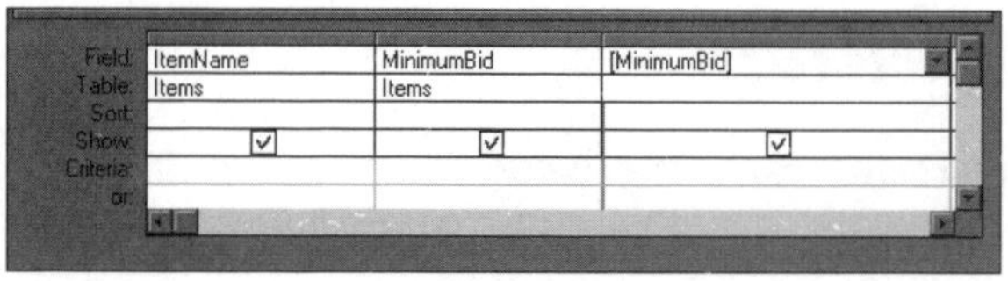

Figure 15-2:
Using square brackets tells Access that you are discussing a field.

You can now type the rest of the formula in the field; however, you may not be able to see all your formula at one time. You have two choices: Either keep typing and trust that what you are typing is actually going into the field, or enlarge the field so that it is wide enough to display the entire formula. Figure 15-3 shows the entire formula for calculating the expected price displayed in the field.

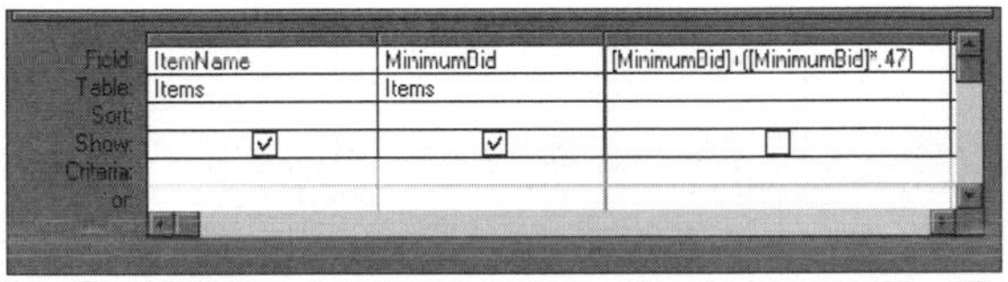

Figure 15-3:
The formula for the expected price of your sale items.

Field	ItemName	MinimumDid	[MinimumDid] : [[MinimumBid]*.47]
Table	Items	Items	
Sort			
Show	☑	☑	☐
Criteria			
or			

Because Access 97 isn't smart enough to recognize the percent sign, you need to convert any percentages to decimals. In this case, you write 47% as **.47**. In order to convert a percent to a decimal, just divide it by 100.

You have to type each field name into your formula; you can't just drag the field name down from the table list. Dragging down the field name adds it as a field itself.

When you run this query, it produces a table showing the item name, the minimum bid, and an expected price for each entry (see Figure 15-4). If you want, you can take a calculator and check that Access 97 did its job correctly. You should find that if you take the value in the MinimumBid field and multiply it by 1.47, you get the result shown in the new calculated field.

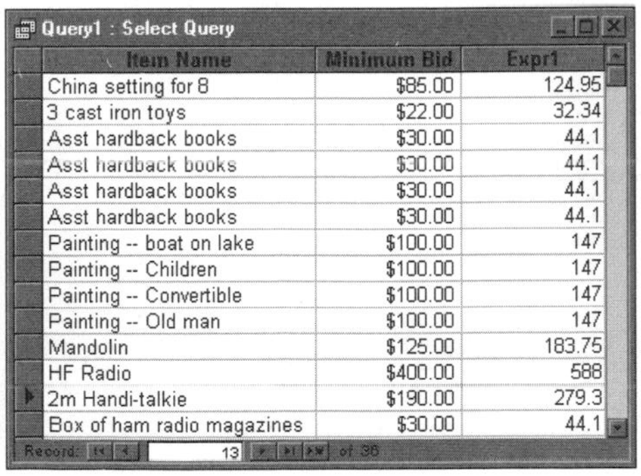

Figure 15-4:
The calculation actually works!

Item Name	Minimum Bid	Expr1
China setting for 8	$85.00	124.95
3 cast iron toys	$22.00	32.34
Asst hardback books	$30.00	44.1
Asst hardback books	$30.00	44.1
Asst hardback books	$30.00	44.1
Asst hardback books	$30.00	44.1
Painting -- boat on lake	$100.00	147
Painting -- Children	$100.00	147
Painting -- Convertible	$100.00	147
Painting -- Old man	$100.00	147
Mandolin	$125.00	183.75
HF Radio	$400.00	588
2m Handi-talkie	$190.00	279.3
Box of ham radio magazines	$30.00	44.1

Record: 13 of 36

In Figure 15-4, notice that the column for the expected price is labeled a little strangely — Expr1 (which stands for *Expression 1*) is the default name for the first *expression,* or formula for a calculation, that you create. Changing the expression heading is easy. If you look at the grid after creating an expression, you find that Access 97 inserts the default field name and a colon in front of your equation. To give the field a different name, simply highlight the field name and replace it. Figure 15-5 shows the calculated field after it's been given the field name Expected Price.

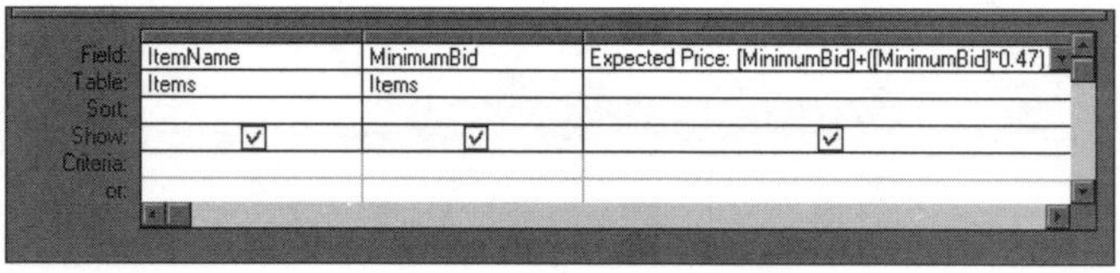

Figure 15-5:
The words before the expression create the label for the field name.

Field:	ItemName	MinimumBid	Expected Price: [MinimumBid]+([MinimumBid]*0.47)
Table:	Items	Items	
Sort:			
Show:	☑	☑	☑
Criteria:			
or:			

In addition to changing the field name, you may want to change its format. To change the format of the field, simply right-click on the field and, from the pop-up menu that appears, select Properties. In the Field Properties dialog box (shown in Figure 15-6), click in the Format line and then click on the button that appears on the right end of the field (the one with the downward-pointing arrow).

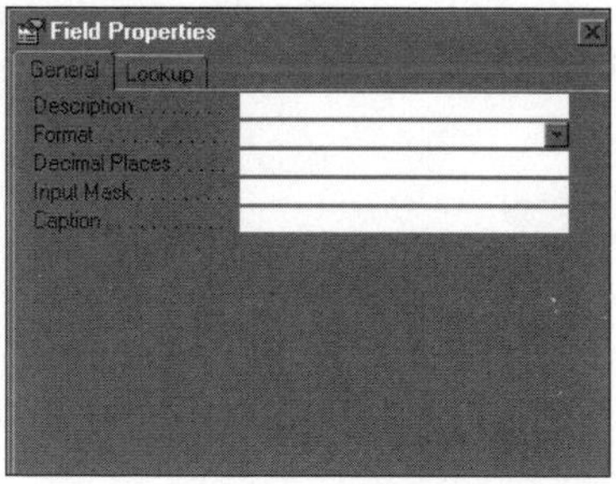

Figure 15-6:
Use the Field Properties dialog box to change the formatting of your fields.

Field Properties

General | Lookup

Description
Format
Decimal Places
Input Mask
Caption

In the drop-down list that appears, select the type of format that you want to use for the field. For this example, select Currency. Figure 15-7 shows the resulting table after you change the name of the field to Expected Price and use the Currency format for all the values.

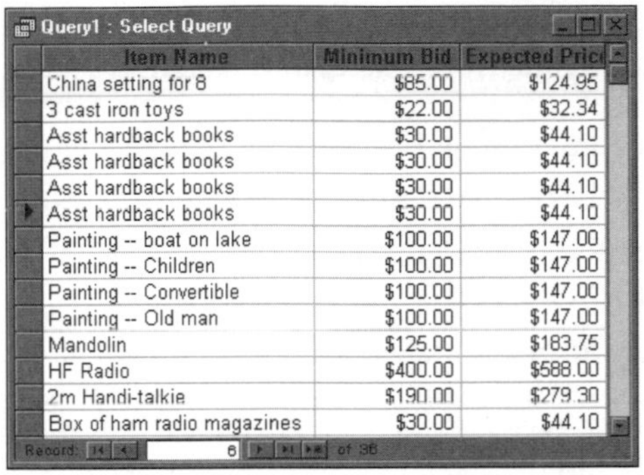

Figure 15-7:
Using the
Format
section of
the Field
Properties
dialog box,
you can set
a particular
format for
any field.

Item Name	Minimum Bid	Expected Price
China setting for 8	$85.00	$124.95
3 cast iron toys	$22.00	$32.34
Asst hardback books	$30.00	$44.10
Asst hardback books	$30.00	$44.10
Asst hardback books	$30.00	$44.10
Asst hardback books	$30.00	$44.10
Painting -- boat on lake	$100.00	$147.00
Painting -- Children	$100.00	$147.00
Painting -- Convertible	$100.00	$147.00
Painting -- Old man	$100.00	$147.00
Mandolin	$125.00	$183.75
HF Radio	$400.00	$588.00
2m Handi-talkie	$190.00	$279.30
Box of ham radio magazines	$30.00	$44.10

After you get the hang of simple calculations, you can more confidently use Access for more powerful operations.

Bigger, Better (And More Complicated) Calculations

You can use more than one field in your calculation to create a result. Figure 15-8 shows the Items table after adding a couple of options. In addition to the fields previously discussed, ActualPrice, DateIn, and DateOut fields are added, and, for many of the records, the DateOut and ActualPrice fields are filled in with dates and amounts as the items have sold. For some items, the Status field is changed from Available to Sold, and two new fields have entries. (You may notice that a couple of items are withdrawn from the auction.)

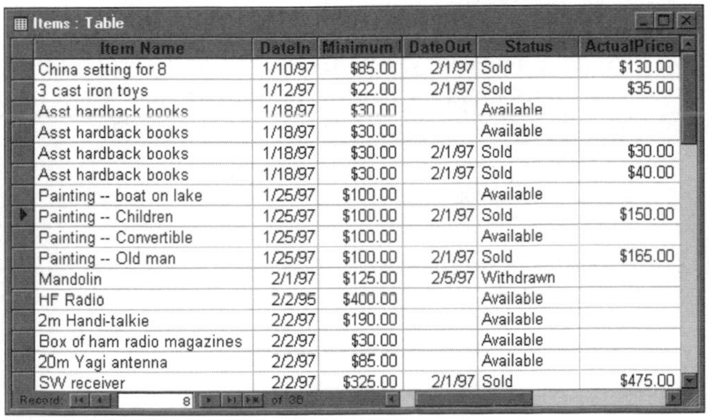

Figure 15-8:
I added the
ActualPrice
field — an
important
field — to
the Items
table.

Item Name	DateIn	Minimum	DateOut	Status	ActualPrice
China setting for 8	1/10/97	$85.00	2/1/97	Sold	$130.00
3 cast iron toys	1/12/97	$22.00	2/1/97	Sold	$35.00
Asst hardback books	1/18/97	$30.00		Available	
Asst hardback books	1/18/97	$30.00		Available	
Asst hardback books	1/18/97	$30.00	2/1/97	Sold	$30.00
Asst hardback books	1/18/97	$30.00	2/1/97	Sold	$40.00
Painting -- boat on lake	1/25/97	$100.00		Available	
Painting -- Children	1/25/97	$100.00	2/1/97	Sold	$150.00
Painting -- Convertible	1/25/97	$100.00		Available	
Painting -- Old man	1/25/97	$100.00	2/1/97	Sold	$165.00
Mandolin	2/1/97	$125.00	2/5/97	Withdrawn	
HF Radio	2/2/95	$400.00		Available	
2m Handi-talkie	2/2/97	$190.00		Available	
Box of ham radio magazines	2/2/97	$30.00		Available	
20m Yagi antenna	2/2/97	$85.00		Available	
SW receiver	2/2/97	$325.00	2/1/97	Sold	$475.00

When items in the auction start selling, knowing how much more than the minimum bid each item earned and how long each item took to sell may be useful. You can find out by creating three calculated fields:

- ✔ One field calculates the number of days an item took to sell by subtracting the DateIn field from the DateOut field.

- ✔ A second field calculates the difference between the amounts in the ActualPrice and MinimumBid fields.

- ✔ A third field calculates the percentage of difference between the minimum bid and the amount above the minimum bid for which the item actually sold. This percentage can be calculated by taking the difference — in this example, Expr2 — and dividing it by the amount in the original MinimumBid field. Notice in Figure 15-9 that the Expr2 reference is treated like a field name and is enclosed in brackets.

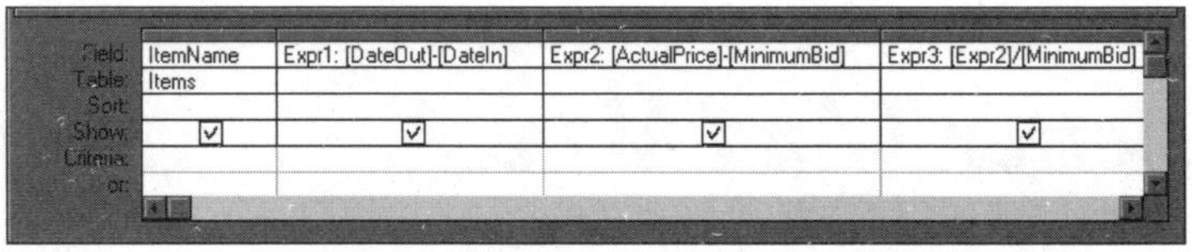

Figure 15-9:
This query uses three different expressions.

Field:	ItemName	Expr1: [DateOut]-[DateIn]	Expr2: [ActualPrice]-[MinimumBid]	Expr3: [Expr2]/[MinimumBid]
Table:	Items			
Sort:				
Show:	✔	✔	✔	✔
Criteria:				
or:				

Although these formulas produce correct results, the fields would be clearer if they had names that were more descriptive and formatting that was more logical. Figure 15-10 shows the query grid after the names of the fields are changed to DaysToSell, AmountAbove, and Increase. Note that if you change the field name for the second field (the one calculating the difference between the actual sale price and the minimum bid), you need to change the reference to that field in the third formula — in this case, from Expr2 to AmountAbove.

After looking at the query for a minute, you may realize that displaying the AmountAbove field isn't necessary — you can just include the information for that field directly in the formula for the Increase field. Instead of having AmountAbove above the divisor, your formula would be

```
([ActualPrice]-[MinimumBid])/[MinimumBid]
```

Whichever way you do it is up to you.

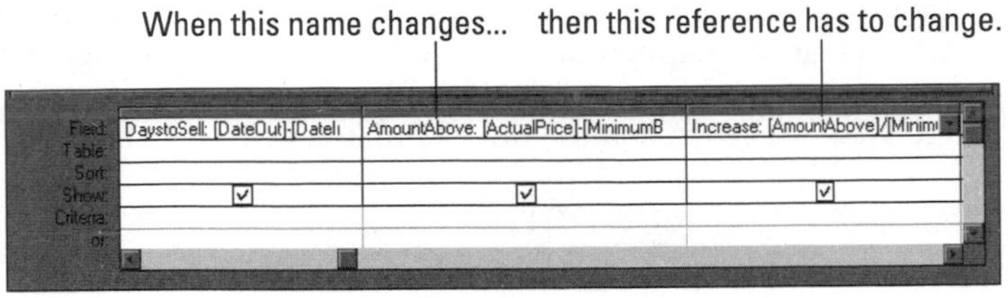

Figure 15-10:
Make sure
references
match in
calculated
fields.

When this name changes...   then this reference has to change.

Figure 15-11 shows the results of the query using these formulas. Rather than show all the items, the list includes only those items that have been sold (and therefore have ActualPrice and DateOut fields). Setting up such criteria is discussed in Chapter 11, but to refresh your memory — just add the Status field and type **Sold** in the Criteria row.

Figure 15-11:
The results
of your
calculations
for auction
items
already
sold.

Item Name	DaystoSell	AmountAbove	Increase
SW receiver	13	$150.00	46.15%
Portable printer	11	$125.00	71.43%
Wedding dress	0	$440.00	57.89%
Miscellaneous men's clothing	0	$5.00	25.00%
Treadle sewing machine	21	$45.00	56.25%
Box of asst silk thread	6	$5.00	10.00%
50 asst laser disks	2	$50.00	25.00%
Board games (5)	0	$5.00	50.00%
China setting for 8	36	$45.00	52.94%
3 cast iron toys	20	$13.00	59.09%
Asst hardback books	42	$0.00	0.00%
Asst hardback books	14	$10.00	33.33%
Painting -- Children	21	$50.00	50.00%
Painting -- Old man	7	$66.00	66.00%

Making Access 97 ask

At times, you may want a value that's not in your database included in a formula. If you already know the value, you can simply type it into the formula, just as you type **.47** for 47 percent (see "A Simple Calculation" earlier in this chapter). But if you'd rather enter that value as you run the query, that's easy to do, too.

Simply create a field name to use within your formula. For example, you may choose to calculate an ExpectedPrice field by using a percentage value that you plan to enter when you run the query. Imagine that this field is called PercentIncrease. You then create your calculated field by using this formula:

```
[MinimumBid]+([MinimumBid]*[PercentIncrease])
```

When you run the query, Access displays a dialog box like the one shown in Figure 15-12. This dialog box lets you enter a value for the increase that you're expecting.

Figure 15-12:
Access asks you to provide a value for your calculation.

When the dialog box appears, just enter the value of your expected increase (as a decimal value), and then Access 97 does the rest. This option means that you can use the same query with different values to see how changing that value affects your results.

Working with words

Number fields aren't the only fields you can use for calculations. In fact, performing the calculation by using a text field is often more useful. Figure 15-13 shows one of the most common database formulas, which is used to combine the FirstName and LastName fields to provide the full name.

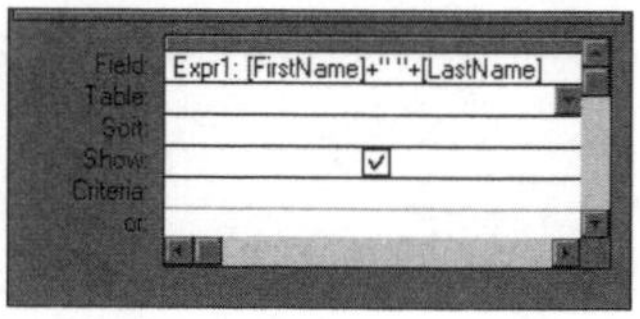

Figure 15-13:
You can turn a name into a calculated field.

This formula consists of the FirstName field, a plus sign, then a single space inside quotation marks, followed by another plus sign, and then the LastName field:

```
[FirstName]+" "+[LastName]
```

When you run this query, Access 97 takes the information from the two fields and puts them together, inserting a space in between them. The results of this query are shown in Figure 15-14.

Figure 15-14: See! You *can* join the names back together again.

Notice that each individual's name appears as it would on a mailing list label. This kind of text calculation makes taking information from your database and turning it into a more readable format easy.

Expression Builder to the Rescue

Creating calculated fields has two basic problems. First, you have to figure out what the formula should say. And then you have to know how to enter the formula so that Access 97 can recognize it.

Unfortunately, Access 97 can't help you with the first problem — but it can help with the second. To get help creating a calculated field the way Access 97 wants it, click on the Build button and bring out the Expression Builder.

The Expression Builder has several parts to it, as you can see in Figure 15-15. The top part is the area where you actually create the expression, and immediately below that are the operators you can use to work with the information in your expression.

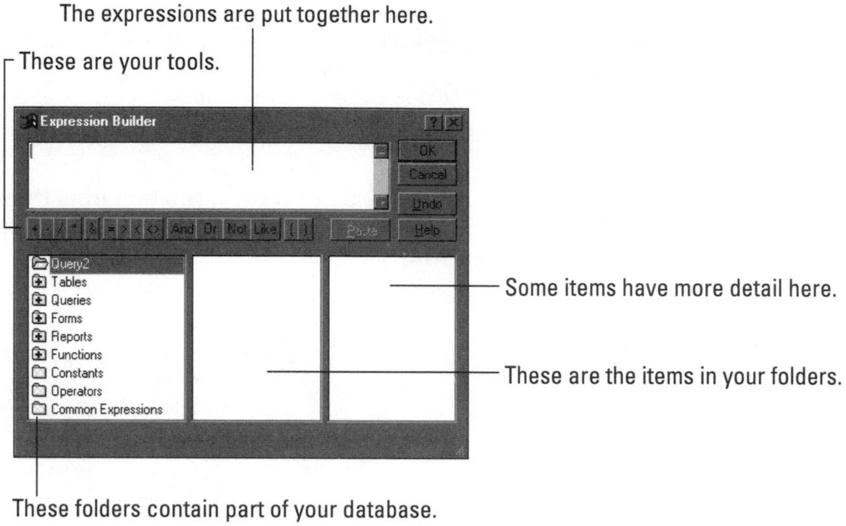

The expressions are put together here.

These are your tools.

Figure 15-15:
The Expression Builder puts it together so that you don't have to.

Some items have more detail here.

These are the items in your folders.

These folders contain part of your database.

The first group of these operators does simple mathematical operations: addition, subtraction, multiplication, and division. The next operator, the ampersand (&), is similar in that it can be used to combine two text fields (in most cases, you can also use the plus sign to add text fields).

The next two groups of operators do logical comparisons. These operators create expressions similar to formulas used in the Criteria field and return a response of True or False. The final two buttons in this collection enable you to enter parentheses. (You can also simply type these symbols directly from your keyboard, which is often much easier.)

The lower half of the dialog box has three windows. The left window contains folders of the various parts of your Access 97 environment, including all the information in your tables.

To add a field from one of your tables, simply open the Tables folder and then open the folder for the table that you want to use. A list of all the fields in that table appears in the middle window. To add a field to the expression, simply double-click on it. Figure 15-16 shows the Expression Builder with the Items folder open and the MinimumBid item already added to the expression.

Notice that when you use the Expression Builder to add a field, it includes the table name in front of the field name with an exclamation mark in between the two. The format for this is

```
[Table Name]![Field Name]
```

Figure 15-16:
You can find
a field in the
lower half of
the builder
and add
it to an
expression
by double-
clicking
on it.

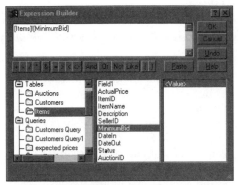

The other folders listed in the left window often contain much more information. In some cases, this information is organized into categories within the folder. For example, the Functions folder contains a variety of built-in functions, as well as some functions that you or others may have defined in your database. These functions can be used to perform calculations using the information in your database.

To use one of the built-in functions, simply open the Functions folder, select a category of functions from those in the middle window, and then look through the list in the right window until you find the function you want to use. Figure 15-17 shows the Built-In Functions folder open, with the Financial functions displayed in the right window. To select a category of functions, simply click on the category name in the middle window. To select a function, double-click on it in the right window.

Figure 15-17:
In the lower
left, you see
a brief
synopsis of
the function
that you've
selected.

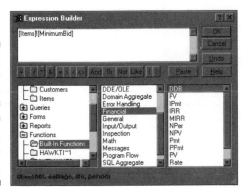

Useful items are in the other folders, as well. The Constants folder contains constants that are defined for use in comparisons, including True, False, and some that can represent empty fields. The Operators folder contains symbols used for creating expressions.

The Arithmetic category (inside the Operators folder) includes the same four operators that are available as buttons. It also includes the caret (^), which is used for exponents (raising a number to a higher power); MOD, which is used to return the remainder of a division operation; and the backslash, which is used for integer division. With integer division, dividing 5 by 2 (5/2) gives you the answer 2, and 5 MOD 2 gives you the result of 1, the remainder.

Finally, Common Expressions enable you to include various common entries. These entries are most useful for creating a report and are discussed in Chapter 20.

One of the advantages to using the Expression Builder is that it helps to remind you what you need to do. For example, when you are creating an expression, the Expression Builder won't let you just add two fields, side by side. Figure 15-18 shows what would happen if you double-click on the DateOut and DateIn fields, one after the other.

Figure 15-18:
The Expression Builder tells you when you need to add an operator to an expression.

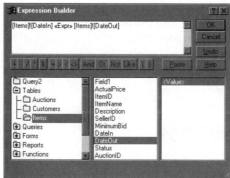

Notice the angle bracket (the two less than signs), Expr, and angle bracket (the two greater than signs)

```
<<Expr>>
```

that appear between the two fields. They remind you that you need to insert an expression between the two fields. If you click on the <<Expr>> entry, the entire text highlights, and then you can click on one of the operators to insert it between the two fields (for example, the minus sign).

Chapter 16

Action Queries to the Rescue

In This Chapter

▶ Replacing data

▶ Deleting data

▶ Updating data

*F*ixing an incorrect entry in an Access 97 table is pretty easy. A couple of clicks, some typing, and {poof!} the problem is gone.

But what if you need to fix 26,281 records? Suddenly, you're talking about a whole bunch of clicking and typing and clicking and typing. Editing an entire table by hand doesn't sound like a {poof!} experience to me — it sounds more like a clean-the-elephant-herd-with-a-toothbrush kind of experience.

Fortunately, Access 97 has a variety of large-scale housekeeping and editing tools. These tools enable you to make widespread changes to your database without wearing down your fingers in the process. This chapter explores the tools available within Access 97 and gives you examples of how to use them to make quick work of the elephant herd in your life.

Quick and Easy Fixes: Replacing Your Mistakes

Before moving on to the elaborate techniques that you can use in queries, you need to know about one particular editing technique: using the Replace command to change a mistake into a different value. When you open a table in the Datasheet view, you can choose the Replace command from the Edit menu to display the dialog box shown in Figure 16-1.

In this dialog box, you can enter the information that is currently in your database (the wrong word) in the Find What box and enter the proper information into the Replace With box. When you have entered text in both fields, the buttons on the right side become available; you can use these buttons to move through your data, making changes as you go.

If you've misspelled "munchkin" throughout your data and need to change all its occurrences to the proper spelling, you can simply put the incorrect spelling in Find What, the proper spelling in Replace With, and click on the Replace All button. Your computer goes off and does your bidding, changing each and every instance of the word in the Find What box to the word in the Replace With box.

You can, however, have greater control over what's going on. Some features that control how Access locates specific records are discussed in Chapter 10 as part of the Find command. Two additional options, though, are unique to the Replace command:

 ✔ One option, Match Whole Field, tells Access to only bother looking for cases where the information in the Find What box is all that is in the field. If you have any additional characters, even a single letter, in the field and the Match Whole Field box has a check next to it, Access skips over that field.

 ✔ The other option gives you both a Find Next and a Replace button to move you through the data. You use the Find Next button to move to the next information that matches what is in the Find What box without changing the current selection. You use the Replace button to change the current selection and move on to the next match.

These two buttons enable you to browse through your database, making changes only in certain cases. Click on Find Next to move on without changing; click on Replace to make the change and move on. (Clicking on Replace All makes each and every change without asking your permission first. Access does tell you how many changes it made when it finishes.)

Different Queries for Different Jobs

Although Select queries are the most useful type of queries within Access, because they answer your questions and you can use them as the basis for reports, other types of queries are also useful (otherwise, Microsoft wouldn't have bothered including them). You can change the type of query that you are using by selecting from the Query menu (found in Query Design View) or by using the Query Type button on the Query Design View toolbar. When you click on the downward-pointing arrow on the right side of the Query Type button, a list of query types drops down, as shown in Figure 16-2.

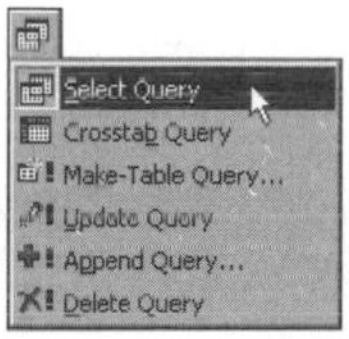

Figure 16-2:
A veritable smorgasbord of query types unfurl from the Query Type button.

I discuss the Crosstab query in Chapter 14 and the Append query and Make Table query types in Chapter 12. To change the type of query you're using, simply choose the type that you want from the list (either the Query menu or the Query Type button list).

 The last four types of queries (Make Table, Update, Append, and Delete) are pictured with exclamation marks to remind you that these types of queries actually change the way your information is organized. When you work with these four types of queries, you can use the Query View button to preview which records are affected by the query. I strongly recommend that you do a preview before running any of these queries, because previewing is the only way to make sure that the changes you're making are really the ones you intend.

 With most types of queries, the difference between using the Run button and the Query View button is minor. But when you use either the Delete query or the Update query, whether you use the Run or the Query View button makes a BIG difference. When you use the Query View button with these two functions, you see the results without really changing your database. If you use the Run button instead, your information is changed for all time and eternity (well, unless you have a backup).

You're Outta Here: The Delete Query

One of the easiest types of editing queries to create is a Delete query. Unfortunately, the Delete query is also one of the most dangerous queries around. When you create a Delete query, you use the same commands and setup as you do for a Select query. In fact, consider doing a Select query first to make sure that you are matching the records you mean to match before converting the query to a Delete query.

 At the very least, click on the Query View button before you use the Run button.

1. **To begin, set up all your criteria in a normal Select query for identifying your records.**

2. **Run the query to make sure that it does, in fact, display the records that you want to work with.**

3. **Return to the Design view and use the Query Type drop-down list to choose a Delete query or choose Delete from the Query menu.**

   You see the Delete Query option on the Query Type list.

 When you switch to a Delete query, the name in the Title Bar changes and the Sort line changes to the Delete line. Figure 16-3 shows a typical Delete Query screen. Notice that information for locating records is already in this query because it was converted over from the query I used to list out these records (the original Select query).

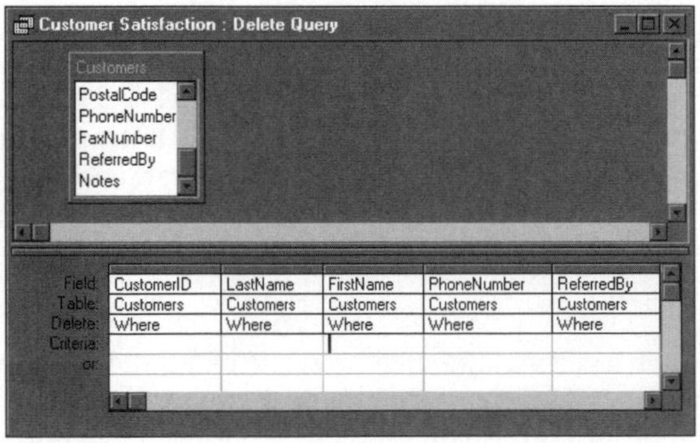

Figure 16-3:
The Delete Query window rubs out the data you don't want.

Access identifies those fields you want to use to select the records with the Where instruction on the Delete line. This instruction simply means, "Find records *where* this criteria is true." After you set up your criteria, if you want to delete all the records that match your criteria, convert to a Delete query and you're ready to go. When you start to run the query, you see a message asking whether you're sure that you want to delete the records and reminding you that you won't be able to get the data back.

You cannot undo the changes made with the Delete query. After you delete these records, they are gone — period. Gone for good, never to be seen or heard from again. Are you sure you really mean to do this?

If you realize that this is all a bad dream and you really want to keep those records in your table, carefully click on <u>N</u>o. If you're *sure* (really sure) that you want to delete the records, click on the <u>Y</u>es button; Access goes out, finds the records that match the criteria, and removes them from the table. That's all you need to do.

You can, in fact, create Delete queries that use more than one table to locate their information. Be very careful when doing so, however, as the number of changes that you are making can go up dramatically. Again, I suggest doing a Select query first to list out the records that you want to delete.

You actually don't need to run a separate Select query before you begin. You can simply click on the Query View button on the left side of the standard toolbar to switch to a Datasheet view and see what records will be affected by your query.

If you want, you can emphasize which records are to be deleted by dragging the asterisk symbol from the appropriate table. When you drag in the asterisk, the information on the Delete line for that field changes to the From instruction, indicating the table *from* which the record will be deleted.

Things get a bit more complicated if you create a query that uses more than one table. When deleting from more than one table, Access can only figure out by itself when it needs to delete records that are linked one-to-one — in other words, each record that is linked only to a single record in the other table. When you look at the relationship grid at the top of the Query screen, one-to-one links are shown with a "1" symbol. If your relationships are one-to-many (indicated with an infinity symbol — ∞ — at the end of the link), you need one query to delete all the matching records from the first table and a second query to delete the single record from the other end of the relationship.

Making Big Changes

There comes a time in every database's life when it needs to change. Fortunately, you can make changes of the large variety automatically by using an Update query. An Update query enables you to use a query to select records and then use instructions to change the information.

As with other types of queries that modify your data, particularly the Delete query discussed previously in this chapter, making sure that your query is working only with the records that you want to change is important. That's why I always suggest setting up your criteria and then running the Select query.

When you select the Update query, either by choosing Update from the Query menu or by choosing Update query from the Query Type list, your query grid changes to resemble the one shown in Figure 16-4.

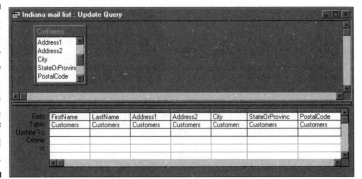

Figure 16-4:
The Update Query Design view gives you a field to update the entries of selected criteria.

The one change to your query grid is the addition of the Update To line. You can use any criteria to select your records, just as you can in a normal query. For example, you may want to select all the records in your auction database that belong to the Allen-Brown family. To do so, set up your criteria with the LastName field and the entry "Allen-Brown" on the Criteria line. You may also want to include the ItemName and its MinimumBid to make sure that you find those records you want. When you run your Select query, your grid resembles the one shown in Figure 16-5.

Figure 16-5:
A Select query shows the items contributed by the Allen-Brown family.

When you run this query, you see that, in fact, you are getting only the records for the items submitted by the Allen-Brown family — four boxes of assorted books.

The Allen-Brown family has decided to raise the price of the books that they have in the auction. You could simply go through and change each record by hand, but using an Update query is much easier. The Allen-Brown family has decided on a price of $35.00 as the MinimumBid. So, your Update query screen looks like the one shown in Figure 16-6. Notice that the new value is in the Update To row for the MinimumBid field.

Figure 16-6:
The Update query enables you to change the values of all the items in a field that correspond to your criteria.

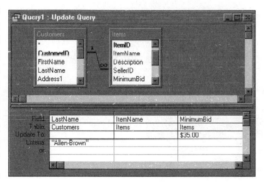

When you run the query, you get a warning message that you are about to update records. Click on Yes to go ahead and make your changes.

You can also make changes based upon the existing value in a field. For example, you may decide to apply a 10 percent discount to all minimum bids over $100. To do that, you simply need to use a calculation in the Update To field.

You can use the Expression Builder, discussed in Chapter 15, to create your calculation. In this case, the MinimumBid is equal to .9 times the MinimumBid. Taking 90 percent of the current cost is the same as taking away 10 percent (100% – 10% = 90%), and .9 is the same as 90 percent. Figure 16-7 shows how this Update query is set up.

When you run this query, Access attempts to update 20 of the Auction records, discounting the MinimumBid price to 90 percent of its original, but only on those records that have a MinimumBid of more than $100.00.

Figure 16-7:
The expression for updating the values of a field can be based on the current contents of the field.

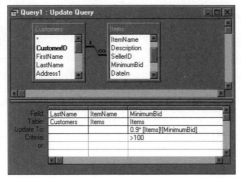

To combine additional tables and criteria, you may want to update the MinimumBids of all the items that will be at one of the auction sites. To do that, you can use a grid like the one shown in Figure 16-8.

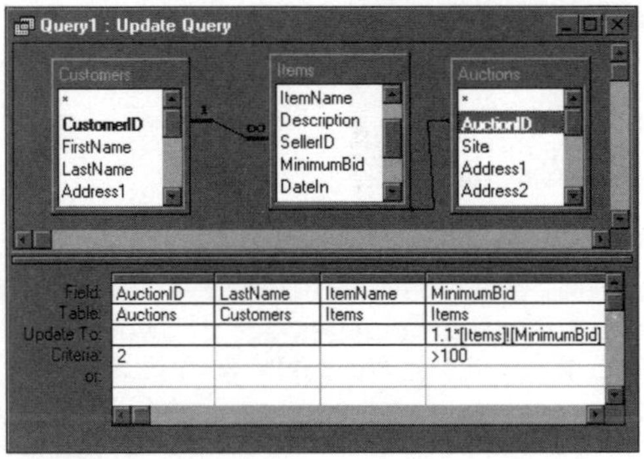

Figure 16-8:
You can update fields by using criteria from more than one table.

In Figure 16-8, the criterion being used is the AuctionID code for the auction, and MinimumBids are getting updated again — in this case, increasing the price of the items by 10 percent (multiply the old price by 1.1).

Part IV
Turning Your Table into a Book

The 5th Wave   By Rich Tennant

Get the Huggies, hon—she's reaching for the Diaper icon

In this part . . .

Someone said that the computer revolution would do away with paper. Needless to say, that person was wrong. (Last I heard, that person is now compiling the annual psychic predictions page for one of the national tabloids.)

So far, this book's shown you how to put the data in and then mixed it up a little. Now it's time to pull the data out, clean it up a bit, and record it for posterity on the printed page. Access 97 has some strong reporting tools to make your multi-thousand-page reports look truly cool. Better still, it offers some great summary tools to make those multi-thousand page reports a thing of the past. Stick your head in this part and see what you can see!

Chapter 17

AutoReport: Like the Model-T, It's Clunky but It Runs

. . . .

In This Chapter

▶ Choosing between Columnar and Tabular AutoReports

▶ Creating an AutoReport

▶ Perusing your report with Print Preview

▶ Customizing your report with Page Layout

. . . .

*A*lthough everyone who survived high school English knows what a report is (usually to their regret), understanding what Access means by "report" is another story. Access considers a *report* to be a component of your database (like a query or a form) used to organize and present your data. Specifically, you use reports to format your information so that you can present it to others in an understandable and sensible fashion. (*Very* different from any of *my* reports in high school, I can tell you.)

What do you do if someone (say, your boss) wants you to share all the revelations you've made using your datasheets, tables, and queries? Odds are, the whole management team doesn't want to crowd around your monitor and study thousands of records and dozens of queries to glean the same information that they're paying you to find.

Lucky for you, Access 97 makes creating and printing reports just another part of the whole database system. Like queries, reports can take information from the other parts of your database (specifically, tables or queries) and organize that information according to your instructions. Access 97 even includes report wizards to walk you through the steps of designing a report to meet your needs.

Creating an AutoReport

One of your first big decisions when creating a new report is determining what *type* of report you want. In this chapter, I focus on the simplest type of Access report: AutoReport. Chapter 18 shows you how to create more complex reports using the Report Wizard, as well as how to turn your data into labels and charts.

One limit to using an AutoReport is that it works with only one table or query, but it's still a very useful tool.

The great Tabular versus Columnar quandary

If you decide to stick with the simple AutoReport format, you still have one more choice to make — no, not paper or plastic — Columnar or Tabular AutoReport? Both reports organize the same data, but they don't organize data the same way.

- A *Tabular AutoReport* places all information for each record on one row, with a separate column for each field.
- A *Columnar AutoReport* organizes the data of each record vertically on the page, in two columns — one for the names of the fields (the *labels*) and one for the contents of the fields. Each record generally starts its own page. (You can adjust the report so that more than one pair of columns appears across the page.)

I don't have a profound answer to the question of when to use one or the other of the two types of AutoReports. The choice is more a matter of personal taste and aesthetics than anything else. The only advice I can offer is that the Tabular format is generally more useful if your report has lots of records with small fields, whereas the Columnar format is often better for reports with large fields but not very many records.

If you know how to put together a Columnar AutoReport, you also know how to create a Tabular AutoReport — because the tools are identical. The only real difference in a Tabular AutoReport is the direction in which you look at your information. The Tabular AutoReport organizes records to run across the page in rows, and columns represent the different fields.

The Tabular AutoReport most closely resembles the Datasheet view for your data. It is most useful when you have many records and your fields are restricted in size, as with a series of numbers or one-word text. All of the tools that you used in Columnar AutoReports work identically in Tabular AutoReports.

A report is born

Follow these steps to create a Columnar or Tabular AutoReport:

1. **Click on the Reports tab of your main database screen to reveal the window shown in Figure 17-1.**

Figure 17-1:
The Reports tab displays all your reports and enables you to create new ones.

2. **Click on New to create a new report.**

   The New Report dialog box appears, showing all the report types from which you can choose.

3. **Click on AutoReport: Columnar or AutoReport: Tabular.**

   When you click on the appropriate AutoReport entry in the list, the little graphic in the New Report window changes so that it looks like Figure 17-2.

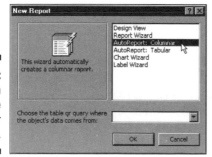

Figure 17-2:
Click on your choice of Columnar or Tabular.

The query advantage

The fact that Access 97 lets you base a report on a query is actually a wonderful thing. When you base a report on a table, you get an entry in your report for each and every record in the table. But what if you only want a few of the records? The answer is to create a query and then base the report upon that query (or, to put it another way, on the query's datasheet).

The advantages don't stop there. If you create a query based on multiple tables, Access neatly organizes your results into a single datasheet. If your query produces the information that you

want in its datasheet, then a report based on that query's datasheet organizes and presents the information in the way you want. (For more on creating queries using more than one table, see Chapter 12.)

But there is one circumstance in which a query datasheet doesn't give you what you need. If you want to create a report with several levels of information, you need to use the techniques discussed in Chapter 18. Reports that are based on a datasheet are always organized with all of the records in a single group.

4. **Click the drop-down list at the bottom of the dialog box to select which table or query you want to use.**

   Scroll through the options until you find the table or query on which you want to base your report. Remember that each AutoReport can only cover one query or table.

5. **Click on OK.**

   You are now the proud owner of an AutoReport. After a bit, Access shows your report in Print Preview. You *could* choose to print your document at this point — and it *may* even turn out well. But I recommend you do a bit more fiddling first.

Previewing Your Report

The Print Preview window, as shown in Figure 17-3, enables you to see what your document will look like when you print it.

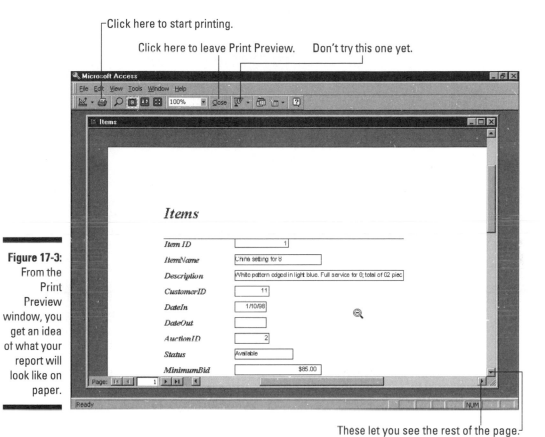

┌Click here to start printing.

Click here to leave Print Preview.　　Don't try this one yet.

Figure 17-3:
From the
Print
Preview
window, you
get an idea
of what your
report will
look like on
paper.

These let you see the rest of the page.

Using the Print Preview toolbar

When you're in Print Preview, you can't *do* a whole lot with your report except print it. But Print Preview does give you the important ability to closely check out exactly what your document looks like. Table 17-1 shows the tools Print Preview provides to help with your inspection.

Table 17-1	Print Preview Tools
Tool	*What It Does*
	To flip between Print Preview and Design view, click here. The button art changes when you're in Design view (the button looks looks like a page with a magnifying glass over it), but don't let that worry you.
	Click on the Print button and your printer begins spewing out your report. Pretty straightforward.

(continued)

Table 17-1 *(continued)*

Tool	What It Does
🔍	Click the on the Zoom button to toggle between viewing the entire page on-screen and viewing the page at 100 percent magnification.
Fit ▾	Use the Zoom Control drop-down list to determine what percent magnification you are currently viewing and to choose a new one.
▣	Select this option to view only one page at a time.
▣▣	Select this option to view two pages at one time.
▦	Select this option to view more than two pages on the screen. (Consult your optometrist before choosing this option.)

If you look back at Figure 17-3, you can see that not all of the page is visible; what you can see is legible, but you can't see the whole record, let alone the whole page. The setting in this figure is 100 percent magnification. That is, it's a life-size representation of a sheet of paper with your data on it.

What if you need to see what the whole page will look like? Click on the Zoom button to display the full-page view shown in Figure 17-4. This view is called the *Fit view,* because Access 97 sizes the view to fit the whole page on your screen. When you click on Zoom, the Zoom Control text box displays the word Fit to indicate this change. The Fit view is a good way to get an idea of the bigger picture. You can't read the text, but you can see what it looks like on the page. When you want to go back to the 100 percent view, click on the Zoom button again, and Access 97 obligingly switches for you.

But what if you want to see a view that fits more of the page in the Print Preview window than 100 percent view, but that is still legible (unlike Fit view)? Not a problem; that's what Zoom Control is for. Click on the Zoom Control arrow to see a drop-down list that shows a variety of percentages. These percentages determine the magnification of your page view. Click on a size other than the one currently in use, and your view changes. If you don't like *any* of your choices, you can use your own setting by typing a percentage into the Zoom Control and then clicking somewhere else on the screen.

Notice that when you move your mouse pointer over the view of your report, your pointer changes to look like a magnifying glass. Access is telling you that if you click on any area of the report, it will switch you to the previous view. Not only that, but if you are increasing the Zoom, your screen automatically shows the area that you clicked on. Click again, and your view changes back.

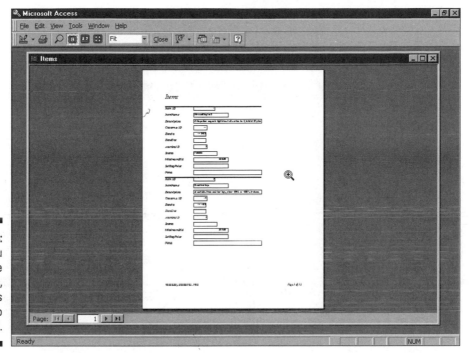

Figure 17-4:
When you
view the
whole page,
the print is
too tiny to
read.

Note that clicking any of the page-number buttons (one page, two page, multiple pages) sets the Zoom view to the Fit view setting. When you have two pages showing, the odd-numbered page is always on the left. (In book publishing, the odd-numbered page is always on the right — unless the production department is having a very, very bad day.)

If you choose View⇨Pages, Access 97 shows you a cool trick — you can see more than two pages simultaneously on the screen. When you choose View⇨Pages, the submenu shown in Figure 17-5 appears.

Figure 17-5:
This menu
enables you
to view up to
12 pages of
your report
at one time.

Clicking on one of the page view options changes your view to display a new, multipage arrangement. For example, Figure 17-6 shows the 12-page configuration.

Figure 17-6:
You certainly can't read it, but a multipage Print Preview can, at a glance, show you how your report will look on paper.

Calling on the pop-up menu

You can right-click anywhere on the Print Preview screen to see a pop-up menu that gives you the choice of switching the Zoom or viewing a specific number of pages. When you select the Zoom command, a submenu appears with the same choices that appear on the Zoom Control. Two other commands are available when you right-click on the Print Preview screen:

- ✔ **Save As/Export:** Choose this command to save your Access 97 report in a format used by another program.

- ✔ **Send:** Choose this command to take a copy of your Access 97 report and send it as a mail message.

Checking out that footer

When you view reports in Print Preview, you can see one more neat feature of AutoReports. Adjust the Zoom so that you can comfortably read the print and then scroll to the bottom of the on-screen page. You see something like Figure 17-7.

Figure 17-7:
The date
and page
number
appear as a
footer in
AutoReports.

Wednesday, October 02, 1996   *Page 1 of 13*

Access 97 automatically inserts a footer with the date the report was generated and the page number. The footer appears at the bottom of each and every page of your report. You can find out more about changing the contents of the footer by hoofing over to Chapter 20.

 If you finish looking at your report but aren't yet ready to print it (perhaps it may need a few *teensy* little changes), click the Close button on the report window (not the one opposite the *Microsoft Access* title because that one closes Access 97 entirely!). Doing so doesn't close you out of the report unless you've already saved it. If you *have* saved your document, it *will* close; otherwise, you go to the Design view for your report.

Designing reports by hand is an odious little task that I personally try to avoid. If you're like me, put off reading Chapters 19 and 20 (which tell you how to design your reports) as long as humanly possible.

Laying Out Your Pages

After looking at your report in the Print Preview window, you have a decision to make. If you're happy with how your report looks, great! Go ahead and print the document. However, a few minutes of extra work can do wonders to even the simplest reports.

You can choose File⇨Page Setup from any Report view in Access 97 to display the Page Setup dialog box. This dialog box provides three tabs of options to insure that your report is as effective and attractive as it can be.

The Page tab

You make some of the most fundamental decisions about how your report will look from the Page tab of the Page Setup dialog box (Figure 17-8).

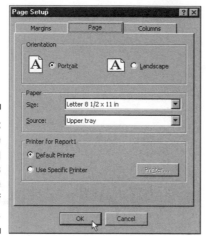

Your first page lay-out decision is which direction you want your paper to go. The default choice is Portrait, with the long side of your paper running from top to bottom of your text (the way most magazines and books appear). Your other choice is Landscape, where the long side of the paper runs horizontally from left to right so that the page is wider than it is tall.

More than just aesthetics goes into this portrait/landscape decision. If you have a Tabular report, Landscape orientation displays a wider column, which can convey more information for each field. The columns will be shorter, however, so there is always a trade-off. (After all, that piece of paper is only so big.) Columnar reports don't do very well in Landscape, because they usually need more vertical space than horizontal space. Figure 17-9 shows you how the same report you've seen before looks if you change the orientation to Landscape.

Your other choices for the Page tab are determined by your printing capabilities. The two drop-down lists in the Paper section of the tab enable you to pick the Size of the paper you want to use (refer to Figure 17-8). The Source drop-down list gives you the option to use your regular paper feed (the AutoSelect Tray choice), another automatic source, or to manually feed your paper into the printer.

The last part of the Page tab is labeled Printer for [your report name appears here], and displays a pair of radio buttons. You can use either the Default Printer or the Use Specific Printer option. Most of the time, you can leave this setting alone; it's only useful if you want to force this report to always come out of one specific printer at your location. If you decide to go with the Use Specific Printer option, the Printer button then becomes available. Clicking on this button displays a dialog box that lets you choose from among your available printers.

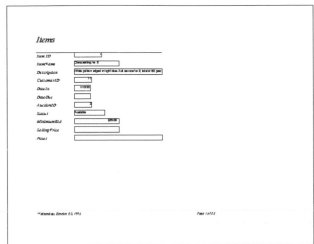

Figure 17-9:
Landscape
orientation
usually
creates
much more
white space
in your
report,
which can
make it
easier to
read.

The Columns tab

After you finish with the Page tab, you're ready to click on the Columns tab (see Figure 17-10). Now you're ready to really get busy.

Figure 17-10:
The
Columns
tab of the
Page Setup
dialog box
lets you
redesign
your report.

The Columns tab of the Page Setup dialog box is divided into three sections:

- ✔ **Grid Settings:** Enables you to control how many columns your report uses and how far apart the different elements are from each other
- ✔ **Column Size:** Enables you to adjust the height and width of your columns
- ✔ **Column Layout:** Defines the way that Access 97 places your data in columns (and uses a very easy-to-understand graphic to *show* you as well)

The default Grid Setting is one column to a page, but you can easily change the setting to suit your particular report. Just keep in mind that with more columns, your reports may show less information for each record. If you use so many columns that some of the information won't fit, you see a warning similar to the one displayed in Figure 17-11.

Figure 17-11: You may not be able to fit more than one column on a page.

If the number of columns you've selected will fit (or if you're willing to lose your view of the information in some of your fields), click on OK to see a view of how your document will look with multiple columns. Figure 17-12 shows a two-page Fit to Screen view of a report where two columns — at least as they are currently formatted — can cause you to lose data.

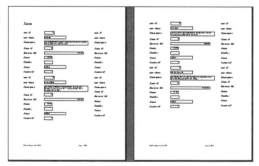

Figure 17-12: Sometimes, two or more columns cause your data to run off the screen.

The Grid Settings section of the Columns tab also lets you adjust row spacing and column spacing:

- ✔ **Row Spacing:** To adjust the space (measured in inches) between the horizontal rows, simply click on the Row Spacing box and enter the amount of space that you want to appear between each row. Again, this setting is a matter of personal preference.

- ✔ **Column Spacing:** Adjust the width of your columns. If you narrow this width, you can make more room, but your entries could be more difficult to read.

The bottom section of the Columns tab, called Column Layout, lets you control how your columns are organized on the page. You have two options here:

- ✔ **Down, then Across:** Access 97 starts a new record in the same column (if the preceding record has not filled up the page). For example, Record 13 will start below Record 12 on the page (provided there's enough room), and then Records 14 and 15 will appear in the second column.

- ✔ **Across, then Down:** Access starts Record 13 across from 12, and then puts Record 14 below 12, and Record 15 below 13, and so on.

The Margins tab

No surprises here. The Margins tab of the Page Setup dialog box is where you control the width of the margins in your report. (The *margin* is the space on each edge of the paper where Access 97 is not allowed to print.) Figure 17-13 displays the Margins tab.

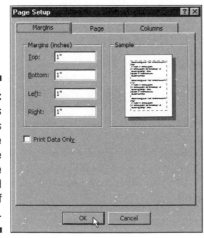

Figure 17-13: The Margins tab controls the space between the edge of the page and the start of your data.

The Margins tab is really straightforward; you have a text box for the Left, Right, Top, and Bottom margins. Double-clicking on each of those boxes highlights the setting and you can type a new setting, using inches as your measurement.

To the right of these boxes is a Sample, which shows you how your current margin settings will appear. Figure 17-14 shows you a Fit to Screen view of the report I've been working on, after I've made a few changes to the margins.

Figure 17-14:
To fit the columns on the page, change the left and right margins to .5". To center the data, change the top and bottom margins to 1.5".

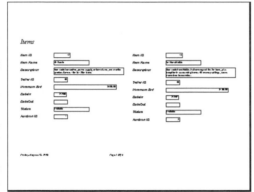

After you make all the changes you want to the layout of the report, go ahead and click on the OK button at the bottom of the dialog box. At this point, you may want to go back to Print Preview and check the report over to make sure that everything looks the way you want it. If it doesn't, simply go back to Page Setup and play with the options until everything looks just right. Then you can click on the Print button (or choose File⇨Print) and let your printer do its job.

The last item on this tab is the Print Data Only check box. If you click on this option (so that a check is showing), Access 97 prints only the data in your records; field headings won't appear on the printed document.

Chapter 18

Wizardly Help with Labels, Charts, and Multilevel Reports

. . . .

In This Chapter

▶ Printing labels with Label Wizard

▶ Adding charts with the Chart Wizard

▶ Organizing your report

▶ Using the Report Wizard

▶ Creating grouping levels

▶ Adding summaries

. . . .

*A*utoReports, covered in the preceding chapter, are just the tip of the Access report iceberg. If you have the inclination, you can use Access 97 to generate much more complex reports. You can even create useful printouts that you probably never even thought of as reports — mailing labels and charts. Don't be daunted — Access provides kind, gentle wizards to help you along your report-creating journey.

Creating Labels

When you need them, there's nothing like a good stack of mailing labels to really make your day. When the bulk-mailing urge strikes, it's time to check out the Access 97 Label Wizard. The Label Wizard creates labels for any number of uses. You may need to create a series of labels for your mailing list (probably sorted by postal code). Or perhaps you need to create labels identifying the price and description of the items for sale at your auction. In these cases, you want each label to be different, with specific information from your records — and the Label Wizard can do it for you with the wave of a wand.

The first step in using the Label Wizard is to decide what data you want to appear on the labels. You may need to create a query to sort through your data before starting on the labels. After you've decided which query or table to use for your labels, follow these steps to create your Label report:

1. **Click on the Reports tab of your main database screen.**

2. **Click on New to create a new report.**

   The New Report dialog box appears, showing you all the report types you can choose from. See Figure 18-1.

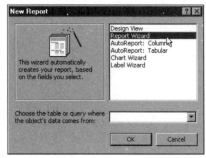

Figure 18-1: The New Report screen is where you tell Access 97 that you need wizardly advice with your reports.

3. **Choose Label Wizard from the list of report types.**

   See, I told you that Access considers labels a report!

4. **In the drop-down list box, choose the table or query that you have created for your labels.**

5. **Click on OK.**

   You see the dialog box shown in Figure 18-2.

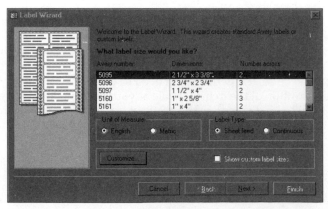

Figure 18-2: The first Label Wizard dialog box determines the size of your labels.

Access 97 is designed to make the process of creating labels as painless as possible. If you're using Avery labels, the Label Wizard already lists your choices by product number. Just scroll down the list until you find the number that matches the one on your label box, highlight that row, and then skip merrily along to Step 14. Lucky you.

If you aren't using Avery labels, your road is a bit rockier.

6. **Click on the Customize button in the Label Wizard dialog box to tell the Label Wizard that you want to set up nonstandard labels.**

Up springs the New Label dialog box, where you can pick from any type of labels that you've used previously. If you're using a new label type, you have to input some measurements so that Access 97 knows how big your labels are.

7. **Click on New to display the dialog box shown in Figure 18-3.**

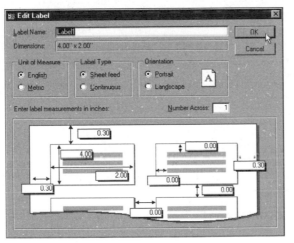

Figure 18-3:
You may need a ruler to measure the dimensions of non-standard labels.

8. **Click in the Label Name text box and create a name for your custom label.**

Choose a descriptive name such as "Custom label" or "Box label."

9. **If necessary, select either English or metric standards in the Unit of Measure section of this dialog box.**

10. **In the Label Type section, tell the program whether your labels are on individual sheets or on a continuous feed form.**

11. **Enter your label measurements in the lower half of the dialog box.**

For this step, you need the measurements of the physical labels to tell Access 97 the size of the label, the margins around the outside of the label, and the interior margins before the text begins. Just look at the arrows in the dialog box to determine which dimension is being measured, take that measurement on the physical label, and type the result next to the arrow.

12. **When you finish with the lower half of the dialog box, click on OK to see the New Label Size dialog box shown in Figure 18-4.**

Figure 18-4:
When you
create a
new label,
Access 97
saves the
settings for
future use.

If you make a mistake, you can correct it by clicking on the Edit button, which returns you to the previous screen. If you change your mind and want to get rid of that type of label, click on Delete. If, the next time you want to make labels, you are using a style that is close to, but not the same as, your customized label, click on Duplicate and make the changes you need on a duplicate label format.

13. **When you're happy with the results of your labors, click on Close to save these settings and return to the Label Wizard.**

Notice the Label Wizard check box called Show custom label sizes (refer to Figure 18-2). If you remove the check from that box, you see the listings for Avery labels. If you put the check in that box, you see your customized label settings. (Using Avery labels is so much simpler, I wonder if Microsoft is planning to buy Avery.)

14. **When you find the label you want to use, click on Next in the Label Wizard dialog box to see the screen shown in Figure 18-5.**

Figure 18-5:
Formatting
your labels
can be
a snap
with this
dialog box.

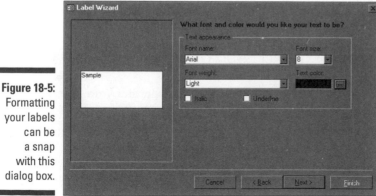

This window of the Label Wizard lets you change the format of your label. You can modify the font name, font size, font weight, italics or underline, and even the text color for your labels (if you have a color printer). Unfortunately, the formatting you choose applies to *all* the text on your label. You can't choose to italicize one field and not the others.

15. When your formatting is complete, click on <u>N</u>ext to see the next screen of the Label Wizard, shown in Figure 18-6.

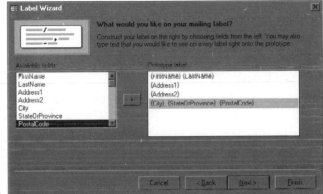

Figure 18-6: At last, you are ready to insert your data onto the label.

Okay, so it's taken a while, but you're almost finished. At this point, you tell the Wizard which data items you want to appear on the label, and how you want the information to appear. You've done this drill before: Select the fields from the Available fields list on the left and click on the > button to transfer the field to the Prototype label box on the right. However, this procedure has one slight twist. The Label Wizard prints your fields *exactly* as you tell it to.

If you want fields on separate rows, press Enter or use an arrow key to move to the next row. When you double-click on a field (or click on the > button), that field always transfers to the highlighted line in the Prototype label box. Access 97 figures out how many lines can print on your label, based upon the label's size and the font size you are using.

If you want a consistent character to appear on your labels, type in that character where it should appear on the label. For example, to insert a comma between the city and state or province on your mailing labels, select the City field, type in a comma, press the spacebar, and then select the StateOrProvince field.

16. When you've entered your fields to your satisfaction, click on <u>N</u>ext.

The next window, shown in Figure 18-7, lets you sort your labels by any field you choose. For example, you typically sort a mailing list by postal code.

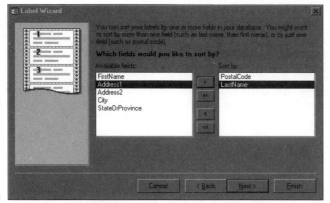

Figure 18-7:
Select the
field on
which you
want to sort.

17. **After choosing the field by which you want to sort your labels, click on Next.**

The last screen (finally!) of the Label Wizard lets you give your report a name for posterity and determine whether you want to see a preview of your labels (which I recommend). If necessary, you can go back and modify your design before printing.

Using the Chart Wizard in Your Report

Generally, reports are just a collection of words and numbers, organized to allow you to make sense of the information. But sometimes, words and numbers are simply not enough. At these times, creating a picture can help others make heads or tails out of all the information in your report. After all, everybody knows that a picture is worth a thousand words (which can be a lot of pages for a single report).

One option for making your Access 97 reports more understandable is to create a chart using the Chart Wizard:

1. **Click on the Reports tab of your main database screen.**

2. **Click on New to create a new report.**

The New Report dialog box appears, showing you all the report types you can choose from. (Refer to Figure 18-1.)

3. **Choose Chart Wizard from the list of report types.**

4. **In the drop-down list box, choose the table or query that you have created for your labels.**

5. **Click on OK.**

To start designing a chart or graph (Access 97 uses the terms interchangeably), you need to select the fields that you want to include. At least one of these fields must be numeric (Access 97 needs at least *some* numbers to plot in your graph), but you can include more than one numeric field if you want. The only limitations are that all of the fields must be from a single table or a single query, and you can use no more than six fields in any single chart.

The purpose of your chart determines what data items you include. For example, if you want to create a Column chart comparing the MinimumBid for each item to the ActualPrice, you need to include both of these fields so Access can use them as data. You also need to include any fields that you are going to use to organize your data into groups, like AuctionID, Description, or LastName.

After you select the fields that you want to appear in your chart, click on Next to select the type of chart you want to create. You can choose from five major types of charts:

- Line charts
- Bar or column charts
- Pie and donut charts (which go well with a steaming cappuccino)
- Area charts
- XY charts

When you click on a chart button, the area to the right of the dialog box provides a brief explanation of how you use that chart. After you pick the chart type, click on Next to reveal a third screen, which lets you organize the chart. This third screen varies depending on the type of chart you select, but some elements are consistent.

- The *Data* area in each screen tells Access 97 which fields to display in the chart.
- Some of the chart types also have an area labeled *Series,* in which you tell Access what field to use when grouping information on the chart.
- Some types of charts have a third slot, labeled *Axis.* The Axis slot is most commonly used in a bar or column chart to identify the field that is used to create the various clusters of objects in the chart.

The next dialog box lets you provide a title for your chart and control various other aspects of the way the chart is organized. After you make these choices, you can go back and make changes or click on Finish. You also have the option to Open the report with the chart to see how it looks.

Creating More Advanced Reports

The AutoReports Wizard (discussed in Chapter 17) creates reports that reflect a single level of organization and that include information from only one query or table. For a more complex report with more levels of organization (or a report that includes information from more than one table), seek help from the Report Wizard. This master of reporting lets you add fields from as many tables as you want, and organize those fields into as many levels as you choose. Each new level creates its own section of the report with its own header and footer.

Using the auction example from Chapter 15, imagine that a company wants to create a report summarizing the items for sale at the auctions. The fields to include on the report are Site (from the Auctions table), LastName (from the Customers table), ItemName, and MinimumBid (from the Items table). Because the company wants this report first grouped by the *auction location,* the Site field is the first level of organization.

The auction company also wants the report to help them track the folks who have contributed items to the auction (because paying your customers is important), so the second level of organization is by the last name of the seller. This way, the printed report first divides all the sale items according to the auction at which they are being sold. Then, within each auction listing, the report groups the items according to the seller's last name.

The first steps

Creating complex reports does involve quite a few steps. This section lists the first batch of steps. You may need to take a breather before moving on to the next section.

1. **Click on the Reports tab of your main database screen.**

2. **Click on New to create a new report.**

   The New Report dialog box appears, showing you all the report types you can choose from.

3. **Choose Report Wizard from the list of report types and click on OK.**

   When you create an AutoReport, this is the point where you would select a table or query for your report to use. But with the full Report Wizard, there's no need to choose a table or query.

   After a moment, the dialog box shown in Figure 18-8 appears, allowing you to add fields from any or all your tables and queries to the report structure.

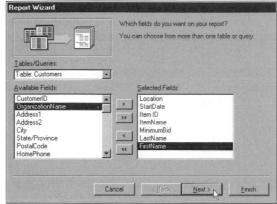

Figure 18-8:
The Report
Wizard lets
you add
fields from
any table or
query in
your
database.

This dialog box may look familiar because it's almost identical to the first dialog box of the Simple Query Wizard from Chapter 12.

4. **In the Tables/Queries drop-down list, pick a table or query that contains some of the fields that you want to use.**

   When the fields appear in the Available Fields box, you can start transferring the ones you want to the Selected Fields box on the right. After getting all of the fields from that source, just select a different table or query from the Tables/Queries drop-down list.

   Probably the easiest way to move a field from one side to another is by double-clicking on it. No matter which side you start on, if you double-click on a field, it moves to the opposite list.

5. **After displaying all the fields you could ever possibly want in the Selected Fields side of the dialog box, click on Next to progress to the next screen, shown in Figure 18-9.**

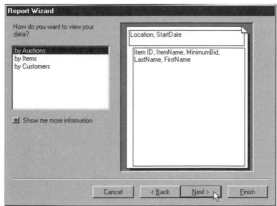

Figure 18-9:
This screen
lets you
choose how
you want
your
information
grouped.

This window appears only if the Report Wizard thinks that you need to see it, so don't panic if your screen looks different than the one shown in Figure 18-9. In that case, skip ahead to the next section.

The dialog box shown in Figure 18-9 lets you pick the field by which to organize the data. It displays a sample organization based on the Report Wizard's analysis of your data. Access 97 may or may not guess correctly about how you want your data to appear (remember, it's only a program). Take a close look at each of the report-organization choices and decide which one displays the information in the most effective way. To see a different organization, click on one of the *by* choices on the left side of the dialog box *(by Auctions, by Items, or by Customers)*.

When you click on one of these choices, that field separates from the other fields and appears at the top of the sample display (refer to Figure 18-9), indicating that all the information in the Details section (the main body) of your report will be organized by the values in that field.

If you don't want the records sorted into groups, that's okay. Just click on the very last entry in the *by* list (in this case, the *by Customers* entry). For reasons beyond my comprehension (but that probably make sense to a demented programmer somewhere), this action makes Access 97 lump all the records together, displaying the records without sorting them into groups.

More groups! More groups!

Up to this point, all of the steps are the same whether you built a single-level or a multilevel report. It's only with the next step that things start to get interesting. Click on <u>N</u>ext to reveal the screen shown in Figure 18-10.

Access 97 lets you further organize the information in a report by additional fields — fields other than the main field that you specify. The dialog box in Figure 18-10 lists all these fields at the left side of the window and lets you pick

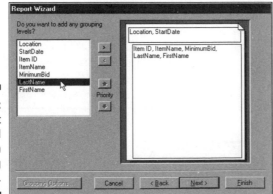

Figure 18-10:
The Report
Wizard
takes an
interesting
turn.

as many as you want. If you want to organize your report within your main group, select the field to use for grouping the records and double-click on the field name to add it to the list at the right.

For example, in the Auction database, it is possible to group the information by the site, then by the seller's name, the seller ID, or even by the type of item. Of course, if you want to use more than one level of grouping, you have to tell Access 97 the order in which the groups should appear.

Because the auction company organizes its records based on the site at which an item is being sold, they use the Location field to set this up. But they also know that a number of families have contributed more than one item to the auction, but they don't need each family listed multiple times. That's why there's a subcategory of the LastName field. By organizing the report this way, the report shows two main groups — one for each of the two auction sites — and within each site, the items are grouped by who donated the auction items. Figure 18-11 shows the dialog box with both levels of organization: Location (set in the previous dialog box) and LastName.

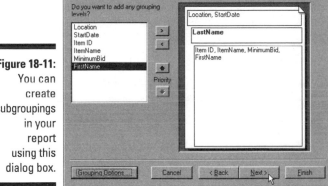

Figure 18-11:
You can create subgroupings in your report using this dialog box.

If you feel daring after creating the first subgroup, you can create reports with more than two levels. In fact, you can create all the subgroups you want until you are left with only one field in the Details section of your report.

What if you realize that you really want to organize the report by last name and *then,* within the last-name grouping, by site? All you have to do is rearrange the fields with the Priority buttons (as shown in Figure 18-11). If you highlight a field and click on the up-arrow Priority button, the field moves up a level in the organization. If you click on the down-arrow button, the highlighted field moves down a level.

If you highlight more than one field, the topmost one moves if you click on the up-arrow button; the lower field moves if you click on the down-arrow button. Then if you repeat the click with the same button, the highlighted field next in line moves accordingly, and so on. You can play with this feature to your heart's content until the report is organized exactly as you want it.

Each of the fields you select to organize your report creates a new section. Each of these sections has its own header and footer area that can hold information from your database, or information that you add directly to the report.

Sorting out the details

After you pick which fields Access will use to group the records in your report, click on <u>N</u>ext to go on to the dialog box shown in Figure 18-12.

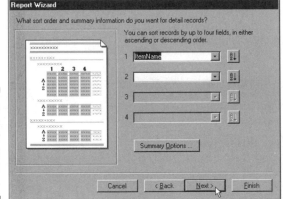

Figure 18-12:
You can sort your remaining fields with this screen.

Access 97 calls the fields that are not grouped as headers *Detail records.* The screen in Figure 18-12 lets you sort those records by the remaining fields, which you can organize in either ascending or descending order. To do that, simply select the field in the drop-down list and then click on the button at the right to change the sorting order from ascending (with the letters going from A at the top to Z at the bottom) to descending (with the letters going from Z at the top to A at the bottom). Don't ask me why the arrow doesn't just change directions. (Sorting on more than one field is discussed in more detail in Chapter 10.)

Notice that in the lower middle of this dialog box contains a button labeled Summary <u>O</u>ptions. You can click on this button to see the dialog box shown in Figure 18-13. (If you don't see a Summary <u>O</u>ptions button on your screen, it's because you didn't include any fields that *could* be summarized in your report.) This dialog box lets you tell Access 97 to summarize your data with a number of statistical tools, including totals (Sum), averages (Avg), minimums (Min), and maximums (Max). Check the boxes next to the operations that you want performed on the fields in your report.

In Figure 18-13, the auction company wants Access 97 to add up all the minimum bids for each group (that's what the *Sum* checkmark does) and display the average minimum bid for each group (the purpose of the *Avg* entry).

Figure 18-13:
Access 97
can do
statistical
calculations
on the data
in your
report.
Better it
than me.

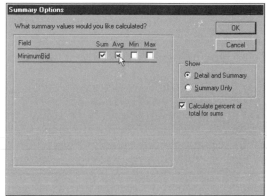

On the right side of the Summary Options dialog box is an option labeled Show. If you want to see both the data *and* the summary, click on the Detail and Summary radio button. If you need to see only the summarized information, click on the Summary Only radio button. The last check box on this dialog box is Calculate the percent of total for sums. If you click on this button, Access 97 calculates the total amount of the field and tells you the percentage of each record's contribution to that total.

The home stretch

After you okay the Summary Options and return to the Report Wizard, click on Next to move along to the next screen (shown in Figure 18-14).

You can use the Layout window of the Report Wizard to organize your report data in any of the organizational styles offered by Access 97. If you click on one of the styles in the Layout box, the window to the left shows how your report will appear. Your choices here vary depending on the data you're trying to present and your personal preferences.

The Orientation page lets you decide between having your report printed in Portrait (long edge along the side) or Landscape (long edge across the top and bottom) orientation. Again, this choice depends on your specific circumstances and preferences. But generally, if you have a lot of fields or the fields are large, you may want to consider the Landscape orientation.

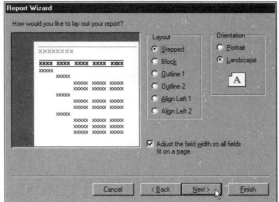

The check box labeled `Adjust field width so all fields fit on a page` is important. If you check this box, Access 97 force-fits all of your fields onto one page, even if it has to squish some of them to do it. This is a dandy feature but it has a little, tiny drawback that you need to understand. During the highly scientific squishing process, the field may end up being too small to display all of the data it contains. For example, a field holding the name *Harriet Isa Finkelmeier* may only display *Harriet Isa Fink* after it gets squished. The rest of the name isn't lost — it just doesn't appear on the report. If you *don't* check the box, then Access 97 packs as many fields onto the page as it can *without* changing any of the field widths. Fields that don't fit are left off the page, but the fields that *do* print appear in their normal, glorious size.

Click on Next one more time to see a dialog box that lets you choose from six predetermined styles for your report. The window at the left gives you a basic idea of what the style looks like. Again, this is a matter of taste, not what is "correct." Pick the one you like the most and move on.

Finally, you're ready to click on Next for the last time. In the final screen, you give your report a name. This action saves your report and provides it with its title. You also have the choice of previewing your report in Print Preview, modifying your report, or simply screaming for help. If you think that you are satisfied with what you've done, go ahead and preview your report. You should see something like the report shown in Figure 18-15.

If you want to make changes to the design of your report, you can click on the `Modify the report's design` button before you click on Finish. If you do so, Access 97 opens the Design view of your report, and you can tinker with the report to your heart's content. Chapter 19 explains how to modify and format your reports to create your own unique look.

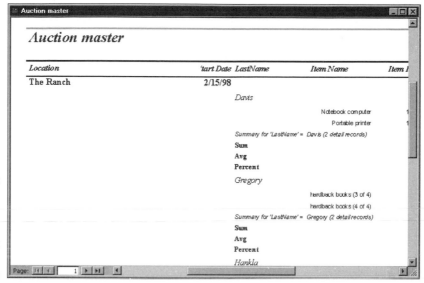

Figure 18-15:
Wow! A
professional
report at
last.

Chapter 19

It's Amazing What a Little Formatting Can Do

. . . .

In This Chapter

▶ Getting into Design view

▶ Working with report sections

▶ Marking fields and labels

▶ Previewing your stuff

▶ Letting AutoFormat do the hard work for you

▶ Drawing lines and boxes

▶ Adding graphics to your reports

▶ Exporting reports to Microsoft Word and Excel

. . . .

*T*he Access 97 Report Wizard is a pretty swell fellow. After a brief round of 20 compu-questions, it sets up an informative, good-looking report for you automatically. Well, at least the report's *informative* — just between you and me, I think Report Wizard could use a little design training.

Although the Access 97 Report Wizard does the best job it can, the results aren't always exactly what you need. Those clever engineers at Microsoft foresaw this problem and left a back door open for you. That door is called *Design view.* In Design view, you can change anything — and I mean *anything* — about your report's design. You can easily reorganize the fields, add some text, or emphasize things with boxes and lines.

This chapter guides you through some popular Design view tweaking and tuning techniques. With this information in hand, your reports are sure to be the envy of the office in no time. (And there's nothing like a well-envied report to start your day off just right.)

Taking Your Report to the Design-View Tune-Up Shop

The first stop in your quest for a better looking report is Design view itself. After all, you can't change *anything* in the report until your report is up on the jacks in the Design view. Thankfully, you can choose from several easy ways to tow your report in for that much-needed tune-up. Precisely how you do it depends on where you are right now in Access 97:

> ✔ After you create a report with the Report Wizard, the wizard asks if you want to preview the report or modify its design (even the wizard knows that its design skills are lacking!). Choose the modify design option to work in Design view.

> ✔ If the report is already on-screen in a preview, hop into Design view by clicking the Design View button on the toolbar.

> ✔ To get into Design view from the Database window, click on the Reports tab and then click on the name of the report you want to work on. Click on the Design button to open the report in Design view.

No matter which method you use, Access 97 sends you (and your report) to a Design view screen that looks a lot like Figure 19-1. Now you're ready to overhaul that report!

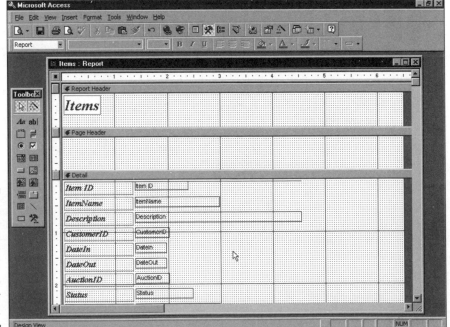

Figure 19-1:
The Design view gives you all the tools you need to modify your reports.

Striking Up the Bands (And the Markers, Too)

When you look at a report in Design view, Access 97 displays a slew of *markers* that are grouped into several bands (or *sections,* as they're called in Access 97). The markers show where Access 97 plans to put the fields and text that will appear on your final report. They also give you an idea of how the program plans to format everything.

Access 97 uses two kinds of text markers, depending on what you want to show in the report:

- **Data boxes:** Boxes that display a particular field's data in the report. Every field you want to include in the final report has a data box in the Design view. If a field doesn't have a data box, the data for that field won't end up in the report.

- **Labels:** Plain, simple text markers that display some kind of text message on the report. Sometimes, labels stand alone (such as "The information in this report is confidential."); often, they accompany a data box to show people who read the report what kind of data they're looking at ("Customer ID" or "Right Shoe Size," for example).

Markers are organized into sections that represent the different parts of your report. The sections govern where and how often a particular field or text message is repeated in your report. The report design in Figure 19-2 displays the three most common sections: Report Header, Page Header, and Detail. Arrows to the left of the section names show you which markers each section contains.

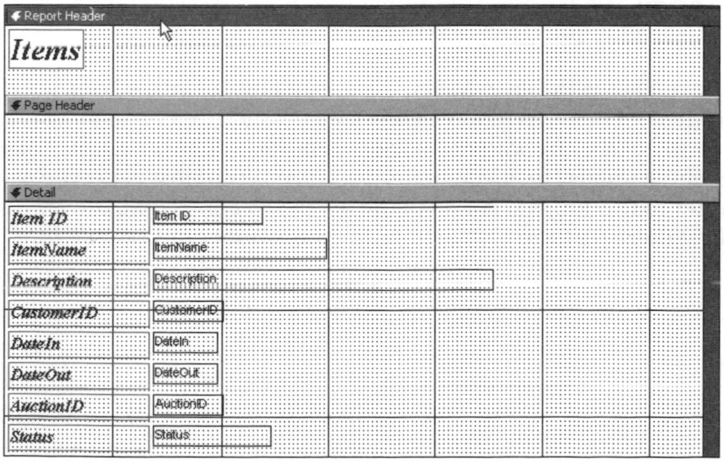

Figure 19-2: Every report has three basic sections: Report Header, Page Header, and Detail.

The sections work in teams that straddle the Detail line. The teams are pretty easy to figure out (Report Header works with Report Footer, and Page Header works with Page Footer, for example). Figure 19-3 displays the mates to the sections shown in Figure 19-2.

Figure 19-3:
The Page
Footer and
Report
Footer
mirror their
headers.

Here's how the most common sections work:

- ✔ **Report Header:** Anything that appears in the Report Header prints at the very start of the report. The information prints only once and appears at the top of the first page.

- ✔ **Page Header:** Information in the Page Header prints at the top of each and every page. The only exception is on the report's very first page, where Access 97 prints the Report Header and *then* the Page Header.

- ✔ **Detail:** The meat of the report, the stuff in the Detail section, fills the majority of each report page. The Detail section is repeated for every record included in the report.

- ✔ **Page Footer:** When each page is nearly full, Access finishes it off by printing the Page Footer at the bottom.

- ✔ **Report Footer:** At the bottom of the very last page, immediately following the Page Footer, the Report Footer wraps things up.

Being familiar with Glenn Miller, Claude Bolling, or John Philip Sousa won't help you when it comes to report bands in Access 97. (Sorry, but I just couldn't let the term *band* go by without making some kind of musical note.) Because the concept of bands (or, if you prefer, *sections*) is so dense, I devote a whole chapter to the subject. For all of the details on controlling the sections and making them perform calculations for you, check out Chapter 20.

Formatting This, That, These, and Those

You can artfully amend almost anything in a report's design with the help of the Formatting toolbar in Figure 19-4. Whether you want to change text color, font size, or the visual effect surrounding a data box, this toolbar has the goodies you need.

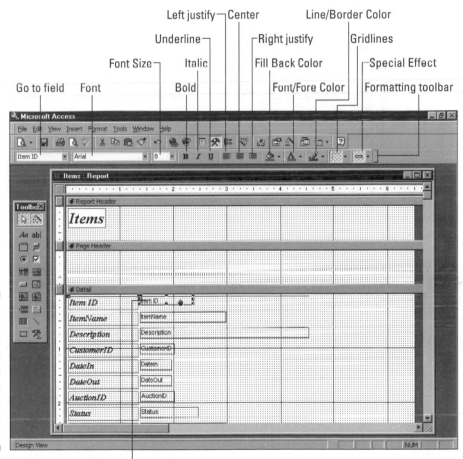

Figure 19-4:
The tools to format the features of your report hop into action when you select a field.

To adjust items in your report with the tools in the Formatting toolbar, follow these steps:

1. Click on the item you want to format.

Any field, label, line, or box will do — Access 97 is an equal-opportunity formatter. When you click on something, a bunch of little black boxes appear around it, much like Figure 19-5. (The boxes are a good sign.)

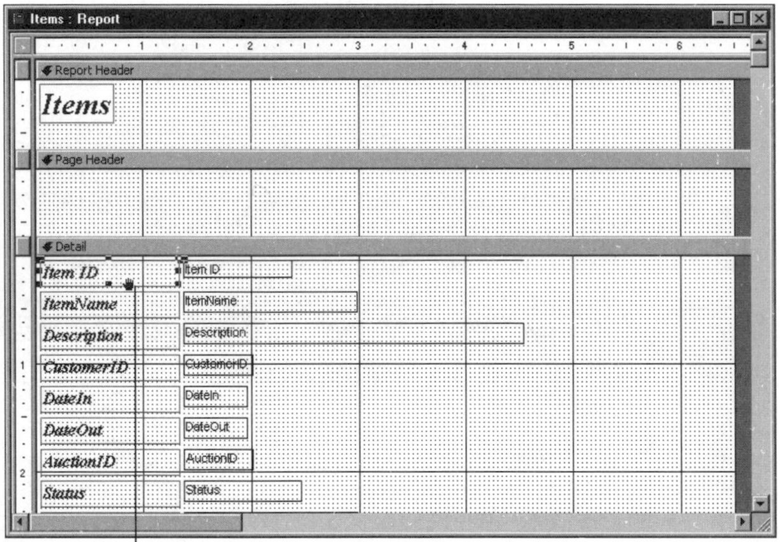

Figure 19-5:
The field marker for the label information is selected.

Selected label

2. Click on the toolbar button for the formatting effect you want.

With most formatting tools, the new format immediately takes effect. Some tools (such as the ones for color, border, and 3D effect) also offer a pull-down list of choices. I cover these options in detail later in the chapter, so don't worry about them right now.

3. Repeat Steps 1 and 2 for all of the fields you want to modify.

If you make a mistake while formatting, just choose Edit⇨Undo Property Setting. Poof! Access removes the last formatting you applied.

The following sections step through some of the most common formatting tasks ahead of you. Just follow the instructions and soon your report will look like a cross between the Mona Lisa and a state tax form (I *think* that's a compliment, but I'll have to get back to you on that).

Taking control of your report

You can put other things besides labels and simple rectangular fields into your report. All the various items you can put in a report are called *controls,* and you add controls to your report by using the Toolbox.

You can use certain types of controls for specific types of fields. For example, you can use a check box with a Yes/No field. Because applying controls isn't as easy as it looks, Access 97 includes several *control wizards.* These wizards, like their brethren elsewhere in the program, walk you through the steps for building your controls in a patient, step-by-step manner. They really do make your life easier! By default, the control wizards automatically come to life after you place a control in the report.

If you create a new control with one of these tools, but the control wizard *doesn't* show up to help, make sure that the Wizard button at the top of the Toolbox (the button emblazoned with a magic wand) is turned on. If it's *on,* the button looks as though it's pushed down a bit. If you aren't sure, click it a couple of times so you can see the difference.

Some of the controls (specifically the Line, Box, Page Break, and image controls) are covered later in this chapter. In the next chapter, I show you how to use controls to create summaries in your report.

Colorizing your report

Nothing brightens up a drab report like a spot of color. Access 97 makes adding color easy with the Font/Fore Color and the Fill/Back Color buttons. These buttons are located on your friendly Formatting toolbar (no surprises there).

Both buttons change the color of text markers in your report, but they differ a little in precisely how they do it:

 The Font/Fore Color button changes the color of text in a data box or label marker.

 The Fill/Back Color button alters the marker's background color, but leaves the text color alone.

To select a color to use, click on the arrow at the right of the Font/Fore Color or Fill/Back Color button. When the menu of colors appears, click the color you want to use. Notice that your color choice also appears along the bottom of the toolbar button, too.

To change the color of a field or label on your report, click on the marker that you want to work with. To change the font color, click the Font/Fore Color button; to change the background, click on Fill/Back Color, instead. The new color settings appear right away on-screen, like the label in Figure 19-6 that proudly sports a new gray background.

Figure 19-6: You can color the background of any item in your report.

You can also use the Font/Fore Color button to change the color of the text in a data box or any label. You can easily create special effects by choosing contrasting colors for the foreground and background, just like the white text floating on a black background in Figure 19-7.

Figure 19-7: Combine and mix colors to create just the effect you want.

Be careful when choosing your colors — if you make the text and background colors the same, the text seems to disappear! If this happens, just choose Edit⇨Undo Property Setting to bring back the original color setting.

Moving things around

You can easily move just about any element (data box, label, line, and such) in a report. In fact, moving things is *so* easy that you need to go slow and take extra care not to move things you shouldn't.

To move a line, box, label, or data box, follow these steps:

1. Click on the item you want to move.

A bunch of black squares surround the item, letting you know that it's selected.

If you have trouble selecting a line, try clicking near its ends. For some reason, Access 97 has a tough time recognizing when you want to grab a line. Clicking right at the line's end seems to help the program figure out what you want to do.

2. Move the mouse pointer to any edge of the selected item.

When you do this step, the mouse pointer turns into a little hand. Too cute, isn't it?

3. Press and hold the left mouse button and then drag your item to a new position.

4. Release the mouse button when the item is hovering over its new home.

If something goes wrong, and you want to undo the movement, choose Edit⇨Undo Property Setting. Access 97 is *very* forgiving about such things.

In some Access 97 reports (specifically the ones created by the Columnar Report Wizard), the data box and label for each field in the report are attached to each other. If you move one, the other automatically follows. In this case, you have to adjust the procedure a bit if you want to move one *without* moving the other. Follow the preceding steps, but instead of moving the cursor to the edge of the marker, move it to one of the big square handles shown in Figure 19-8.

✔ The handle on the far left moves the label.

✔ The handle in the middle of the two markers moves the data box.

As the mouse pointer enters the handle, the cursor changes to a pointing finger. That's your sign that you can proceed with Step 3 — press and hold the mouse button and then start moving. Release the mouse button when you have the field positioned where you want it. If the mouse pointer changes to a double-ended arrow instead of a pointing hand, try moving your mouse pointer onto the big handle again. That double-ended arrow tells Access to *resize* the item, not move it.

Figure 19-8:
Use big handles to move a label or a field separately.

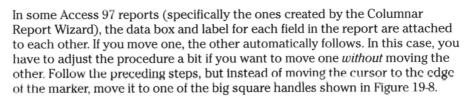

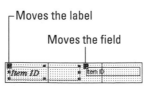

Other types of reports, such as Tabular Reports or Labels, do not combine the label and the field together the way Columnar reports do. In such reports, either no label appears, or the label appears only once in the Page Header section. When labels aren't linked to their respective fields, they each appear separately — without the special large handles shown in Figure 19-8.

Use the smaller handles around the edge of a field to resize the field. For example, if you discover that the information in one of your fields is getting cut off, you can click on the field and use the small handles to make that field somewhat longer. Or if a text field or a memo field (any field where the information is broken into words) contains a lot of information, you can make the field taller. Access wraps the information to more than one line.

The amount of space between the markers controls the space between items when you print the report. Increasing that spacing gives your report a less crowded look; decreasing the space enables you to fit more information on the page.

Bordering on beautiful

Lines and marker borders are wonderful things. They draw your reader's eye to particular parts of the page, highlight certain sections of the report, and generally spruce up an otherwise drab page. The toolbar contains three buttons to put lines and borders through their paces: the Line/Border Color button, the Line/Border Width button, and the ever-popular Special Effects button.

Coloring your lines and borders

The Line/Border Color button changes the color of lines that mark a field's border and lines drawn on your report with the Line tool. This button works just like the Back Color and the Font/Fore Color buttons did for text, so you probably know a lot about using it already. (Comforting feeling, isn't it?)

To change the color of a line or a marker's border, follow these steps:

1. **Click on the marker or line to select it.**

   Remember to click near the end of a line to select it; otherwise, you may end up clicking all around the line, but never highlighting it.

 2. **Click on the arrow next to the Line/Border Color button.**

   A drop-down display of color choices appears on-screen (see Figure 19-9).

3. **Click on your choice from the rainbow of options.**

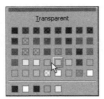

Figure 19-9:
Choose from
an entire
palette of
colors.

Widening your lines and borders

In addition to colorizing lines and borders, you can also control their width:

1. **Click on the line or text marker you want to work with.**

2. **Click on the arrow next to the Line/Border Width button to display line- and border-width options.**

   Your choices for line and border width are represented in terms of *points* (a geeky publishing word that means $\frac{1}{72}$ *inch*). The menu offers options for a hairline (half-point) line, 1 point, 2 points, 3 points, 4 points, 5 points, and finally the 6-point Monster Line that Devoured Toronto. (A 6-point line is $\frac{1}{12}$ of an inch thick, but actually appears quite heavy on a report.)

3. **Click on the line- or border-width option you want.**

   That's all there is to it! As with everything else, choosing Edit⇨Undo Property Setting repairs any accidental damage, so feel free to experiment with the options.

Adding special effects to your lines and borders

You can change the style of a marker's border by using the Special Effects button. Six choices are available under this button, as shown in Figure 19-10.

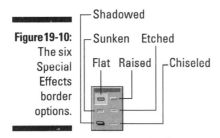

Figure 19-10:
The six
Special
Effects
border
options.

The Sunken and Raised options actually change the colors on two sides of the field, but the effect makes the field look three dimensional. Selecting a sunken border makes the label or field appear as though it is pushed into your text; a raised border makes it seem as though your field is rising out of your text. Figure 19-11 shows an example of a raised border and a sunken border. Striking difference, isn't it? (Yes, I *am* kidding.)

Figure 19-11:
Can you
tell the
difference?

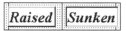

The Chiseled option gives a field the appearance of having the bottom portion of its border raised upward, and the Etched option gives the effect of the border being etched into the background around the field. The colors of your field and of your report background affect how these borders look. Figure 19-12 shows examples of these two types of borders.

Figure 19-12:
You can't
miss the
difference
between
these
effects.

The Shadow option places a shadow around the lower-right of the field. The Flat option simply puts a standard, single-line border around the entire field.

To add special effects to a markers border, follow the same basic steps as you would for changing a border's color or width:

1. **Click on the marker whose border you want to change.**

2. **Click on the arrow next to the Special Effects button to display your six options.**

3. **Click on the special effect you want to add.**

If you have trouble reaching all the buttons on the drop-down Special Effects list, you can tear the list off the menu bar. Simply click on the down-arrow to display the list and then click on the bar at the top of the drop-down display area. When you drag the pointer down and to the left (outside the border of the list), a dotted rectangle the same size and shape as the list follows the pointer. When you can see all of the rectangle, release the mouse button. Ta da! A floating toolbar that displays the Special Effects options.

Tweaking your text

The tools on the left side of the Formatting toolbar enable you to change the style of text within a selected field. You can choose the font (the actual shape of the characters used to display text), the size of the font, and whether the font is **bold,** *italic,* or <u>underlined</u> — just use the formatting buttons shown in Figure 19-13.

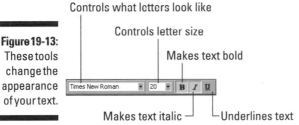

Figure 19-13:
These tools change the appearance of your text.

To change the font or the font size, simply click on the arrow to the right of the Font or Font Size list box and select from the drop-down list that appears. To turn on or off the bold, italic, or underline characteristics, select a block of text and click on the appropriate button. If the feature is off, clicking on the button turns it on. If the feature is on, clicking on the button turns it off. When one of these formatting features is turned on, the button appears to be pressed into the surface of the toolbar.

You can also control the alignment of the text within labels and fields. To change the alignment of the text for a label or data box, simply select the marker and then click on one of the three alignment buttons on the toolbar.

 ✔ Aligns left

 ✔ Aligns right

 ✔ Centers text

In Figure 19-14, the labels are both left-aligned, but the data fields vary a bit. The top one is right-aligned, but the bottom one is left-aligned. As you can see, badly aligned fields are a little distracting. To make the best looking report possible, pay attention to the little details like label and data alignment. Your effort may mean the difference between a hard-to-read report and an object of informational beauty.

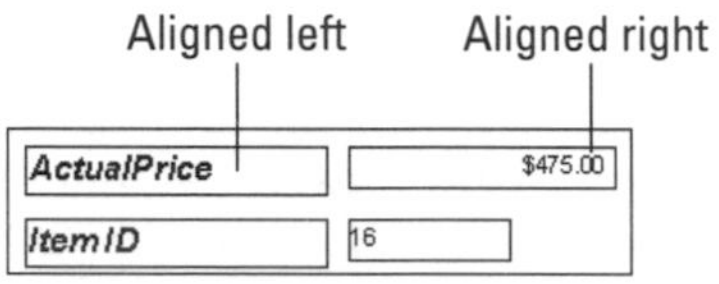

Figure 19-14:
You can change the text alignment for fields and labels.

Aligned left   Aligned right

| *ActualPrice* | $475.00 |
| *ItemID* | 16 |

Taking a Peek

After fiddling around long enough in design view, you inevitably reach a point where you want to view the *actual* report, rather than just looking at the technical magic being used to create it. No matter how good your imagination, it's difficult to visualize how everything will actually look when it all comes together in the printed report. Access 97 provides two distinct tools for previewing your report.

- ✓ **Layout Preview:** When you select the Layout Preview, Access 97 takes a portion of your data and arranges it to give you an idea of how your data will appear in the finished report. The preview shows only a sampling of your data (without performing any final calculations that you included). The idea is to see what the report *looks like,* not to review your calculations. To view Layout Preview, click the down-arrow next to the Report View button and then select Layout Preview from the drop-down list, as shown in Figure 19-15.

 - ✓ **Print Preview:** If you want to see a *full* preview of your report, complete with the calculations and all the data, select Print Preview by clicking on the Print Preview button. (Or you can go the long way around and click on the down-arrow next to the Report View button and then select Print Preview from the drop-down list shown in Figure 19-15.)

Figure 19-15:
Choose
Layout
Preview to
see how the
report will
look; choose
Print
Preview to
see the
report in full.

Regardless of which approach you use, you see a Print Preview screen similar
to the one shown in Figure 19-16. The various items of your report appear as
they will when you print the report. You can then use the controls at the top of
the Print Preview window to change the appearance of the screen.

For more information about using Print Preview and Layout Preview, see
Chapter 17.

Figure 19-16:
Print
Preview
shows you
exactly how
your report
will look
when you
print it.

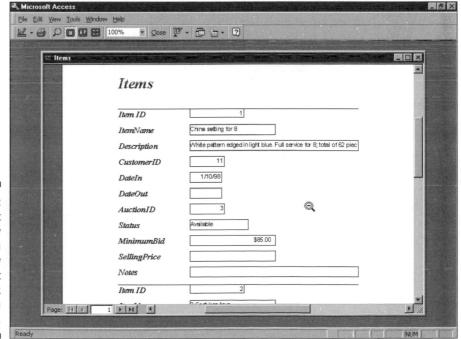

AutoFormatting Your Way to a Beautiful Report

When you want to change the look of the whole report in one (or two) easy clicks, check out the AutoFormat button. When you click this button, Access 97 offers several different format packages that reset everything from the headline font to the color of lines that split up items in the report.

To use AutoFormat, follow these steps:

1. **Click in the empty gray area below the Report Footer band.**

   This may sound like a strange first step, but there's reason behind my peculiarity (or at least there is *this* time). Clicking in this area is the easiest way to tell Access 97 that you don't want *any* report sections selected. If any one section is selected when you do the AutoFormat command, then AutoFormat *only* changes the contents of that one section. Although that kind of precision may be nice sometimes, most of the time you want AutoFormat to redo your whole report.

2. **Click on the AutoFormat toolbar button.**

   A dialog box appears, listing your various package-deal formatting choices.

3. **Click on the name of the format you want and then click OK (see Figure 19-17).**

   Access 97 updates everything in your report with the newly selected look.

   If just a few fields in one section change, but the majority of the report stays the same, go back to Step 1 and try that *click in the gray area* step again. The odds are good that you had one section selected when you clicked AutoFormat.

Figure 19-17: Pick the look that you like and apply it to the whole report.

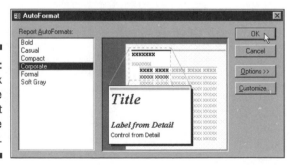

You can use the Customize button to create your own formats, which Access then stores on the AutoFormat page. Simply format your report using a consistent set of fonts, colors, and borders for everything on the report; then click on AutoFormat. In the AutoFormat dialog box, click on Customize. At this point, you have the option of adding your new format to the list or replacing one of the existing formats with your new definition. Don't redefine any of the default formats; instead, if you want to add your own format to the list, create a new AutoFormat for it. Give your new format a name and then click on Close to make the dialog box go away.

Lining Everything Up

When you start moving various items around on your report, you can easily wind up with a report that's out of alignment. For example, you may have put the column headings in the Page Header and the actual information farther down the page in a Detail line. Of course, you want the data fields to line up with the headers, but simply moving the items around the page by hand and eyeballing the results may not do the trick.

The grid in the background of the screen can help you position screen elements by aligning them with the vertical lines or with the various dots on the Design screen. When you move an object on the report, you can choose Format⇨Snap to Grid to control whether the object stays lined up with these dots that are "snapped to the grid," or whether you can move the object freely between the dots.

When you move an object with Snap to Grid turned on, the object's upper-left corner always aligns with one of the dots on the grid. Choose this command when you resize an object, and the side of the object that you move stays aligned with the dots on the grid.

Figure 19-18 shows several objects that I moved into position on-screen. I positioned the items in the left column with the help of the Snap to Grid command; I positioned the items in the right column freehand, without Snap to Grid steadying my hand. Notice how the label markers in the left column are lined up nicely, but the data boxes on the right are all over the page. So much for my dream of becoming a surgeon.

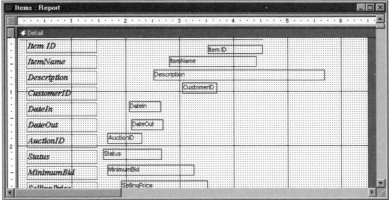

Figure 19-18:
The Snap to
Grid feature
helps you
keep your
reports neat
and aligned,
without
driving
yourself
crazy.

Other commands on the Format menu that you may find useful for arranging objects on your reports include:

- **Align:** You can choose two or more objects and align them to each other or to the grid. Selecting Left, Right, Top, or Bottom causes the left, right, top, or bottom sides of the selected items to line up. For example, if you select three objects and then choose Format⇨Align⇨Left, the three objects move so that their left edges line up. By default, Access 97 moves objects to line up with the object that is the farthest to the left.

- **Size:** You can change the size of a group of objects by selecting the objects and then selecting an option from the Size submenu. For example, you can choose Size⇨to Fit, which adjusts the size of the controls so that each one is just large enough to hold the information it contains. Choose Size⇨to Grid to adjust the controls so that all control corners are positioned on grid points.

  Or adjust the controls relative to each other. If you choose Size⇨to Tallest, Size⇨to Shortest, Size⇨to Widest, or Size⇨to Narrowest, each box in the selected group is adjusted to that characteristic. In other words, if you select a group of controls and then choose Size⇨to Tallest, each of the selected controls is resized to the same height as the tallest control in the selected group.

- **Horizontal Spacing, Vertical Spacing:** Use these commands to space a selected group of objects equally. This feature can be very useful if you're trying to spread out the title items for a report. Simply select the items in your group and then choose Format⇨Vertical Spacing⇨Make Equal to have Access 97 space the items equally.

  Figure 19-19 shows four labels and fields in the top of the figure that are somewhat mushed together, and a duplicate set of four labels and fields lower down on the page that have been distributed with the Make Equal command.

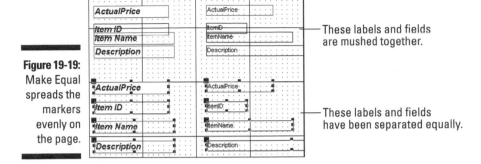

These labels and fields are mushed together.

These labels and fields have been separated equally.

Figure 19-19: Make Equal spreads the markers evenly on the page.

Drawing Your Own Lines

An easy way to make your report a bit easier to read is to add lines that divide the various sections. To add lines to your report, follow these steps:

1. **Open the Toolbox by clicking the Toolbox toolbar button.**

   Bet you can't say that five times fast!

2. **Click the Line tool from the Toolbox.**

   When you select the Line tool, your cursor changes to a cross-hair with a line trailing off to the right.

3. **Click where you want to start the line, drag to the location where you want to end the line, and release the mouse button.**

   Access adds a line along the path you draw.

You can use the various toolbar buttons (discussed earlier in this chapter) to dress up your lines. For example, to change the line's color, thickness, and appearance, use the Line/Border Color, Line/Border Width, and Special Effects buttons.

You can use the Box tool to draw boxes around separate items on your report. Click on the point that you want to be the upper-left corner of your box, and drag the box shape down to the lower-right corner. When you release the mouse button, presto, you have a box.

Inserting Page Breaks

Most of the time, page breaks aren't high on the list of report priorities. Instead, you worry about things like making the summaries work, lining the data up into neat columns and rows, and selecting the proper shade of magenta (or was that more of a pinky russet?) for the lines and label borders.

Occasionally, though, you get the urge to tell Access 97 precisely where a report page should end. Maybe you want to end each page with a special calculation, or just keep some information grouped on the same page. Regardless of the reason, inserting a page break into your report is as quick as a click.

To insert a page break into your Access 97 report, follow these steps:

1. **Click on the Page Break button in the Toolbox.**

   The mouse pointer changes into a crosshair with a page next to it, signifying that you're about to do something that involves a page. (Someday, I want to be the person that gets paid to design mouse pointers for Windows programs. Can you imagine explaining that job to your kids' class on Parents Day?)

2. **Position the crosshair wherever you want the page break, and then click the left mouse button.**

   A couple of small black marks appear on the left side of the report. This little notation, believe it or not, is the page break marker. From now on, a new page will always begin here.

If you want to remove a page break that you so carefully added, click on the page break marker and then press Delete. That page break's outta there. If you want to move the page break, click on it, press and hold the mouse button, and then drag the page break marker to its new home. When the page break is hovering over the right spot, release the mouse button to place the page break.

Sprucing Up the Place with a Few Pictures

A sure-fire way to spruce up a report is to add an image to it. You can use the Image button in the Toolbox to create a frame into which you can paste an image from your clip-art collection.

Images are great, but I strongly encourage you to add images only to the Report Header or Page Header. If you put an image in the Detail section, for example, the image would repeat so many times that the report would look as though you wanted a little information with your graphics, instead of a few graphics to perk up the information.

If you don't have an image that you're ready to use, but rather have an image in progress, you may choose to use the Unbound Object Frame to add an OLE object. *OLE* (which stands for object *linking and embedding*) enables you to put an object onto your page, while maintaining the object's link to its original file. Any changes to that original file are reflected in the object you place into the report. You can link to an image or to *any* type of file that supports OLE.

When you click on either the Image or the Unbounded Object Frame tool, you get a plus-sign pointer, with the button's image to the lower-right. You can then use this tool to draw a box onto your screen.

> ✔ **If you're using the Image tool:** Access opens the Insert Picture dialog box, which you can use to locate the image you want to insert.
>
> ✔ **If you're using the Unbound Object Frame tool:** Access opens the Insert Object dialog box so you can select the type of object to insert. This option enables you to insert objects ranging from graphic images to digital sound files — you can even include a whole Microsoft Excel worksheet! (For more about the magic of OLE, see *OLE For Dummies,* by John Mueller and Wallace Wang.)

 You can also add an image to your report by cutting or copying the image from another program, storing it on the Clipboard, and then pasting it onto your design. This technique is the only easy way to include *part* of an image from a file.

Passing Your Reports around the (Microsoft) Office

You can do an awful lot with Access 97, but sometimes a different program can get the job done better and make your life a little easier. The engineers at Microsoft are aware of this fact, so they gave Access 97 the ability to send information directly to other programs. Which other programs? Why, other Microsoft programs, of course! (Why does this not surprise me?)

The button that you use to move information out of Access 97 is called the OfficeLinks button, and it's the same as the Tools➪OfficeLinks command. Just as the submenu for the OfficeLinks command has three choices, its toolbar button has three different faces.

From Access to Word

 On several Access toolbars, you see the Publish It with MS Word button. This button takes whatever you are working on and formats it as a Word document. When you click on this button, the various items in your report are formatted as a new Word document, with tabs separating the columns. In fact, Access even opens the document for you in Word — automatically. (That's assuming that you own a copy of Word and that you have enough memory in your computer to run both programs at the same time.)

(Of course, if you *do* own a copy of Word, you probably have *Word 97 For Windows For Dummies,* by Dan Gookin. Right?)

 What the folks at Microsoft don't want you to know is that the Publish It with MS Word button creates a file in a format that most word processors can read. If you don't own Microsoft Word, the only problem you may encounter is trying to figure out where Access 97 stored your file.

From Access to Excel

 Analyze It with MS Excel takes your report (or whatever information you were working on in Access 97), creates a datasheet, and then formats the data as an Excel worksheet. Each line of the report is placed in its own row, and the information that forms columns in your Access 97 report become separate columns on your Excel worksheet. Your system then runs Excel and displays your newest creation. You can then use any of the Excel tools (including charting) to analyze, interpret, and generally abuse your data.

For more about making Excel 97 do some rather impressive tricks, pick up a copy of *Excel 97 For Windows For Dummies,* by Greg Harvey.

From Access to Mail Merge

 The Merge It button is available only when you are working with a table or datasheet. Unlike the other buttons, which just take your information and run with it, clicking the Merge It button (or selecting the Merge It command) starts the Mail Merge Wizard. This wizard guides you through the steps of linking your database with a Word Mail Merge document. If you don't already have a Mail Merge document, the wizard helps you create one.

Chapter 20

Headers and Footers for Groups, Pages, and Even (Egad) Whole Reports

· ·

In This Chapter

▶ Getting into sections

▶ Grouping and sorting your records

▶ Adjusting the size of sections

▶ Fine-tuning the layout of your report

▶ Controlling your headers and footers

▶ Putting expressions into your footers

▶ Adding page numbers and dates

· ·

*W*izards are great for creating reports, but they can only do so much for you. Even when you're working with a wizard, you still need to know a little something about how to group the fields of your report to get the optimum results. And someday after you've created your report, you may need to alter its organization or fine-tune its components to meet your changing needs. To tweak an existing report, you need to go into Design view and manually make the changes you want.

Don't despair! This chapter is designed to help you through these thorny issues. In this chapter, I explain the logic behind grouping your fields in a report, and I show you several options for your groups. I also walk you through the Design-view thicket — a thorny place if ever there was one.

Everything in Its Place

The secret to the organization of a report lies in the way you position the markers (known to programmers as *controls*) for the labels and fields within the report design. Each and every report design is separated into *sections* (called *bands* in other database programs) that identify different portions of the report. Which parts of the report land in which section depends on the report's layout.

- ✔ **Columnar:** In a standard Columnar report (see Figure 20-1), field descriptions print with every record's data. The layout behaves this way because both the field descriptions and data area are in the report's Detail section. Because the report title is in the Report Header section, it prints only once, at the very beginning of the report.

- ✔ **Tabular:** The setup is quite different in a standard Tabular report, such as the one in Figure 20-2. The title prints at the top of the report, just as in the Columnar report, but the similarity ends there. Instead of hanging out with the data, the field descriptions move to the Page Header section. Here, they print once per *page* instead of once per record. The data areas are by themselves in the Detail section.

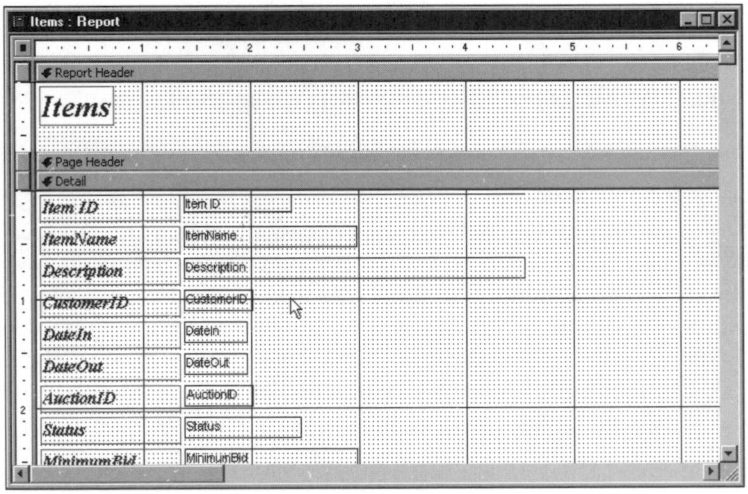

Figure 20-1:
The sections in Design view. In a Columnar report, the labels are to the left of the fields and repeat for each record.

Understanding the whole *section* concept is a prerequisite for performing any serious surgery on your report or for running off to build a report from scratch. Otherwise, your report groupings don't work right, fields are out of place, and life with Access 97 is less fulfilling than it should be.

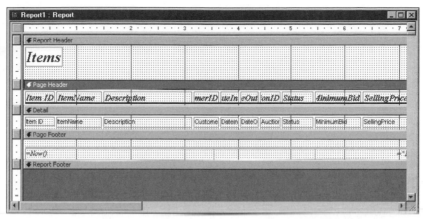

The most important point to understand about sections is that the contents of each section are printed only when certain events occur. For example, the information in the Page Header is repeated at the top of each page, but the Report Header only prints on the *first* page.

Getting a grip on sections is easy when you look at the innermost section of your report and work your way outward, like so:

- ✓ **Details:** At the center of every report is the Details section. Access prints items in this section each time it moves on to a new record. Your report includes a copy of the Details section for each and every record in the table.

- ✓ **Group headers and footers:** Moving outward from the Details section, you may have markers for one or more *group sections.* In Figure 20-3, information in the report is grouped by AuctionID, and then by LastName (you can tell by the section bars labeled `AuctionID Header` and `LastName Header` — the section bars identify which field is used for grouping).

  Group sections always come in pairs: the *group header* and the *group footer.* The header section is above the Details section in the report design; the footer is always below Details. Information in these sections is repeated for every unique value in the group's field. For example, the report in Figure 20-3 will reprint everything in the AuctionID Header for each unique auction number. Within the section for each auction, Access repeats the information in the LastName Header for each customer.

- ✓ **Page Header and Page Footer:** Above and below the group sections, you find the Page Header and Page Footer. These sections appear at the top and bottom of every page. They're among the few sections not controlled by the contents of your records. Use the information in the Page Header and Footer sections to identify the pages of your report.

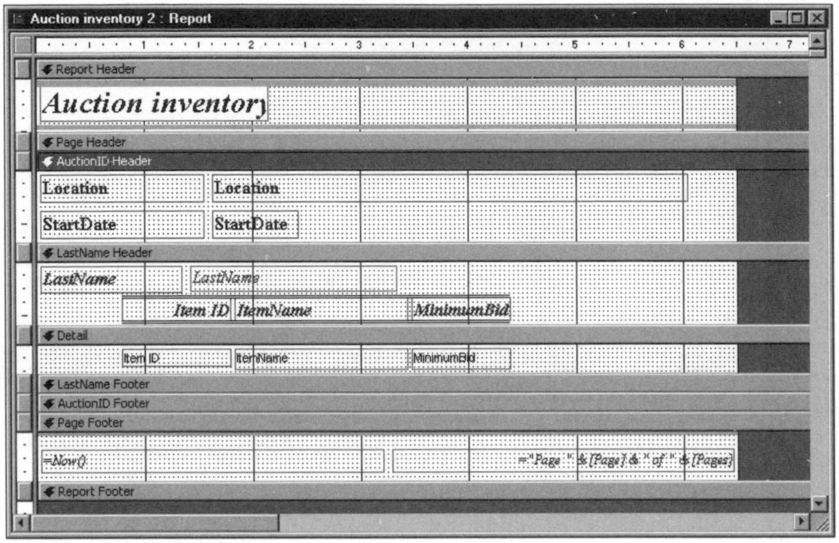

Figure 20-3:
Grouping
records by
AuctionID,
and then by
LastName.

✔ **Report Header and Footer:** The outermost sections are the Report
Header, which appears at the start of your report, and the Report Footer,
which appears at the end of your report. Both the Report Header and the
Report Footer make only one appearance in your report — unlike the
other sections, which pop up many times.

So when Access produces a report, what does it do with all these sections? The
process goes a little something like this:

1. Access begins by printing the Report Header at the top of the first page.

2. Next, it prints the Page Header, if you choose to have the Page Header
   appear on the first page. (Otherwise, Access reprints this header at the top
   of every page except the first one.)

3. If your report has some groups, the Group Headers for the first set of
   records appear next.

4. When the headers are in place, Access finally prints the Detail lines for
   each record in the first group.

5. After it's done with all the Detail lines for the first group, Access prints that
   group's footer.

6. If you have more than one group, Access starts the process over again by
   printing the next group header, and then that group's Detail lines, and then
   that group's footer.

7. At the end of each page, Access prints the Page Footer.

8. When it finishes with the last group, Access prints the Report Footer —
   which, like the Report Header, only appears once in a given report.

Having all these headers and footers is great, but what do you *do* with them?

- ✔ The Report Header often provides general information about the report. This is a good place to add the report title, printing date, and version information.

- ✔ The Page Header contains any information you want to appear at the top of each page (such as the date, your company's logo, or whatever).

- ✔ The headers for each group usually identify the contents of that group and the field names.

- ✔ The footers for each group generally contain summary information, such as counts and calculations. The footer section of the Auction ID group, in this example, may hold a calculation that totals up the Minimum Bids.

- ✔ The Page Footer, which appears at the bottom of every page, traditionally holds the page number and report date fields. If the information is very important to your company, consider typing something like **Company Confidential** in the footer (won't your corporate lawyers be proud!).

- ✔ By the time the Report Footer prints, about the only information left is a master summary of what happened during the report. You may also include contact information (whom to call with questions about the report) if you plan to distribute the report widely throughout the company.

Grouping your records

If you're designing a report from scratch, you can use the Sorting and Grouping dialog box to create your groups and control how they behave. Perhaps more importantly, however, if you use a wizard to create a report for you, you can still use this dialog box to control how that report behaves and where information appears.

When the Report Wizard creates a report for you, it automatically includes a header and footer section for each group you want. If you tell the Report Wizard to group by the field AuctionID, it automatically creates both the AuctionID Header and the AuctionID Footer sections. You aren't limited to what the wizard does, though — if you're a little adventuresome, you can augment the wizard's work with your own grouping sections.

The key to creating your own grouping sections is the Sorting and Grouping dialog box in Figure 20-4. This dialog box controls how Access organizes the records in your report. Each grouping section in your report is automatically included in the sorting and grouping list (regardless of whether you created the section or the wizard did). You can also have additional entries that sort the records, although these entries don't generate their own section headers.

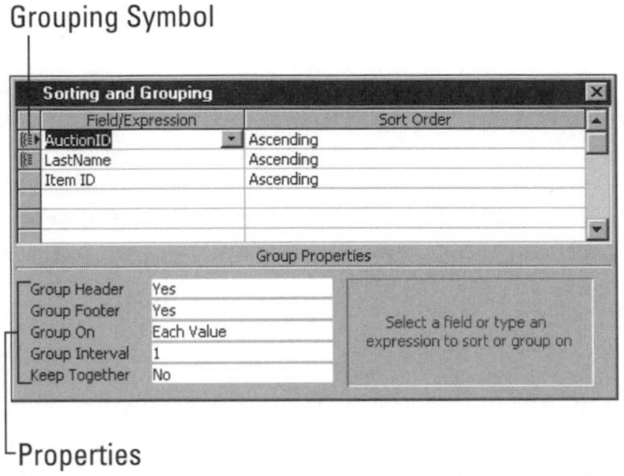

Grouping Symbol

Figure 20-4:
You can adjust the organization of your report without going back to see the wizard.

Sorting and Grouping

Field/Expression	Sort Order
AuctionID	Ascending
LastName	Ascending
Item ID	Ascending

Group Properties

Group Header	Yes
Group Footer	Yes
Group On	Each Value
Group Interval	1
Keep Together	No

Select a field or type an expression to sort or group on

Properties

To build your own groupings, follow these steps:

1. **Choose View⇨Sorting and Grouping.**

   The Sorting and Grouping dialog box appears.

2. **Click on a blank line under Field/Expression.**

   The blinking toothpick cursor appears there, along with a down-arrow button.

3. **Click on the down-arrow to display a list of fields you can use for the group. Click on the field of your choice.**

   Access 97 adds a new line for that field to the Sorting and Grouping list. By default, Access plans to do an ascending sort (smallest to largest) with the data in that field.

4. **To tell Access 97 that you want the entry to be a full-fledged group, click in the Group Header area at the bottom of the dialog box. Click the down-arrow that appears in the box and then select Yes from the drop-down menu.**

   Behind the scenes, Access 97 adds a new group section to your report design. To include a footer for your new group as well, repeat this step in the Group Footer entry of the dialog box.

5. **When you're finished, close the dialog box.**

   That's it — your new group is in place.

To remove a group, click on the gray button next to the group's Field/Expression line and then press Delete. When Access frantically asks whether you really want to delete the group, click on Yes.

Notice that the first two entries in Figure 20-4 have a special symbol next to them. The symbol indicates that other groups are sorted or organized within *this* group. If you group records by more than one field (as this report does), the symbol is repeated in the list for each of the grouping fields.

If you want to change the order of the various groups, just dash back to the Sorting and Grouping dialog box (choose <u>V</u>iew⇨<u>S</u>orting and Grouping). Click on the gray button next to the group you want to move; then click and drag the group to its new location. Access automatically adjusts your report design accordingly.

Be *very* careful when changing the grouping order! It's easy to make an inno-cent-looking change and then discover that nothing in your report is organized correctly anymore. Before making any big adjustments to the report, take a minute to save the report (choose <u>F</u>ile⇨<u>S</u>ave). This way, if something goes wrong and the report becomes horribly disfigured, just close it (<u>F</u>ile⇨<u>C</u>lose) without saving your changes. Ahhh. Your original report is safe and sound.

The properties for the currently selected group appear at the bottom of the Sorting and Grouping dialog box.

- ✔ The first two properties — Group Header and Group Footer — specify whether you want this group to include a section for a Group Header, a section for a Group Footer, or both in your report.

- ✔ The Group On setting determines how Access 97 creates the groups for that value. For more about this feature, check out the nearby "Group on, dude!" sidebar.

- ✔ The last property, Keep Together, controls whether all the information within that group must be printed on the same page, whether the first Detail line and the headings for that group must be printed on the same page, or whether Access can split the information any which way it wants, as long as it all gets printed on one page or another.

  You have three choices under the Keep Together property:

  - **No:** Tells Access to do whatever it pleases.

  - **Whole group:** Tells Access to print the entire group, from Header to Footer, on the same page.

  - **With first detail:** Tells Access to print all the information from the Header for the group through the Detail section for the first entry of the group in that group on the same page. Choose this option to ensure that each of your pages starts with a set of headings.

TIP

Group on, dude!

Groups are one of the too-cool-for-words features that make Access 97 reports so flexible. But wait — groups have still *more* untapped power, thanks to the Group On setting in the Sorting and Grouping dialog box. This setting tells Access when to begin a new group of records on a report. The dialog box contains two settings for your grouping pleasure: *Each Value* and *Interval*.

The Each Value setting tells Access to group identical entries together. If any difference exists between values in the grouping field, Access puts them into different groups. Each Value is a great setting if you're grouping by customer numbers, vendor numbers, or government identification numbers. It's not such a great choice if you're working with names, because every little variation (Kaufield instead of Kaufeld, for example) ends up in its own group.

The Interval setting works a little differently. It tells Access that you're interested in organizing by a range of entries. Exactly how Access interprets the Interval setting depends on whether you're grouping with a number or text field.

If you're grouping a number field with the Interval setting, Access counts by the Interval setting when making the groups. For example, if your Interval is 10, then Access groups records that have values from 0 to 9, 10 to 19, 20 to 29, and so on.

To understand how the Interval setting works with a text field, think back to the way your grade-school teacher taught you to alphabetize words. You look at the first letter of the words, putting the As first, followed by the Bs. If two words start with A, you use the second letter in each word to break the tie. If those letters are identical, too, you try again with the third, and so on until the list is in perfect order or until recess time.

So what do blissful memories of childhood grammar lessons have to do with how the Interval setting works with a text field? In a nutshell, the Interval setting is the number of characters Access 97 reads from each record when it's grouping them. An Interval of one makes Access 97 group the entries by the first letter only; an Interval of two tells Access 97 to consider the first and second letters of each entry.

For example, if you choose 1, 2, or 3 for your Interval setting, the words *abandon* and *abalone* would land in the same group because they start with the same three letters. You'd need an interval setting of 4 or more to split the words into separate groups.

Changing a section's size

One problem you may have with designing your own report is controlling how much space appears in a section. When you print a section — be it a Page Header, a Section Header, or a Detail line — it normally takes up the same amount of space as shown on the Design screen. You generally want to tighten the space within the group so that little space is wasted on your page, but your section needs to be large enough to contain all the markers and such that go into it. (To find out how to create sections that change size based on the information in them, flip ahead to the next section, "Fine-Tuning the Layout.")

Fortunately, changing the size of a section is quite easy. Figure 20-5 shows the Resizing cursor that appears when you position your pointer over the top portion of the bar representing the section. This resizing trick works a bit oddly, in that the bar you move increases or decreases the section *above* it, not the section for which it is labeled.

┌The Resizing cursor

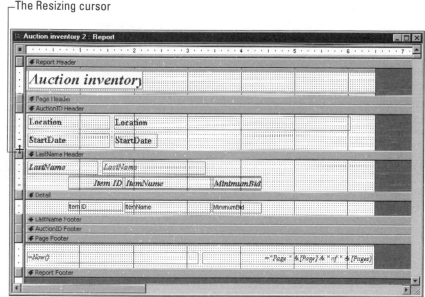

Figure 20-5:
The Resizing cursor enables you to change the size of header, footer, and details sections.

Fine-Tuning the Layout

Most of the control you have over your report comes from setting the report's properties. Although *setting properties* is a formatting topic, it becomes useful only after you start dividing your report into sections.

Dressing up your report as a whole

To adjust the formatting of an entire report, double-click on the small box in the upper-left corner of the report window in Design view. Up pops the dialog box shown in Figure 20-6.

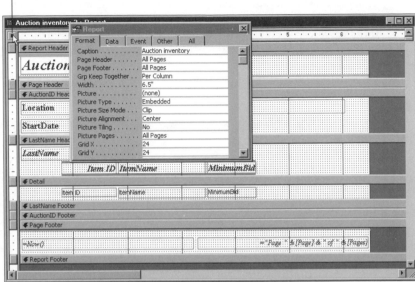

Properties button

Figure 20-6:
In Design
view,
double-
clicking on
your report's
Properties
button
opens the
Report
properties
dialog box.

Playing with page headings

Of particular interest in the Report properties dialog box are controls on the Format Tab that affect when the Page Header and Page Footer will print. The default setting for the Page Header and Page Footer is All Pages, meaning that Access prints a header and footer on every page in the report. Choose Not with Rpt Hdr (or Not with Rprt Ftr for the footer) to tell Access to skip the first and last pages (where the Report Header and Report Footer are printed), but print the Page Header on all the others.

The Page Header itself comes with a bunch of options, too. Double-click on the Page Header to bring up the Page Header properties dialog box, which probably looks quite similar to the one shown in Figure 20-7.

Figure 20-7:
You can
control how
your page
header
looks with
the Page
Header
properties
dialog box.

✔ **Visible:** You can use this dialog box to control whether the Page Header appears at all.

✔ **Height:** Access automatically sets this property as you click and drag the section header up and down on the screen. To specify an exact size (for example, if you want the header area to be *precisely* 4 centimeters tall), type the size in this section. (Access automatically uses the units of measurement you chose for Windows 95 itself.)

✔ **Back Color:** Although setting this property seems easy at first blush, Access 97 couldn't let you get away with just typing **blue** as a color choice. No, it wants a big, technical number describing the color in gory, computerized detail. Luckily, generating that number is easy. If you want to adjust the section's color, click in this box and then click the small gray button that appears to the right of the entry. This button brings up a color palette. Click your choice and then let Access worry about the obnoxious color number that goes into the Back Color box.

Although you can control the color of your Page Header's background from the Report properties dialog box, an easier method is to click on the section in Design view and use the drop-down lists on the Formatting toolbar.

✔ **Special Effect:** This property adjusts the visual effect for the section heading, much as the Special Effect button does for the markers in the report itself. Your choices are somewhat limited here, though. Click in the Special Effect box and then click the down-arrow to list what's available. Choose Flat (the default setting), Raised, or Sunken.

Keeping the right stuff together

The Grp Keep Together option on the Format tab of the Report properties dialog box affects the Keep Together entry, which you set in the Sorting and Grouping dialog box (see "Grouping your records," earlier in this chapter).

Choose Per Page to apply the Keep Together criteria to pages. Or, in a report with multiple columns, choose Per Column to apply the Keep Together criteria to columns.

Formatting individual sections of your report

What if you don't want to change the format of the whole report, but just of one section of the report — for example, the header for one group? Simple. In Design view, double-click on the Group Header to call upon the dialog box shown in Figure 20-8.

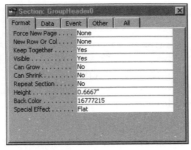

Figure 20-8:
This dialog
box lets you
fiddle with a
single
section of
your report.

With the Force New Page option, you can control whether or not the change for that group automatically forces the information to start on a new page. When you set this option, you can determine whether this page break occurs only before the header, only after the footer, or in both places. Similarly, you can control the way in which section starts and endings are handled for multiple column reports (such as having the group always start in a separate column). As with the previous dialog boxes, you can control whether or not the group is kept together and whether or not the section is visible.

Perhaps the most important settings in this dialog box are Can Grow, Can Shrink, and Repeat Section.

✔ When the Can Grow option is turned on, the section expands as necessary, based upon the data within it.

Can Grow is particularly useful when you're printing a report that contains a Memo field. You set the width of the field so that it is as wide as you want. Then you can use the Can Grow property to enable Access 97 to adjust the height available for the information.

✔ With Can Shrink turned on, the section can become smaller if, for example, some of the fields are empty. In order to use the Can Grow and Can Shrink properties, you need to set them for both the section and the items within the section that are able to grow or shrink.

✔ You can use the Repeat Section option to control whether or not, when a group is split across pages or columns, Access 97 repeats the heading on the new page (or pages, if the section is so big that it covers more than two pages).

Taking it one item at a time

Double-clicking doesn't just work for sections. When you want to adjust the formatting of any item of your report — a field, a label, or something you've drawn on your report — just double-click on that item in Design view. Access 97 leads you to a marvelous dialog box from which you can perform all manner of technical nit-picking.

Filling in Those Sections

Although Access includes several default settings for headers and footers, those settings aren't very personalized or imaginative. You can do much more with headers and footers than simply display labels for your data. You can build expressions in these sections or insert text that introduces or summarizes your data. Now that's the kind of header and footer that impresses your friends, influences your coworkers, and wins over your boss.

At the head of the class

How you place the labels within the report's Header sections controls how the final report both looks and works, so you really oughta put some thought into those Headers. You want to make sure that all your headings are easy to understand and that they actually add some useful information to the report.

When you're setting up a report, feel free to play around with the header layouts. Experiment with your options and see what you can come up with — the way that information repeats through the report may surprise you.

For example, Figure 20-9 shows a common header configuration in Design view. Figure 20-10 shows the same report in action. In this case, the column headings are printed above the site name. The descriptions for the column headings appear at the top of each and every page because they're in the Page Header section. This example is certainly not a bad layout, but you can accomplish the same goal in other ways.

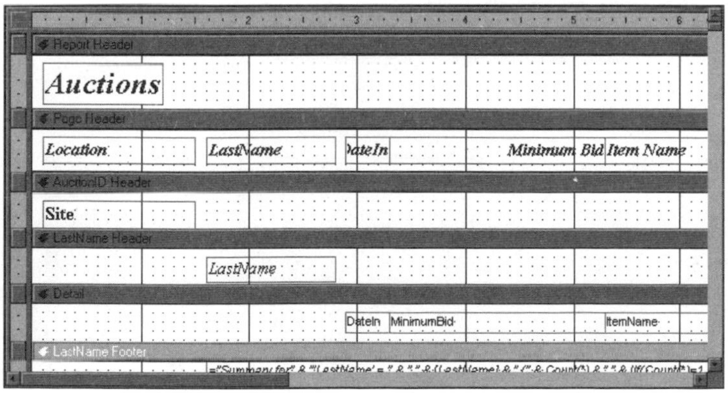

Figure 20-9:
The Design View of the Auctions report.

Auctions				
Location	LastName	DateIn	Minimum Bid	Item Name
The Ranch				
	Abercrombie			
		2/22/97	$80.00	Treadle sewing mac
	Summary for 'LastName' = Abercrombie (1 detail record)			
	Sum		$80.00	
	Min		$80.00	
	Max		$80.00	
	Allen-Brown			
		1/18/97	$30.00	Asst hardback book
		1/18/97	$30.00	Asst hardback book

Figure 20-10:
What the Auctions Report actually looks like.

Figures 20-11 and 20-12 show an alternate arrangement. In this case, the DateIn, Minimum Bid, and Item Name headings repeat every time the LastName Header is printed. This is a little easier to read than the version in Figure 20-10 because the column descriptions are right above their matching columns.

Figure 20-11:
Another arrangement for the Auctions report. Notice the new positions for the headers.

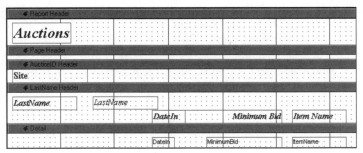

Figure 20-12:
How the new arrangement looks in Print Preview. Compare this report to Figure 20-10.

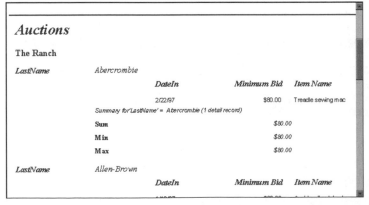

In comparing the figures, you may notice that some of the labels (such as LastName) were also moved, and the various sections were resized. In addition, the pair of lines used to mark the top and bottom of the Page Header were removed in order to close that space.

Expressing yourself in footers

Footers are most often used to produce summary statistics and general information. Figure 20-13 shows some of the markers that commonly appear in a simple Access 97 report.

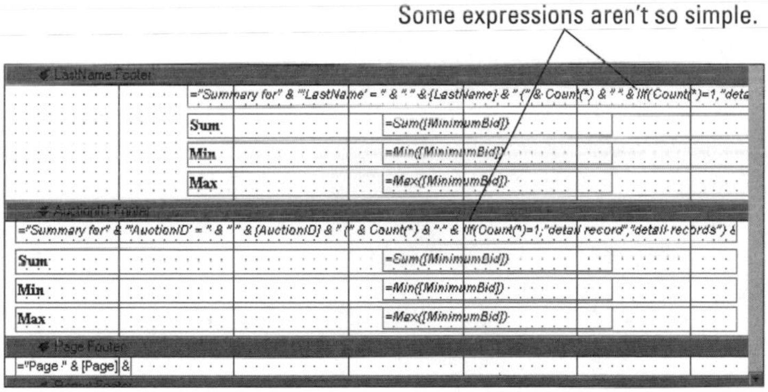

Some expressions aren't so simple.

Figure 20-13: You can select from a plethora of footers to include in your reports.

Most of the time, the markers in the footer simply print the page number or some other kind of text. That doesn't mean that you *can't* put something more complex in there, however. Notice the first field in each of the footer sections in Figure 20-13. These fields involve a somewhat complex-looking formula. This formula mixes some text with the current value of a field in the report to produce an informative note for the report. Figure 20-14 shows the results of this complicated bit of computer wizardry.

In the example, the actual last name is inserted along with some standard text ("Summary for"), and a function is used to count the number of records being reported in the group. The expression at the end is just used to determine whether the sentence ends with "record" or "records." In order to help you better understand the formula used for this last bit of magic, Figure 20-15 shows the expression in the Expression Builder.

Complex calculations build these sentences.

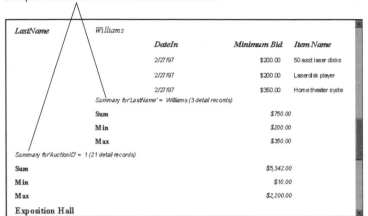

LastName	Williams			
		DateIn	Minimum Bid	Item Name
		2/27/97	$200.00	50 asst laser disks
		2/27/97	$200.00	Laserdisk player
		2/27/97	$350.00	Home theater syste

Summary for 'LastName' = Williams (3 detail records)

Sum	$750.00
Min	$200.00
Max	$350.00

Summary for 'AuctionID' = 1 (21 detail records)

Sum	$5,342.00
Min	$10.00
Max	$2,200.00

Exposition Hall

Figure 20-14:
The results
of the work
shown in
Figure 20-13.

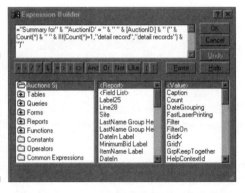

Figure 20-15:
Some
expressions
you don't
want to
develop
yourself.

Remember that the names enclosed in square brackets represent fields from the database. The last portion of the expression, starting with the *If,* controls whether the sentence ends with the singular *detail record* or the plural *detail records*, and it does this by determining whether the count of records is equal to one or to some other number (that is, more than one). If there were no records, the section wouldn't have been printed at all, so no summary for it would appear.

These feet were made for summing

Access 97 contains many functions, but the ones listed in Table 20-1 win the award for Most Likely to Be Used in a Normal Human's Report. These functions create different summaries of the fields in your report.

Table 20-1	Summary Functions	
Function	*Description*	*Example*
Sum	Adds up all of the values in the field	Sum([MinimumBid])
Maximum	Finds the largest value in the values listed in this section for this field	Max([MinimumBid])
Minimum	Finds the smallest value in the values listed in this section for this field	Min([MinimumBid])
Average	Finds the average value of all of the values listed within this section for this field	Avg([MinimumBid])
Count	Counts up how many values are listed in this section for this field	Count([MinimumBid])

By double-clicking on a calculated field in a report, you open the Properties dialog box, like the one shown in Figure 20-16. You can use the first line of the Format tab to select a format for displaying the information in the field. This control is the most useful for setting the look of your report. You also have options for whether duplicates within the field are shown or whether the fields after the first instance of the same entry are left blank. These options are most useful in the Detail section, where you may want to show only the first record of several records with the same entry in a field.

Figure 20-16:
The
Properties
dialog box
lets you
control more
settings
than you
ever thought
possible.

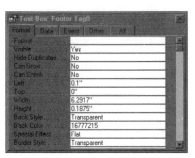

The Data tab contains four entries, one of which is the Control Source that provides the calculation's information. The easiest way to get to this card is to double-click on the field itself, which brings up the Properties dialog box, and then click on the Data tab.

At the bottom of the Data tab is an option for whether or not the entry is a Running Sum. This feature controls whether the value is reset at zero each time the corresponding Header appears, or whether the value from the previous group is carried through. If this is set to No, then every time the Header for the group is printed (every time the entries in the grouping field change), the total is reset to zero.

If Running Sum is set to Over Group or Over All, then the value from the previous group is carried forward across all the groups. This setting can be useful for giving a grand total or a grand average of a group of records. Use it to obtain such calculations as the average across regions in a report summarizing information about regions.

With the Over Group option, the calculation is continued across all the groups contained within that section (any sections that fall between the header for the group and the footer for the group). With Over All, the calculation continues no matter how the group changes.

Page numbers and dates

Access can insert certain types of information for you in either the headers or the footers. Most notably, Access can insert page numbers or dates, using the Page Number command and the Date and Time command under the Insert menu.

Hey, what page is this?

Choosing Insert⇨Page Number displays the dialog box shown in Figure 20-17.

Figure 20-17:
From this dialog box, you can fiddle with how your reports generate their page numbers.

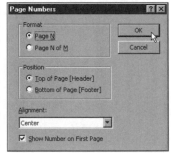

From this dialog box, you have several options for your page-numbering pleasure:

- **Format:** Choose Page N to tell Access to print the word "Page" followed by the appropriate page number. Or choose Page N of M to have Access count the total number of pages in the report and print that number in addition to the current page (as in "Page 2 of 15").

- **Position:** Tell Access whether to print the page number in the Page Header or the Page Footer.

- **Alignment:** Set the position of the page number on the page. Click the arrow at the right edge of the list box to scroll through your options.

- **Show Number on First Page:** Select this check box to include a page number on the first page of your report. Deselect it to keep your first page unnumbered and pristine.

If you want to change the way that the page numbers work on your report, first manually delete the existing page number field by clicking on it and pressing the Delete key. Once the number is gone, choose Insert⇨Page Numbers to build the new page numbers.

When did you print this report, anyway?

Choosing Insert⇨Date and Time displays the dialog box shown in Figure 20-18. The most important options to consider here are Include Date and Include Time.

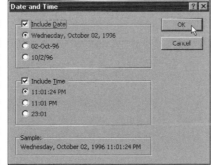

Figure 20-18:
You can even tell Access how you want the date displayed on your report.

You then can select the format for both the date and the time from a somewhat limited set of choices.

You don't have a choice of where the date and time go — Access always puts them in the Page Header. But, if you're feeling a bit sneaking, here's a tip: Use the Cut and Paste commands to move the date and time markers to the section where you want to place them.

Part V
Wizards, Forms, and Other Mystical Stuff

In this part . . .

Part V defies rational explanation. (How's *that* for a compelling tag line?) Its four chapters introduce a wide range of stuff that's all individually useful, but collectively unrelated. When you get down to it, the only thing tying these topics together is the fact that they're not related to anything else.

Chapter 21 (appropriately enough) takes you and your databases into the 21st century with Internet integration — one of the much-heralded features of Access 97.

Also, be sure to check out Chapter 22 to find out all about forms in Access 95. (Uh oh — my *inner nerd* is starting to get excited. . . .) Forms are really powerful and flexible . . . and they're fun to make — that's right, I said *fun*.

Chapter 23 delves into the wonderful world of importing and exporting data. Chapter 24 shows you how to analyze the heck out of your tables. (Perhaps you should just go ahead and read the part while I try to get the nerd back under control before it's too late.)

Chapter 21

Spinning Your Data into (and onto) the Web

. . . .

In This Chapter

▶ What Access 97 knows about the Internet

▶ Entering and using hyperlinks

▶ Publishing stuff on the Web

▶ Advanced topics to challenge your hair retention

. . . .

Yes, it's true — I couldn't make something like this up by myself. Yesterday, Access was merely a database, another tool for shoving data around your hard drive or local area network. Today, Access 97 is a powerhouse of Internet and intranet information. If you're itching to join the online revolution, or if you yearn for fun and profit on the electronic superhighway, then Access 97 (and the rest of the Office 97 suite, for that matter) is ready to get you started.

This chapter takes a quick look at the technology behind Access 97's new-found online capabilities and then discusses some of the details of hyperlinks and online database publishing. The chapter closes with some advanced topics for your further research pleasure. (Trust me, these topics are just too high on the old techno-nerd scale for this book.)

Right from outset, this chapter dives headlong into things like the Internet, corporate intranets, and the World Wide Web. If these terms remind you of some technology-based conspiracy theory, you need to relax a little (after all, they're not out to get *just* you). When you're nice and rested, pick up a copy of the popular *The Internet For Dummies,* 3rd Edition, by John Levine, Carol Baroudi, and Margaret Levine Young (published by IDG Books Worldwide, Inc.). To try out the Internet in an easy, low-stress environment, get *America Online For Dummies,* 3rd Edition, by Yours Truly, and get ready to join the fun. Either way, invest some time to discover more about the online world — it's vital information for the coming years of your career. (Yes, it really is *that* important.)

Access 97 and the Internet: A Match Made in Redmond

These days, it seems that all software makers are touting their products' cozy linkage with the Internet. Whether it's a natural fit or the marketing equivalent of a shotgun wedding, everyone's joining the rush to cyberspace.

Thankfully, Internet integration with Access 97 is on the *natural fit* end of the scale. Databases are a perfect fit for the Net's popular World Wide Web information system. The Web has always offered lots of interactivity and a flexible presentation medium. But until now, publishing a database on the Web was a complex process requiring time, effort, and a willingness to cheerfully rip your hair out by the roots.

To make the data-publishing process much easier and less hair-intensive, Microsoft came up with a way to bring the Net right into Access 97. The key to the behind-the-scenes magic is a new Microsoft technology called ActiveX.

ActiveX is Microsoft's answer to another recent Internet innovation: Java. Don't stress out yet about the technology — I have some good news. You don't need to know *anything* technical about either ActiveX or Java to make Access 97 sing on the Net. Just make a mental note that ActiveX is like a super-duper version of *Object Linking and Embedding* (OLE), the technology that lets you store an Access database inside a Microsoft Word document and perform other equally amazing feats of technological magic. ActiveX has capabilities that go beyond OLE, because ActiveX knows how to do its thing over the Internet instead of being limited to your hard drive.

If anyone asks you about ActiveX or Java, just say something about how "ActiveX and Java are both very robust and promising technologies." Be sure to use the term *robust* in your answer — it's one of those amazing buzzwords that nobody understands but everybody agrees with.

Access 97's Internet power comes directly from the latest release of the Microsoft Web browser, Internet Explorer 3.0, through a cool ActiveX pipeline. When you work with hyperlinks, browse the Net from a form, or search your company's intranet, Internet Explorer is doing all the work. Even when it *looks* as though Access 97 is in the thick of things, the Internet information is coming directly from Internet Explorer. It's the ActiveX technology that makes everything look so seamless.

To make Access 97 do its Internet tricks, you *must* install Internet Explorer 3.0. In addition, you need a connection to the Internet (or to your company's intranet) that uses the built-in Windows 95 32-bit Winsock file. (Internet Explorer 3.0 doesn't work with a 16-bit Winsock — sorry, but it's a fact of life.) Winsock is yet another special piece of Windows 95 code that helps Windows applications talk to the Internet.

If you don't know what this stuff means, that's okay — you're allowed to ask questions. In that case, I suggest consulting your company's computer nerds before going any further. If you're on your own and don't have a corporate techweenie department handy, try calling your Internet Service Provider for help, because you pay them to know stuff like this.

Can't Hyperlinks Take Something to Calm Down?

Sitting right in the center of the whole Internet discussion is the term *hyperlink*. Although "hyperlink" sounds vaguely like a frenzied game show host, hyperlinks are actually the special storage compartments for whatever you want to link with. Hyperlinks can connect to a variety of Internet or intranet locations, as Table 21-1 shows.

Table 21-1	Hyperlinks in Access 97
Link	*Description*
file://	Opens a local or network-based file
ftp://	File Transfer Protocol; links to an FTP server
gopher://	Links to a Gopher server on the network or Internet
http://	Hypertext Transfer Protocol; links to a World Wide Web page
mailto:	Sends e-mail to a network or Internet address
news:	Opens an Internet newsgroup

Table 21-1 contains the most popular and commonly used tags. For a complete list of the hyperlink tags that Access 97 understands, press F1 to open the Access 97 Help system and then search for the term *hyperlink*.

If you regularly surf the World Wide Web, many of these tags should look familiar. Although most of them are geared toward Internet/intranet applications, Access 97 can also use hyperlinks to identify locally-stored Microsoft Office documents. This technology is so flexible, the sky's the limit.

Adding a hyperlink field to your table

You can't let hyperlinks just stand around without a permanent home, so Access 97 sports a new field type specifically for this special data. As you probably guessed, this type is called the *hyperlink* field. Figure 21-1 shows a table design containing a hyperlink field. Notice that the hyperlink field is no different from the other mundane fields surrounding it.

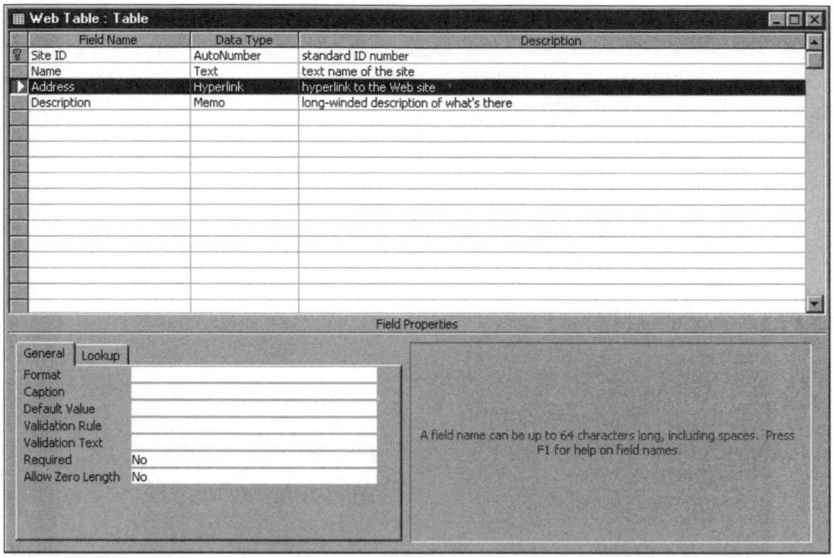

Figure 21-1:
This table
contains a
hyperlink
field.

There aren't any special steps for adding a hyperlink field to a table. Just use the same steps you would for adding *any* new field to a table:

1. **Open your table in Design view.**

   A window that shows the table's structure appears on-screen.

2. **Click the spot where you want the new field and then choose Insert⇨Rows from the main menu.**

   A blank row appears in your table design, as shown in Figure 21-2.

3. **Type a name for the field and then press Tab to place the cursor in the Data Type column.**

   Hyperlink fields have names just like all the other fields. Goodness knows you don't want them to feel left out.

4. **Click the down arrow in the Data Type column, select Hyperlink from the pull-down menu, and press Tab when you're done.**

   So much for the mystique — you use the same steps for *any* new field. (Even though they're special, hyperlink fields behave just like all the other fields in Design view.)

5. **Type a field description if you want one.**

6. **Choose File⇨Save from the main menu to save your design changes.**

   The new hyperlink field proudly takes its place in your table, just as in Figure 21-3.

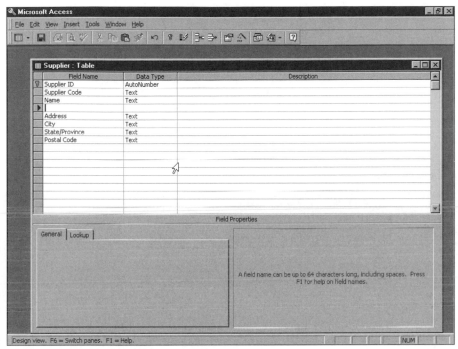

Figure 21-2:
A space opens for the new field.

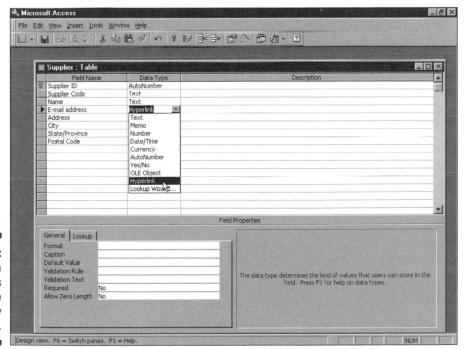

Figure 21-3:
Adding a hyperlink is just like adding any other field.

Typing hyperlinks (and using them, too)

Hyperlinks are just data, so you don't have to do anything special to coax them into your tables. In fact, all you have to do is type! Granted, hyperlinks *look* a little different than normal data (see Figure 21-4), but that's okay. They're just like plain fields most of the time — they need to have *some* fun.

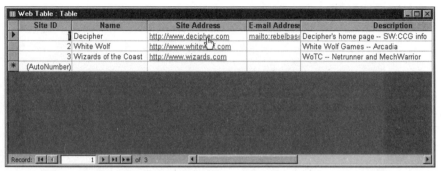

Figure 21-4:
Hyperlinks
automatically
dress up in
special
formatting.

Although most hyperlinks store World Wide Web or other Internet addresses, they can point to just about anything in the known world. Thanks to their flexible tags, hyperlinks understand Web pages, intranet servers, database objects (reports, forms, and such), and even plain Microsoft Office documents on your computer or another networked PC.

Using the hyperlink is easy, too. Here are the steps:

1. **Either log onto your network or start your Internet connection.**

   Internet Explorer needs to see that everything is up and running before it consents to making an appearance. (Silly prima donna software.)

2. **Open the Access 97 database you want to use and then open the table containing those wonderful hyperlinks.**

   The fun is about to begin!

3. **Click the hyperlink of your choice.**

   After a few moments of thought, Internet Explorer leaps on-screen, displaying the Web site from the link, just as in Figure 21-5. If the link leads to something other than a Web site, Windows 95 automatically fires up the right program to handle whatever the link has to offer. (Isn't technology amazing when it works?)

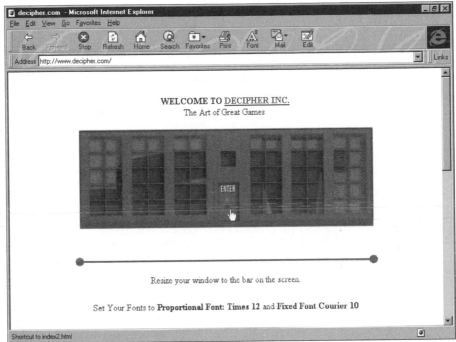

Figure 21-5:
One click
later, the
Web site
appears.

A few words about the World Wide Web (and why you should care)

Although this whole hyperlink thing may seem like just so much techno-hype, it really *is* important. More and more businesses are moving information to the World Wide Web. Companies are also creating in-house *intranets* (custom Web servers offering information to networked employees).

Access 97's new abilities put it in the middle of the Web and intranet excitement — and that presents a cool opportunity for you.

Everything about the Web and intranet technology is so new that it cuts across all kinds of organizational boundaries. Duties that used to

belong exclusively to *those computer people* are landing in graphic arts, marketing, and almost everywhere else. New jobs are born overnight as companies wrestle with the Web's powerful communication features. It may sound a little chaotic, and that's okay — it is.

If you're looking for a new career path in your corporate life, knowledge of the Web may just be the ticket. Whether you move into Web site development, information management, or even your own Web-oriented consulting business, this is an exciting time full of new possibilities. Dive in and discover what's waiting for you!

Pushing Your Data onto the Web

Now that Access 97 contains all of your coolest information, why not share your stuff with others in your company — or even publish it for the world? Whether you're building a commercial site geared toward fame and online fortune, or a cross-department intranet to supercharge your company, Access 97 has a new Publish to the Web Wizard feature that whips your data into shape in no time at all.

By far, this wizard's best trick is converting Access 97 datasheets, query results, forms, and reports into *Hypertext Markup Language* (or HTML), the dialect of the World Wide Web.

Although you don't need to know anything about HTML to build Web pages with the wizard, you probably *will* need to know some HTML before your project is done. For a painless introduction to HTML, check out *HTML For Dummies,* 2nd Edition, by Ed Tittel and Steve James. Or pick up a copy of *Creating Cool Web Pages with HTML,* 2nd Edition, by Dave Taylor (both published by IDG Books Worldwide, Inc.).

The wizard does two kinds of translations: static and dynamic. The one to choose for your project depends on the equipment, goals, and expertise available in your immediate surroundings. Here's a quick comparison of the options:

- ✔ **Static:** This option is a straight conversion from Access 97 into HTML. Its name reflects the fact that the stuff you convert doesn't change over time — it's a lot like taking a picture of your data. If you add more records to your table and want to include them in your Web-based stuff, you need to re-create the Web pages. Static conversion is a great option for address lists and catalogs. It's also a good place to start when you're exploring the possibilities of the Web.

- ✔ **Dynamic:** Instead of creating a simple HTML page, the Dynamic option builds a special query. Anytime someone wants to see your information through the Web, Access 97 works with your Web server to extract the data, format it, and present it. Because all this technical magic requires some serious cooperation between the Web server, Access 97, and your data, building dynamic Web pages isn't a task for beginners. For more about this, see the sidebar "What about this dynamic Web page thing?" later in this chapter.

Although the Dynamic Web page option is best left to trained (and, like me, often balding) computer professionals, literally anyone can create static Web pages with the wizard. Here's how it works, step by step:

1. Open the database destined for the Web.

The database window hops to the screen.

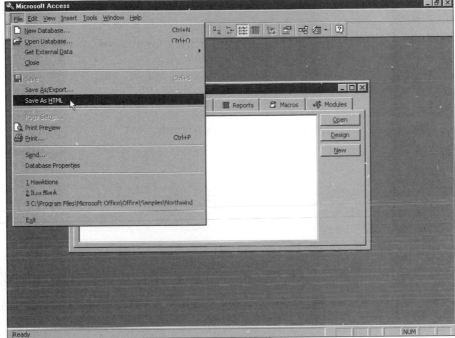

Figure 21-6:
Click here
to summon
forth the
Publish
to Web
Wizard.

2. **Select File⇨Save As HTML from the menu bar (as shown in Figure 21-6).**

   After a gratuitous amount of hard drive activity, the Publish to the Web Wizard ambles forth.

3. **The Publish to Web Wizard's first page contains a quick overview of Web publishing, so click Next to continue.**

   The wizard's item selection page appears, looking a whole lot like the standard database window.

4. **Click the check box next to each item you want export (see Figure 21-7). Click Next when you're done.**

   To flip between lists (Tables, Queries, and so on), click the appropriate tab above the item list.

   If you don't want to mess with flipping from tab to tab, click the All Objects tab to compile a master list of the database's tables, queries, forms, and reports. All the items are listed in tab order (tables first, then queries, forms, and reports). This option is much faster if you have a wide variety of items to export.

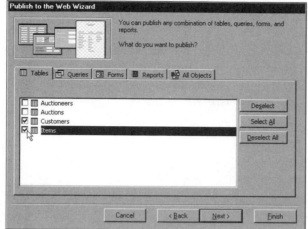

Figure 21-7:
To select a
table, click
in its
check box.

5. **If you already built an HTML template document, point it out to the wizard on this page. Otherwise, click Next to continue.**

   You don't need an HTML template, but having one saves you a lot of time if you're building a bunch of Web pages. See the following section for more info about researching and creating HTML templates.

6. **Now the wizard wants to know whether this is a static HTML page or a dynamic one. The default is static, so simply click Next to move along.**

   Only change this option if you researched dynamic pages and are sure you're ready for the experience. (If you still aren't quite clear about whether you're ready for dynamic Web pages, see the following sidebar for more details.)

7. **Pick a folder to store your new HTML documents and then click Next.**

8. **If you want the wizard to build a simple, yet ugly, home page that leads to the other pages you're creating, click in the Yes, I want to create a home page check box. Type a name for the home page into the text box (as shown in Figure 21-8). Click Finish when you're done.**

   Now that the wizard knows all the details, it begins building your HTML documents. If your tables are large, this may take a while. When it's done, the wizard unceremoniously drops you right where it found you, back at the database window. Whew — what a ride!

   If you plan to rebuild these particular pages every now and then, have the wizard create a Web publication profile for you. To build one, click Next instead of Finish in this step. In the next wizard page, click in the publication profile check box and then type a name for the profile into the text box. Finally, click Finish and proceed with the next step.

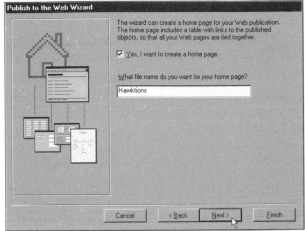

Figure 21-8:
The wizard
is ready
to go.

9. **Test your new pages by running your Web browser and loading the pages up for a quick look (as shown in Figure 21-9).**

   If this page is destined to be part of a big commercial Web site, check the page in a variety of Web browsers. The file may need some adjusting before it looks right (or at least looks passable) when viewed from the many different Web browsers out there.

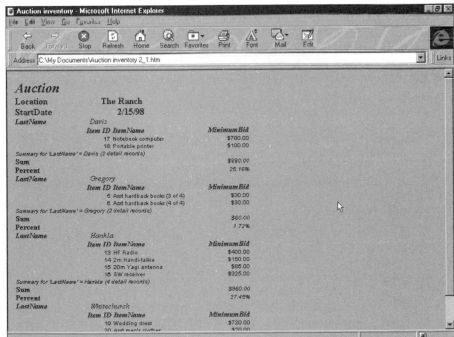

Figure 21-9:
This is good
work,
considering
it came
from a mere
piece of
software.

What about this dynamic Web page thing?

Dynamic Web pages are pretty cool. They offer totally current, up-to-the-second data through the Internet's most popular information system. What else could you ask? Well, frankly, you *could* ask for the implementation process to be a little less complex.

It takes a bevy of Microsoft products working together behind the scenes in sweet harmony to make dynamic Web pages work. Even though you already have the first piece, Access 97, that's only half the story.

Next on the shopping list is your Web server itself. A high-volume system — a Web server connected directly to the Internet, for example — requires Microsoft Windows NT Server running Microsoft's Internet Information Server product. (If you think that sounds expensive and technical, you're right.) The odds are good that you'll also need some help assembling, tweaking, and generally beating the system into submission.

If your sights are set a little lower, though, you just may be able to do this yourself. For a small Web server running on a local area network, try using Microsoft's Personal Web Server product. It uses a networked Windows 95 computer as the base for a fully functional Web server. Don't expect to attach a Personal Web Server to the Internet, though — it's strictly a low volume, local network type of product. The good news is, if you bought Microsoft Office 97 on a CD-ROM, you may already have the software.

For more details about either of these options, press F1 or click the Office Assistant; then type **web server** and press Enter.

Advanced Topics for Your Copious Nerd Time

If all the stuff in this chapter doesn't quell your technological impulses, don't worry — there's plenty more where this came from. Here are a few ideas to keep your mind active, your Web pages sharp, and your Access 97 forms looking truly cool.

Each item includes a brief summary, plus a term to give the Office Assistant if you want all of the details.

- ✔ Put hyperlinks right into your reports and forms. Access 97 lets you attach them directly to command buttons, labels, or images. Search for: **add hyperlink to form**.

- ✔ Build HTML template files to make your exported tables look, act, and dress the same. If you're building the mother of all database Web sites, template files are a big time-saver. Plus, they give your site a consistent, professional feel. Search for: **HTML template files**.

- ✔ Add a Web browser to any Access 97 form. Navigate through Web documents directly from a form — no need to switch between Access 97 and your Web browser! This feature has incredible possibilities for corporate intranets, plus a lot of promise on the Internet, too. Search for: **Web page on a form**.

- ✔ Export datasheets, reports, and forms directly to HTML with the File⇨ Save As/Export menu selection instead of working through the wizard. This feature requires more knowledge of the Web and how it works, but it offers you a lot more control over the results. This option is great when you're fluent in HTML and want to quickly generate a few pages of information that are ready for manual tweaking. Search for: **export to HTML**.

These features just scratch the surface of Access 97's special capabilities. In addition to working with the Net, Access 97 also works very closely with the other members of the Microsoft Office 97 suite. There's so much to know about how the programs interact that Microsoft created a whole huge informational file on the subject. Amazingly, it's available for free through the Internet. To get all the details, ask the Office Assistant for information about the Office 97 resource kit.

Chapter 22

Making Forms That Look Cool and Work Great

*P*aper forms are the lifeblood of almost every enterprise. If they weren't, life would probably be simpler, but that's beside the point. Because real life is the mirror that software engineers peer into (and frequently faint while looking at) when they're designing programs, Access 97 includes the ever-cherished capability to view and work with forms.

The dreaded PBF *(paper-based form)* is not nearly as friendly as its electronic counterpart. In fact, you may even discover that you *like* messing around with forms in Access 97. (If that happens to you, don't tell anyone.) This chapter looks at what forms can do for you, explores a couple different ways to make forms, and tosses out some tips for customizing forms so that they're exactly what you need.

Tax Forms and Data Forms Are Very Different Animals

All forms are *not* created equal. Paper forms make cool airplanes, take up physical space, are hard to update, and (depending on the number of forms involved) can constitute a safety hazard when stacked. Access 97 forms, on the other hand, are simple to update, easy to store, and are rarely a safety risk (although designing a form *can* be hazardous to your productivity, because it's kinda fun).

Forms in Access 97 are something like digital versions of their paper cousins, but the similarity ends with the name. Access 97 forms have all kinds of advantages over old-fashioned paper forms — and they'll spoil you if you're used to wandering through your data in Datasheet view. Here's just a sampling of how forms in Access 97 make viewing your data easier:

- **Escape the clutches of Datasheet view:** Instead of scrolling back and forth through a datasheet, you focus on one record at a time, with all the data pleasantly laid out on a single screen.

- **Modify at will:** When your needs change, take the form into Design view and update it. And, unlike with its paper cousins, you don't have to worry about recycling 10,000 leftover copies of the old form.

- **See your data any way you want:** Access 97 lets you take one set of data and present it in as many different forms as you want — all without re-entering a bit of data for the new form. Create a special form for the data-entry folks, another for your analysts, and a third for yourself. Well-designed forms give the right information to the right people *without* revealing data they don't need to.

- **View the entries in a table or the results of a query:** Forms pull information from tables or queries with equal ease. Forms based on queries are especially flexible because they always display the latest information.

- **Combine data from linked tables:** One form can display data from several related tables. Forms automatically use the relationships built into your database.

Like reports and queries, forms are stored in the database file under their own tab, as Figure 22-1 shows. Forms are full-fledged Access 97 objects, so you can do all kinds of cool tricks with them.

Figure 22-1:
Knowing the forms are just where I left them is comforting.

Depending on your needs, you can use any of three ways to make forms. The *Form Wizard* offers a take-you-by-the-hand approach, walking you through a series of questions and then proudly producing a rather bland-looking form. The three *AutoForm* tools make the same forms as the Form Wizard but don't ask any questions. Finally, in the *by-hand* approach, Access 97 sets up a blank form, drops off a toolbox full of form-related goodies, shakes your hand, and then wanders off to do something fun while you make a form from scratch.

I don't believe in doing any more work than necessary, so this chapter explains how to use the Form Wizard and the AutoForm tools to make the software build basic forms for you. The chapter closes with tips and tricks for manually tweaking these Masterpieces of Vanilla into Truly Cool Forms.

Creating a Form at the Wave of a Wand

The easiest path to the best in computer-designed forms (notice that I didn't say *stunning forms* or *especially useful forms*) is through the Form Wizard. As with all the other Access 97 wizards, the Form Wizard steps you through the creation process, bombarding you with questions to the point that you sometimes want to tell it to just grow up and start making its own decisions.

To get the Form Wizard up and running, follow these steps:

1. **Open your database file and click on the Forms tab.**

   Access 97 displays a list of the forms currently in your database. Don't fret if the list is currently empty — you're about to change that.

2. **Click on <u>N</u>ew.**

   The New Form dialog box appears.

3. **Double-click on the Form Wizard choice in the dialog box (see Figure 22-2).**

   At this point, the computer's hard disk usually sounds like it's having a massive fight with itself. When the noise dies down, the Form Wizard poofs into action.

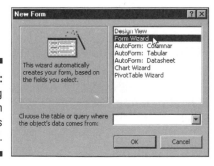

Figure 22-2:
Ringing
the Form
Wizard's
bell.

4. **Click on the down arrow in the Tables/Queries box to list the tables and queries in your database, and then select the one that contains the fields you want to view with this form.**

   The Form Wizard lists the available fields. Now tell the wizard what you want to display in the form.

5. **Double-click on a field name in the Available Fields list to include the field in your form.**

   If you want to see *all* the fields, click the >> button in the middle of the screen. To remove a field that you accidentally picked, double-click on its name in the Selected Fields list. The field jumps back to the Available Fields side of the dialog box.

6. **Repeat the process on each field destined for the form. When you're done with all the fields, click on Next (see Figure 22-3).**

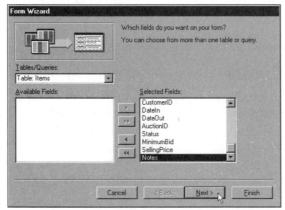

Figure 22-3:
The fields are ready, so it's time to move along.

7. **If you select fields from more than one table, the Form Wizard takes a moment to ask how you want to organize the data in your form. Click on your choice in the by (fieldname) list on the left side of the dialog box and then click on Next.**

   If the Form Wizard asks about form layout at this point, go on to the next step.

8. **The Form Wizard wants to know how you want to display the data on the form. Leave the option set to Columnar (or Datasheet, if that's the default option on your screen) and then click on Next.**

   This is another one of those points where Access 97 has too many options for its own good. If you saw the dialog box that I mention in Step 7, your screen probably shows only two options: Tabular and Datasheet. On the other hand, if you skipped Step 7 and came directly to Step 8, you should have four options on-screen: Columnar, Tabular, Datasheet, and Justified. The Report Wizard offers only the options that it thinks are most appropriate for your data. (Of course, this kind of *help* often leads to confusion, which is why I get to write these cool books. Keep up the good work, Microsoft!)

The other formats (Tabular and Justified) are interesting, but they create really complicated forms that aren't very easy to work with or customize. Sometime in the future, when you're all caught up on work and want to spend some intimate moments with Access 97, give one of the other formats a try.

9. **In the name of sprucing up a bland form, the wizard offers to use some interesting color and background styles to display your data. For now, click on the Standard option (shown in Figure 22-4) and click on Next to continue.**

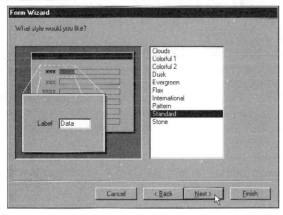

Figure 22-4:
Even though the options are tempting, stick with simplicity at first.

Most of the color and background combinations *really* slow down the performance of your forms. If you absolutely *must* have some color in your forms, try the Colorful or Stone settings. They provide some lively highlights without affecting your form's performance.

10. **Type a descriptive title for your form in the What title do you want for your form? box at the top of the Form Wizard screen.**

By default, the Form Wizard offers you the name of the table that you used to feed the form, but *please* use something more descriptive than just that.

11. **Click on Finish when you're done.**

After a few moments (or a few *minutes,* if you have a slow computer), your new form appears on-screen, ready for action (see Figure 22-5).

The Form Wizard automatically saves the form as part of the creation process, so you don't need to manually save and name it.

Mass Production at Its Best: Forms from the Auto Factory

When I was a kid, I became fascinated with business and how it worked. The move from hand-built products to Henry Ford's automated assembly line particularly amazed me. (Yes, I *was* a little different. Why do you ask?) The assembly line had its good and bad points, but the quote that always defined the Ford assembly line for me was, "You can have any color you want, as long as it's black."

With that thought in mind, let me welcome you to the AutoForm Factory. Our motto: "You can have any form you want, as long as it's one of the three we make." Ah, the joys of flexible production management. . . .

Access 97 claims that the AutoForms are wizards, but because they're so limited — er, I mean *focused* — I don't think of them as full-fledged purveyors of the magical arts. Semantics aside, each of the three AutoForms builds a different kind of form:

- *Columnar* assembles a classic, one-record-per-page form.

- *Tabular* makes a rather cool, multiple-record-per-page form, but be ready for some cosmetic surgery to grind away the rough edges and make the form truly useful (see Figure 22-6).

- *Datasheet* creates (hold on tight for this one) a *form* that looks, acts, smells, and feels just like a classic *datasheet.* Check out Figure 22-7 to see for yourself. Did the world *need* a form that pretends to be a datasheet?

Using the AutoForms is a quick process. Despite their alleged *wizard* status, AutoForms are more like office temps: Just point them at data, stand back, and before you know it, the form is done. Here are the details of the process:

1. With your database open, click on the Form tab and then click on New.

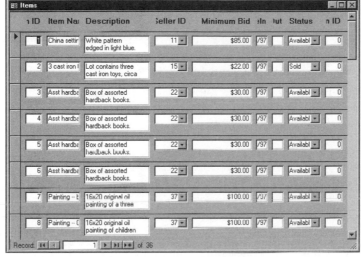

Figure 22-6:
Tabular
forms are
more avant-
garde, but
those
headings
are a mess.

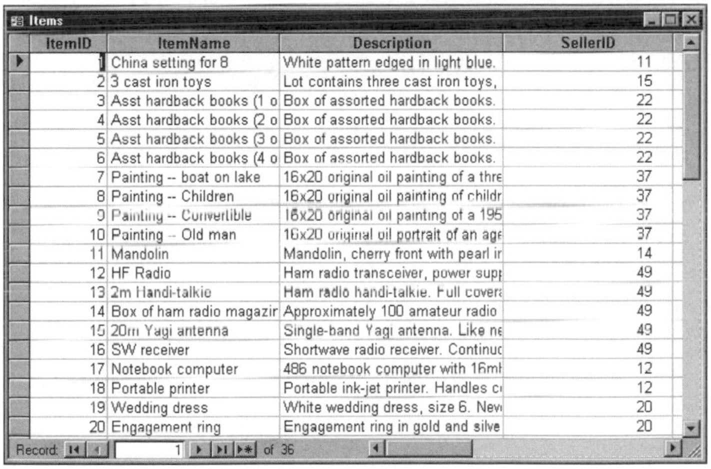

Figure 22-7:
Is it a
datasheet or
a form
pretending
to be a
datasheet?
Only its
properties
know for
sure.

The New Form dialog box hops onto the screen, ready to help.

2. **Depending on which look you're after, click on AutoForm: Columnar, AutoForm: Tabular, or AutoForm: Datasheet.**

   Access 97 highlights the appropriate mini-wizard name.

3. **Click on the down arrow next to the text box below the Wizard list.**

   A drop-down list of tables and queries in the current database appears.

4. **In the drop-down list, click on the table or query that you want to provide information for this form. When you're done, click on OK.**

The appropriate mini-wizard begins its focused little job, and your new form appears on-screen in a few moments.

5. **If you like the form, preserve it for posterity by choosing File⇨Save or by clicking on the Save button on the toolbar. When the Save As dialog box appears, type a name for the form and then click OK.**

Unlike the Form Wizard, AutoForms *don't* automatically save the form they create, so you have to save the form manually. The form is added to your database in the Forms tab.

Ultimate Beauty through Cosmetic Surgery

I have a question for you. Tell me the brutal truth, okay? Don't hold back. I want your honest opinion on this. Ready? Would you rather slavishly toil away in the data-entry sweatshop of Figure 22-8 or casually pop a few records into Figure 22-9 between tennis sets? Take your time to answer.

Figure 22-8:
Before: An unimaginative form created by a mindless software automaton.

Items							
ı ID	Item Nai	Description	Seller ID	Minimum Bid	ıln ıut	Status	n ID
1	China settir	White pattern edged in light blue.	11	$85.00	/97	Availabl	0
2	3 cast iron I	Lot contains three cast iron toys, circa	15	$22.00	/97	Sold	0
3	Asst hardbː	Box of assorted hardback books.	22	$30.00	/97	Availabl	0
4	Asst hardbː	Box of assorted hardback books.	22	$30.00	/97	Availabl	0
5	Asst hardbː	Box of assorted hardback books.	22	$30.00	/97	Availabl	0
6	Asst hardbː	Box of assorted hardback books.	22	$30.00	/97	Availabl	0
7	Painting -- ł	16x20 original oil painting of a three	37	$100.00	/97	Availabl	0
8	Painting -- (	16x20 original oil painting of children	37	$100.00	/97	Availabl	0

Record: 1 of 36

Believe it or not, those images are the *same form*. Yup, it's true. The *Before* image in Figure 22-8 is a standard columnar form straight from the AutoForm Factory of the previous section. The Figure 22-9 *After* image emerged poised, beautiful, and easy to use after just one visit to Dr. John's School for Operationally Inept Forms. To bring about the transformation, I moved the fields around, added some graphics to segment the form, and changed the tab order to make data entry more intuitive.

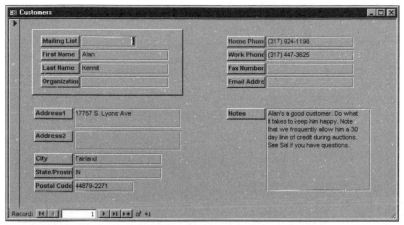

Figure 22-9:
After: The
same form
rescued
from the
depths of
digital
despair,
thanks to
cosmetic
surgery.

Because the school is a small, private institution, it doesn't have enough space for the thousands upon thousands of forms that desperately require this treatment. So instead of sending your forms to my school, I'm sending the school to you. This section outfits you with the basic tool kit used by top form surgeons around the country. In no time at all, your frumpy forms will be sleek data-entry machines, both functionally useful and visually appealing.

Taking a form into Design view

Before you can make *any* of these changes, the form has to be in Design view. Access provides two easy ways to get there, depending on where you happen to be right now:

- ✔ **From the database window:** Click on the Forms tab to list the available forms. Click on the form you want to change and then click on <u>D</u>esign.
- ✔ **From a form window:** Click on the Design button on the toolbar or choose <u>V</u>iew⇨Form <u>D</u>esign from the menu.

Don't let Design view stress you out. It *looks* more complicated than normal life, but that's okay. If something goes wrong and you accidentally mess up your form, just choose <u>F</u>ile⇨<u>C</u>lose from the menu. When Access 97 asks about saving your changes, politely click on <u>N</u>o. This step throws out all the horrible changes you just made to the form. Take a few deep breaths to calm your nerves, and then start the design process over again.

Moving fields

To move a field around in the form design, follow these steps:

1. **Put the mouse pointer anywhere on the field that you want to move.**

   You can point to the field name or the box where the field's value goes. Either place is equally fine for what you're doing.

   If the field is already selected (the name has a box around it that's decorated with small, filled-in squares), click on any blank spot of your form to deselect the field; then start with Step 1. Otherwise, Access gets confused and thinks you want to do something *other* than just move the field.

2. **Press and hold the left mouse button.**

   The mouse pointer turns into a hand, which is how Access 97 tells you that it's ready to move something. Strange response, isn't it?

3. **Drag the field to its new location.**

   As you move the field, a pair of white boxes moves along with the cursor to show you precisely where the field will land.

4. **When the field is in position, release the mouse button.**

   The field drops smoothly into place.

   If you don't like where the field landed, either move it again or press Ctrl+Z to undo the move and start over from scratch.

Adding lines and boxes

Two buttons near the bottom of the the form design toolbox enable you to add lines and boxes:

 ✔ Creates lines on your form.

 ✔ Creates boxes (or borders) on your form.

Here's how to use these tools:

1. **Click on the tool of your choice.**

   To show you that it's selected, the tool visually *pushes in,* just like a toggle button.

2. **Put the mouse pointer where you want to start the line or place the corner of a box; then press and hold the left mouse button.**

   Aim is important, but you can always undo or move the graphic if the project doesn't work out quite right.

3. Move the cursor to the spot where the line ends or to the opposite corner of your box and then release the mouse button.

The line or box appears on-screen.

When adding line or box graphics, remember that several *special effects* are available to you, depending on what you're adding:

- ✓ Lines can be *flat* or *raised*. Even though the other options seem to be available, they don't look any different from *raised* when you're working with a line.

- ✓ Boxes respond to *all* the special effects options, as you can see in Figure 22-10.

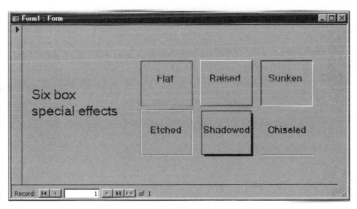

Figure 22-10: Boxes are by far the more stylish graphic element.

To use these special effects, draw your line or box and then right-click on it (if it's a line, right-click on one end). Choose Special Effects from the pop-up menu and then click the particular effect you like best.

If you want to customize your line or box a little further, give the Border settings a try. Begin by opening the Properties dialog box as described above and then click the Format tab.

- ✓ *Border Style* adjusts how the line looks, with options ranging from solid to dotted.

- ✓ *Border Color* changes the line's color.

- ✓ *Border Width* makes the line anything from a wispy hairline to a bold 6-point behemoth.

Experiment with the settings to come up with the best combination for you. As with the special effects settings, click the X button to close the Properties box when you're done.

Changing the field tab order

Changing the field tab order isn't quite as simple and fun-loving as the other options in this section, but changing the order is extremely rewarding. If you move the fields around on the form and then try to use the form, you quickly discover that the fields remember their *old* order when you move from one field to the next with the Tab key. To fix this problem, you need to change the Tab Index property of the fields.

Changing the field tab order is a slightly more technical undertaking than drawing boxes, but it doesn't hold a candle to flying a Boeing 747 aircraft. Now that the issue is in perspective, here's how to change the tab order:

1. **With the form open in Design view, choose <u>V</u>iew⇨Ta<u>b</u> Order.**

   The Tab Order dialog box opens, listing the fields in their current tab order.

2. **Click on the small button to the left of the field you want to work with (as shown in Figure 22-11).**

   The field highlights in response to your click. (Isn't that special?)

Figure 22-11: The HomePhone field is ready to go.

To have Access 97 automatically set the tab order for all the fields in the form, click the <u>A</u>uto Order button at the bottom of the Tab Order dialog box. Access 97 sets the order according to where the field is in the form. It starts from the upper-left side of the form and goes across, and then moves down one line and repeats the process. Fields end up in order horizontally (fields on line one, fields on line two, and so on).

3. **Click and drag the field to its new position in the tab order.**

   As you drag the field, a dark gray bar moves with it, showing where the field will fit into the tab order. When the bar is in the right place, release the button. Access moves the field into its new position in the tab order.

4. **Repeat Steps 2 and 3 for any other fields you want to change.**

   Access doesn't care how much you work with the tab order, so play to your heart's content.

5. **When you're done adjusting the tab order, click on OK.**

   The Tab Order dialog box runs off to wherever dialog boxes hang out when they're not on-screen.

6. **Click on the Form View button on the toolbar and test your work.**

   If any fields are still out of order, note which ones they are and then work back through these steps to fix the order.

Chapter 23

If Love Is Universal, Why Can't I Export to It?

In This Chapter

▶ Pulling data into Access 97

▶ Deciding when to import and when to link data

▶ Speaking in foreign data tongues

▶ Pushing your comfortable data into the cold, cruel outside world

*T*o achieve true success these days, speaking only the tongue of the country that bore you isn't enough. You need to be comfortable with several languages before the pinnacle of achievement is within your grasp. I, for example, am fluent in *American English*, a language that the British view as a poor excuse for grunting and knocking rocks together. To excel at my work, I also studied several variants of the vernacular *Nerd*, including *Windows, DOS*, the pictorial troubleshooting tongue *$%@&#!*, and the esoteric *Macintosh* dialect (which is particularly challenging because all the words in it look and act alike).

Access 97 is multilingual as well, because its electronic world is filled with more disagreeing tongues than the UN Security Council. It understands a couple of spreadsheets, several competing databases, and even plain old text files. Because of this capability, you can exchange data with almost any source out there. I have to say that Access 97 is one of the most flexible programs I've ever seen (and I've seen a *bunch* of programs).

This chapter looks at the import and export capabilities of Access 97, how they work, and what you can do with them. If you work with Access 97 and almost *any* other program, you need this chapter, because sometime soon some data will be in the wrong place — and guess whose job it is to move it. . . .

Importing Only the Best Information for Your Databases

Access 97 really has two ways of sucking data into its greedy clutches. *Importing* involves translating the data from a foreign format into the Access 97 database file format (which, according to Microsoft, all the world's data should be stored in). The other method is *linking*, where you build a temporary bridge between the external data and Access 97.

If you worked with older versions of Access, *linking* used to be called *attaching*. The concept is the same; only the name has been changed to confuse the innocent.

Translating file formats

Regardless of whether you import or link the data, Access 97 understands only certain data formats. Table 23-1 lists the most common file types that Access interacts with. Believe it or not, the entries in this table cover the majority of data stored on PCs around the world.

Table 23-1	The Access 97 List of Language Fluencies		
Program	*DOS extension*	*Versions*	*Notes*
Access	.MDB	2.0, 7.0	Even though they share the same name, these versions use slightly different file formats than Access 97.
dBASE	.DBF	III, III+, IV, V	One of the most popular formats out there; many programs use the dBASE format.
FoxPro	.DBF	2.0, 2.5, 2.6, 3.0	Microsoft's *other* database program; not *directly* compatible with dBASE in some cases.
Paradox	.DB	3.*x*, 4.*x*, 5.*x*	A competing database from Borland.
Excel	.XLS	2.0, 3.0, 4.0, 5.0, 7.0, 8.0	Although it's a spreadsheet, many people use Excel as a simple flat-file database manager.

Program	DOS extension	Versions	Notes
Lotus 1-2-3	.WKS, .WK1, .WK3	1.*x*, 2.*x*, 3.*x*, 4.*x*	The most popular DOS spreadsheet is also the home of many tortured flat-file databases.
ASCII	.TXT	N/A	The "if all else fails" format; Access 97 understands both delimited and fixed-width text files.
SQL	N/A	Sybase, Oracle, Microsoft	This is nerd country, but you may run across SQL when working with the company's *big* databases.

Although Access 97 is pretty intelligent about the translation process, you need to watch out for some quirks. Here are some specific tips to keep in mind as you play The Great Data Liberator and set the imperiled information free to enjoy a new life in Access 97:

✓ When working with dBASE and FoxPro files, make sure that you keep careful track of the associated index files. Access 97 needs the index to work with the table. If Access can't find the index or if it is corrupt, your table is gibberish.

✓ Access 97 has problems linking to Paradox tables that don't have a primary key. Specifically, it can't write changes to the unkeyed Paradox table. To fix the problem, use Paradox to create a primary key in the table and *then* link the table to Access 97.

✓ Remember that data in Paradox tables *isn't* stored in a single file. Having a .PX (the primary index) and a .MB (memo data — I don't know what the *B* is supposed to stand for) file lurking around the .DB file is common. If you copy a Paradox table from one computer to another, take care to copy *all* the associated files!

✓ Double-check information coming from any spreadsheet program to be sure that it's *consistent*. Above all, ensure that the data on each row of a column (field) is the same type. Otherwise, the import won't work right (and you know how forgiving software is of such "little" problems).

✓ For ASCII or SQL data, getting a computer guru's help the first (and possibly the second) time is probably best. Many niggling little details stand between you and a successful data import.

Importing or linking your files

The precise details of importing and linking depend greatly on the type of file you're importing, but here are the general steps to get you started in the right direction. Although the instructions are written mainly for importing, I include supporting notes about linking as well:

1. **Open the Access 97 database you're pulling the data into.**

   If you're not familiar with this step, *stop* — don't go any further. Flip to Chapter 1 and spend some time getting comfy with Access 97 before attempting an import.

2. **Choose File⇨Get External Data⇨Import.**

   The dialog box in Figure 23-1 appears.

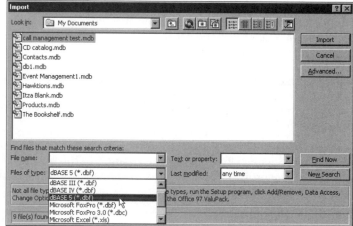

Figure 23-1:
Make sure
that you
pick the
correct data
type.

To make a link, choose Link Tables from the submenu instead of Import. When you make that selection, the dialog box in Figure 23-1 is labeled Link instead of Import, but the choices are exactly the same.

3. **Click on the down arrow in the Files of type box and click on the kind of data you're importing. If necessary, use the Look in list box to navigate your way to the files.**

   The dialog box displays the matching files for your selection pleasure. Make sure that you choose the correct file type. Otherwise, Access doesn't list the file you're looking for in the dialog box!

   If your database file has a strange, nonstandard extension on the end of the filename (like .FOO, .DTA, or .XXX), Access 97 may not be able to make heads or tails of the file. In that case, seek help from your technical support people or local computer jockey.

4. Double-click on the file that you want to import.

Here's where the process takes off in wildly different directions depending on the file format you're importing and whether you're doing a link or an import. The only sage advice I can give is to cross your fingers, follow the instructions on-screen, refer to the preceding tips, and hope for the best.

One final thought: If you're importing and the process is taking *forever,* Access is probably struggling with errors in the inbound data. Press Ctrl+Break to stop the import process and check the data that's being imported for obvious errors (bad or corrupt data, badly organized spreadsheet data, invalid index, and so on).

Sending Your Data on a Long, One-Way Trip

In the interest of keeping you awake, I'll keep this explanation short. Exporting is just like importing, except where it's different.

Hmm . . . perhaps that explanation was a little *too* short.

Exporting a table involves reorganizing the data it contains into a different format. Like importing, Access 97 can translate the data into a variety of "languages," depending on your needs. The master list of export formats is the same one governing imports, given earlier in the chapter.

The main problem to keep an eye out for when exporting is *data loss.* Not all storage formats are created equal (after all, Microsoft didn't come up with them *all,* which is arguably a good situation). Just because the data looked glorious in your Access 97 table doesn't mean a suitable home is waiting when you ship the information off to, say, Paradox or FoxPro. Special Access 97 data types such as *AutoNumber, Yes/No, Memo,* and *OLE* are almost sure to cause problems. Be ready for some creative problem-solving to make the data work just the way you want it to.

Likewise, field names can be trouble. Access 97 is very generous about what you can put into a field name. dBASE, on the other hand, is downright totalitarian about field names. This attitude can lead to multiple fields with the same name — a frustrating (if slightly humorous) problem. If you export an Access 97 table with fields called Projected1997Sales, Projected1997Net, and Projected1997Overhead, ending up with three fields named *Projected1* is distinctly possible — *not* a pleasant thought. Be ready to spend some time tuning the export so that it works just the way you thought it would.

NOTE

To import or to link — the answer is, *It depends*

Because Access 97 offers two different ways to get data in, a logical question comes up: *Which method should I use?* Because this question involves a computer, the simple answer is *It depends*.

The answer mainly depends on the other program and its fate within your organization. Are you still using the other program to update the data? Do other people use the program to access the data? If so, use a link with Access 97.

This option lets you play with the data while keeping it in the original format so that everyone else can use it as well.

On the other hand, if the other application was mothballed and you're doing data rescue duty, import the data permanently and give it a comfortable new home. Preserving a data format that nobody cares about anymore makes no sense.

The steps to exporting a table are much simpler than they are for importing. Here goes:

1. **With the database open, click on the table you want to export.**

   As you may expect, the table name is highlighted for the world to see.

2. **Choose File⇨Save As/Export from the main menu.**

   The little Save As dialog box shown in Figure 23-2 bounds merrily onto the screen.

Figure 23-2:
Here's an easy one — click on OK to continue.

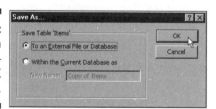

3. **Make sure that the radio button promising to ship your data To an External File or Database is selected; then click on OK.**

   The little dialog box does its job, and a big honking dialog box takes its place.

4. **Click on the down arrow in the Save as type box to list the available exporting formats; then click on the one you want (see Figure 23-3).**

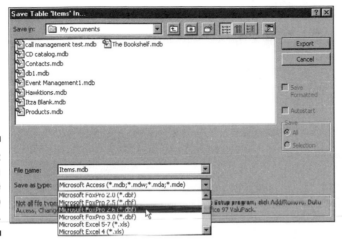

Figure 23-3:
I think that a
FoxPro file
would do
just fine.

If the format you're looking for is in Table 23-1 but is *not* in your list on-screen, run the Access 97 setup program again (oh joy, oh rapture!) and install that format on your system. This procedure may require the help of your Information Systems folks, depending on where your copy of Access 97 is stored and who has custody of the installation disks.

What if you try these steps and Access 97 *still* doesn't understand your data file? Here's one last trick you can try, but be forewarned: This is *truly* a last resort. Go back to your old program (where you created these data files in the first place) and see if that program has an *export* option. If the old program does, try exporting your data to one of the formats that Access 97 understands (see Table 23-1 earlier in this chapter for a complete list).

There's danger here, though — every time you export and import data, you risk messing up part of it. The export/import process isn't perfect, so tread carefully (and make a couple backup copies of the original data file before you begin!).

5. To use a different name for the table, click on the File name list box, highlight the existing table name, and then type a new name.

If the table is headed back to an old DOS or Windows 3.*x* world, remember to limit yourself to eight letters, numbers, or combination thereof. Don't worry about the extension (the three-character part after the period in an old filename), because Access 97 handles that automatically.

6. If you want to stow the newly exported file in a different folder from the current one, use the Save in list box at the top of the window to explain the destination to Access 97.

To leave the file in the folder you're in, just skip this step and forge ahead.

7. Brace yourself and click on Export (see Figure 23-4).

In true computer style, if the process is a success you get absolutely *no* feed-back from Access 97. You only hear about it if something dreadful goes wrong. Luckily, few things ever go wrong with exports, so your computer is probably sitting there looking smug even as you read this.

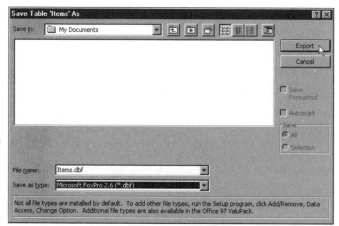

Figure 23-4:
Crossing
your fingers
helps, too.

Chapter 24

The Analyzer: Your Data's Dr. Freud, Dr. Watson, and Dr. Jekyll

• •

In This Chapter

▶ Becoming relational with the Table Analyzer

▶ Making the database document itself

▶ Steering clear of the Performance Analyzer

• •

*I*f I didn't know better, I'd file this chapter under the heading *Oh Sure, That's What It Does* (said with heavy sarcasm). After all, the Analyzer promises to do the three tasks that are nearest to a database person's heart: automatically convert flat files into relational databases; document the database and all its sundry parts (including tables, queries, forms, reports, and more); and analyze the structure of your tables to make sure that everything is set up in the best possible way. If the Analyzer does all that and cooks, too (or at least orders pizza), a nearsighted technoweenie may accidentally fall in love!

Even though technology has come a *long* way in recent years, it's not as advanced as you expect. That caveat is true of the Analyzer, too — it promises more than it delivers. On the bright side, it does deliver a great deal, so the Analyzer gets a chapter of its very own, a place to extol its two virtues and reveal its shortcoming. (I guess one out of three isn't bad.)

It Slices, It Dices, It Builds Relational Databases!

Arguably, the Analyzer's biggest promise is hiding under the Tools⇨ Analyze⇨Table. This piece of software claims it can turn a flat file table into a relational database with minimal human intervention *and* check for spelling errors in the data at the same time.

Truth be told, the Analyzer *tries* awfully hard to convert the flat file into a relational database. But like most software, sometimes it gets confused and vaults off in the wrong direction. I still recommend giving it a try, simply because it *may* work on your table, and if it does, you just saved a ton of time and effort.

The Analyzer works best with a flat file table that contains plenty of duplicate information. For example, imagine a flat-file table that stores video rental information. Each record contains customer and video data. If the same customer rents six tapes, the table has six separate records with the customer's name, address, and other information duplicated in each one. Multiply that by 100 customers and you have precisely the kind of flat-file mess that the Analyzer is designed to solve.

With that thought in mind, here's how to inflict — er, invoke — the Table Analyzer Wizard:

1. **With your database open, choose Tools⇨Analyze⇨Table from the main menu.**

    After a period of thought punctuated with hard-disk activity, the Table Analyzer Wizard dialog box appears on-screen (see Figure 24-1).

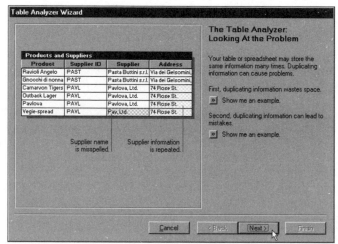

Figure 24-1:
So far, so good — the wizard shows up.

2. **The first two screens are interesting, but strictly educational. Read them if you want and then click on Next.**

    Stop clicking on Next when you get to the screen in Figure 24-2 (which should be precisely two Next clicks from Step 1).

3. **Click on the name of the flat file you want to do the relational magic on and then click on Next.**

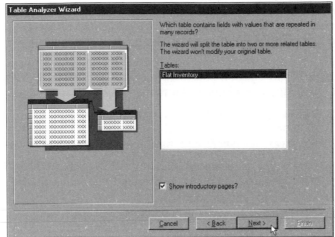

Figure 24-2:
Getting
ready to do
the deed.

Although some call it superstition, I firmly believe in crossing my fingers at moments such as this.

4. **The wizard wants to know whether it can analyze the table and offer suggestions on how the table ought to work. Click on the Yes radio button (if it's not already selected) and then click on Next.**

This step is the pivotal one in the whole process. The wizard leaps into the task, displaying a couple of horizontal bar charts to show how the project's progressing. When the Analysis Stages bar gets all the way to the end, the wizard's done. With the analysis complete, the results look like those shown in Figure 24-3.

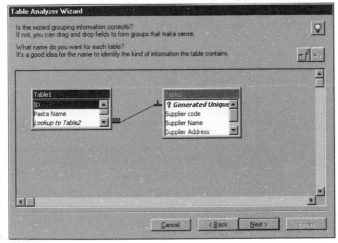

Figure 24-3:
The results
are a little
odd, but not
bad for a
piece of
hardware.

5. **If you like what the wizard came up with, name the tables by clicking on each table and then clicking on the Name Table button (the one that looks like a pencil doodling on a table). When you're done, click on Next.**

If you're not sure about what the wizard wants to do or if the plan just makes no sense, click on Cancel and seek human help. (See the sidebar "When in doubt, ask a human" for more about that option.)

If the wizard recommends that you don't split your table, carefully click the Cancel button and pat yourself on the head for a job well done. That's the wizard's way of saying that it thinks your table is fine just as it sits.

6. **The wizard wants your input about key fields for the tables. To designate a key field, click on a field in the table and then click on the Key button.**

This step lets you replace many of the Generated Unique ID entries that the wizard put in the tables.

Make sure that each table has a key field before continuing!

7. **The structure is basically complete, so the wizard turns its attention to typographical errors within the database. If it finds records that *seem* to be the same except for minor changes, it asks for your help to fix them (see Figure 24-4). Follow the on-screen instructions to effect the repairs.**

Depending on the condition of your data, you may have *many* records to correct. Be patient — the wizard really *is* helping!

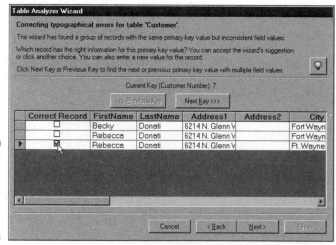

Figure 24-4:
What seems to be a little trouble is easily fixed.

8. **After the correction process is done, the wizard offers to create a query that looks and acts like your original table. If you have reports and forms that work with the flat file, let the wizard create the query for you (the default action). Otherwise, click on the No radio button. Click on Finish when you're through.**

When in doubt, ask a human

The Table Analyzer may not be able to make heads or tails of your table. The Analyzer always tries, but it may fail rather spectacularly. If it does, the project falls back into your lap.

If you're trying to split a flat file database into a relational database and you don't know where to start, a good place to begin is the snack food aisle at the local food store. Get some goodies (preferably chocolate) and use them to bribe your local database nerd into helping you.

If this database is important to your business or life (and it *must* be, or you wouldn't be haggling with it so much), it's important enough to get some live, human help to put it together correctly.

Documentation: What to Give the Nerd in Your Life

Pardon me while I put on my technoweenie hat and taped-together glasses for a moment. One thing the world needs more of (can't ever have enough of, in fact) is *documentation*. If life were a little better documented, things would be different.

(I'm taking off the technoweenie outfit now. Thanks for your patience.)

In truth, documentation is probably the furthest task from your mind right now, but it's still important, especially if you're creating something for your business. I know that you barely have time to get the database running and tested, but you *absolutely* need to document what you're doing.

Like many problems, documenting your work is a trade-off between a dire need and a lack of time. What's a person to do? Call the Documentor!

This second piece of the Analyzer puzzle steps through everything in your database (and I do mean *everything*) and documents the living daylights out of it. This thing collects information so obscure that I'm not even sure the programmers know what some of it means.

But the neat part of the Documentor is that it works *by itself.* Really. You start it, sic it on a database, and nip off for a spot of lunch. When you come back, its report is done and waiting. {Poof!} Instant documentation.

Here's how to put the Documentor to work on your database:

1. **With the database file open, choose Tools⇨Analyze⇨Documentor from the main menu.**

   The Database Documentor rises from the hard drive like a digital Phoenix and appears on-screen. (Okay, so I'm in a poetic mood — I'm still giddy about the prospect of the program doing my documentation for me.)

2. **In the Select Objects dialog box, click on the All Object Types tab and then on Select All to document your entire database (see Figure 24-5). When you're ready, click on OK to start the process.**

Figure 24-5:
One click ensures that everything gets included.

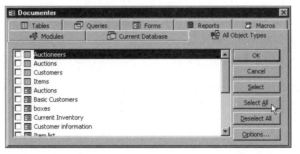

The Documentor begins by examining all the objects in your database, starting with the tables and moving on to the queries, forms, reports, and so on. During the process, your forms appear on-screen for a moment — that's normal.

The process often takes a while, so this is a good time for lunch or a little coffee break.

3. **When the Documentor finishes, it leaves a report packed with information about your database (Figure 24-6). Click on the Print button on the toolbar or choose File⇨Print to get a paper copy.**

   If you want to store the report for posterity, choose File⇨Save as Table and then give the table a name.

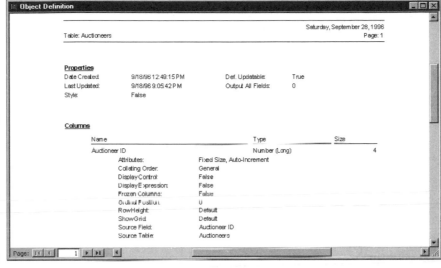

Figure 24-6:
The info's all here in black and white — and you barely lifted a finger!

Let the Performance Analyzer Work on Someone Else's Tables

I don't usually come right out and drop a great big *hands off* notice in your lap, but I'm afraid that the Performance Analyzer deserves to be the exception to the rule.

Don't get me wrong — this feature shows great promise. After all, who wouldn't like something that claims to dig around in your tables, ferret out the technoid tweaks that are the key to better performance, and then implement them for you? But at least for now, forgo the temptation to tinker and instead let someone *else* (preferably someone you don't like) use the Performance Analyzer on his or her data first.

In my tests, the analyzer came up with some pretty lame ideas, such as an ever-present suggestion that I change the postal code field from text to a long integer type. For as smart as the software is, it certainly *ought* to find some more impressive suggestions than that. I tried several combinations, including some with obvious problems in field type. The Performance Analyzer never came up with anything really useful to say.

Keep this feature in the back of your mind and try it out when Access 99 comes out on the market in a couple years.

Part VI
The Part of Tens

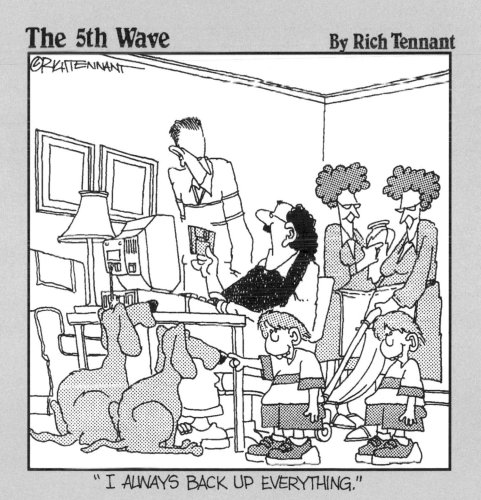

"I ALWAYS BACK UP EVERYTHING."

In this part . . .

All hail the traditional Part of Tens, purveyor of numerically organized information, keeper of the sacred decimal count, and upholder of the proud . . .*For Dummies* tradition.

Every . . .*For Dummies* book closes with a Part of Tens. I guess it's the *Dummies* version of denouement. Anyway, this book's final part includes stuff you can use today, stuff you may need tomorrow, and stuff for *way* on down the road. I tried to include a little something for everyone, so read every chapter *very* closely and see if you can find the stuff I put in just for you.

By the way, no animals were harmed in the quest to bring you this information. One technoweenie was slightly miffed, but I'm sure he'll get over it.

Chapter 25

Ten Timesaving Keyboard Shortcuts

. . . .

In This Chapter

▶ Keystrokes to save you time, energy, and hair

. . . .

*J*ust because Windows 95 is supposed to be the ultimate graphical user environment doesn't mean that you won't need the keyboard anymore. In fact, Access 97 has some cool shortcuts up its sleeve that are available only through this special, keyboard-based offer.

This chapter highlights ten cool shortcuts designed to make your life a little easier. Some keystroke combinations enter data automatically, some make editing quicker, and others are for fun.

Select an Entire Field — F2

This shortcut is particularly handy when you're replacing a lengthy address or description field. Instead of wrestling with the mouse to make sure that you have *everything* in the field highlighted, simply press F2 and you *know* that it's done. The keystroke works in both Datasheet view and Form view.

Insert the Current Date — Ctrl+; (semicolon)

This keystroke combination and the one following not only save time but also increase accuracy. Ever mistyped a date because you were in a hurry (or because the keyboard couldn't spell)? Ctrl+; resolves the issue completely by doing the work for you. The keystroke works in Datasheet view and Form view.

Insert the Current Time — Ctrl+: (colon)

This one is another nod to accuracy. To insert the current time, you actually press Ctrl+Shift+; (semicolon), even though Ctrl+: is the keystroke. To get a colon, you have to do the Shift+; (semicolon) routine.

Insert a Line Break — Ctrl+Enter

When a long entry in a memo or large text field feels like it's never going to quit, end the monotony with a line break. Well-placed line breaks make your data more legible, too. The keystroke is available in Datasheet view and Form view.

Add a New Record — Ctrl++ (plus sign)

Although Ctrl++ looks funny (just how *do* you write *plus* + without spelling it out?), this keyboard shortcut keeps you on the go when you're in a hot-and-heavy edit mode. Because you don't have to keep switching between the keyboard and the mouse to insert new records, your speed increases, as does your accuracy. No doubt to your surprise, this shortcut works in Datasheet view and Form view.

Delete the Current Record — Ctrl+− (minus sign)

Do you suffer from pesky, unsightly, or unneeded records in your tables? Ctrl+− painlessly excises the records that you want to delete. And just like this shortcut's cousin, Ctrl++, this shortcut works in both Datasheet view and Form view.

Save the Record — Shift+Enter

After a long, hard edit, make sure that the record is saved with a quick Shift+Enter. That signals Access 97 that you're truly done working on this one and are ready to store it for posterity. The software takes the cue and saves your changes immediately. Use this key combo in Datasheet view or Form view.

Undo Your Last Changes — Ctrl+Z

Everyone should have this one memorized. The Undo keystroke is a golden oldie. With Access 97's propensity to automatically save things every time you turn around, it can really save your bacon. When something goes wrong, don't panic — try Ctrl+Z instead. This keystroke combination works almost everywhere in Access 97.

Open the Selected Object in Design View — Ctrl+Enter

Hey, what's this? Ctrl+Enter does *two* things in Access 97? You're right. When you're editing a table in Datasheet view or Form view, Ctrl+Enter inserts a line break. When you're in *Database* view, use Ctrl+Enter to whip open something into Design view. Let the *ordinary folks* use the mouse — be different and do it from the keyboard!

Quit for Good — Alt+F4

If you're having a *bad Access 97 day*, reaffirm your power over the software with a good, old-fashioned Alt+F4. Look at Access 97, raise your hand to the keyboard, and wave good-bye as the program goes away and leaves you alone for a while.

Chapter 26

Ten Common Crises and How to Survive Them

*W*here there are computers, so also is there software, because a computer is nothing without its software. Where there is software, so also are there problems, because software without problems is obviously outdated and in need of replacement.

Problems are a part of life. When the problems strike in or around your precious data, they seem all the more fearsome. This chapter touches on only ten problems you may encounter while using Access 97. If your problem is covered here, try the solution I outline. If your particular trouble isn't on the list, refer to Chapter 3 for some other spots to seek help.

And good luck. (I mean it!)

You Built Several Tables, but Put Them in Different Databases

Misplacing your tables is an easy mistake to make at first, especially if you have experience with one of those *other* database programs such as Paradox or FoxPro. Those systems store each table in a separate file. Working from that experience, it's only natural to start creating databases right and left, each one containing a single table.

Of course, separate tables make a great deal of extra work for you in Access 97 because the confused program can't figure out what you're trying to accomplish. Rather than setting up all kinds of links among a slew of different database files, pull your tables together into a single database, the way Access 97 is designed to work with them.

To pull all your tables together, open a database file, right-click on the table you want to move, and select Copy from the pop-up menu. Now open the database you're moving the table to. Click on the Tables tab, right-click in the Table list, and select Paste on the pop-up menu. The table hops into the database. Repeat the process for all the orphan tables rattling around in their own database files.

If you're feeling really rambunctious and adventuresome, try feeding your new database to the mighty Access 97 Analyzer. For more about the Analyzer, flip back to Chapter 24.

You Type 73.725, but It Changes to 74 by Itself

Automatic rounding can frustrate the living daylights out of you, but fixing it is easy. By default, Access 97 sets all number fields to accept *long integers* — numbers without decimal places. You need to change the setting to *single*, which is short for *single precision number*, not *hey you swinging text field, let's go party with the forms*.

To fix the problem, open the table in Design view and then click on the field that's giving you fits. On the General tab of the Properties area at the bottom of the screen, click in the Field Size box. Click on the down arrow that appears on the end of the box; then select *single* from the drop-down menu. Save the table and (voilà!) your automatic rounding problem is over.

The Case of the Missing Database

Sometimes you feel like you just can't trust those database files. Here today, AWOL tomorrow. Access 97 knows how slippery the files are, so it offers a very powerful file finder built right into the Open Database window. When one of your database files tries to make a run for it (or if you just can't quite remember where you left it), use the Find File option to track it down. Everything you need to know about it is in the sidebar "Bo Peep needed the Find Files option" in Chapter 6.

If you're on a network, remember to check the network storage areas, too!

You're Almost Completely Sure That's Not the Question You Asked

Remember the old saying, "Kids say the darnedest things"? Well, this problem falls under the heading, "Queries return the darnedest results." Every now and then, one of your queries returns the most *fascinating* answers. In fact, they're *so* fascinating that you begin to wonder precisely what color the sky is in the query's world, because the query's world is obviously different from the one you're in.

Because the actual cause can be any number of things, this problem doesn't have a tried-and-true solution, but I can offer some steps to send you in the right direction:

1. **Make sure that no stray characters are in the query.**

   A single misplaced keystroke can send Access 97 on a wild data chase. Tidy things up and then try the query again. If you still get flaky results, go on to the next step.

2. **Double-check the query logic itself.**

   Are you asking the question that you *think* you're asking? Access 97 always tries hard to get the query right, but if it misunderstands the question, all its work is for naught. If you're doing one incredibly complex query, try to split it into a few simple queries that build on each other instead.

3. **Try closing the query and rebuilding it from scratch.**

   Every now and then, queries simply freak out (after all, it's *just* a computer). If nothing seems to help, make a backup of your data and call your friendly neighborhood computer guru.

If the query *still* doesn't work right, enlist your local database nerd for a quick consultation. Something very subtle may be wrong with either your query or (horrors!) your tables.

And When You Looked Again, the Record Was Gone

"The record was there — right there!" The key word in that sentence is the verb, because it indicates that the record *isn't* there now. Precisely *where* the record went is a moot point because only the computer knows, and machines have a code of silence about these details. (It's a subset of the rules that make all the copiers break at the same time.)

First, *don't panic*. Panicky people do strange things, and you need your wits about you for the next few minutes. You can panic later after the dust settles.

Before doing anything technical with Access 97 (or hitting the computer with a baseball bat), press Ctrl+Z. That's the Undo key. If the record comes back, you're done. In that case, close the table and go have a panic attack in the break room.

If the Undo key didn't accomplish anything, you're in slightly more trouble. The next best solution is to copy the record from a backup of the database file. This solution works only if you backed up your database at some point. If you have a paper copy of the data, you can always manually re-enter it into the database. If that record was your only copy of the information, then raise your hand, look at the computer, and wave good-bye, because it's gone now (you have my deepest sympathy).

Please, oh *please,* keep current backups of your information. You never know when bad things will happen (insert eerie organ music here).

The Validation That Never Was

Validations are one of my favorite features of Access 97. But like anything, validations can cause problems if they're not used properly.

The biggest concern is a validation rule that *can't* be valid. For example, suppose that someone (certainly not you or I, but *someone*) wants to limit a particular field so that it only accepts entries between 0 and 100. To accomplish that, the person creates a validation that says `<0 And >100`. Unfortunately, that rule won't work — ever! The person mixed up the symbols and created a rule that only accepts a number that's less than 0 *and* greater than 100. According to my college math professor, not too many numbers like that are running loose in the world.

Don't let this problem happen to your validations. To avoid such crises, write your rule on paper and then test it with some sample data. Be sure to include examples of both good and bad entries to make sure that the rule works just like it's supposed to.

You Can't Link to a FoxPro or dBASE Table

In this bet on the cause of the failed link, the odds-on favorite is a bad index file. Access 97 has a specific problem linking to FoxPro and dBASE tables that have bad indexes. Before getting frustrated — even before panicking — go back to the original program, rebuild the table's index, and then try the link again. Most of the time, that procedure solves the problem.

If this snag happens to be the one time in 10,000 where the index file *isn't* at fault, pick up a bag of nacho chips at the convenience store and invite the guru over for a snack and some troubleshooting.

Be *really* careful when updating a FoxPro or dBASE file through Access 97. Make sure that you attach the index — otherwise, you're crawling around on your knees, begging for trouble.

You Get a Key Violation While Importing a Table

When you get a key violation while importing a table, Access 97 is trying as hard as it can, but the data you're importing contains a duplicate key value. Because Access 97 can't arbitrarily change the data in question, you need to do the repair. Go back to the master program, find the offending record, and build a good key to replace the duplicated one. After you're sure that the key values are all unique, then try, try again.

Try as You Might, the Program Won't Start

This dilemma is often a spectacularly fun problem. After picking Access 97 from the Start menu, the oh-so-cool Access 97 splash screen (the pretty picture that keeps you entertained while the program takes too long to load) flows smoothly onto the screen. Suddenly, the serene moment shatters as a small warning box bursts in. `Can't find ODD_ESOTERIC_FILE.MDB`. The Access 97 splash screen fades and you're left facing the Windows 95 desktop once more.

This sequence really does happen from time to time. Honestly, such events are just part of life with computers. I teach my troubleshooting classes a simple mantra to cover precisely this problem: *It's a file. Files go bad.*

Because the error message was kind enough to give you a filename (not all errors are so generous), use the Explorer to look for the file. If it's there, odds are that the file is corrupt. If the file isn't there, well, at least you know why Access 97 didn't find it.

Either way, you need to replace the file with a healthy version from your original Access 97 program disks. If you have a CD-ROM copy of Access 97, this process is easy. Just point the Explorer at the installation CD-ROM, find the file, and copy it to the Access 97 subdirectory.

Doing this process from floppy disks is more complicated because the files on floppies are compressed, and you have to use Microsoft's special decompression program to make them usable. Your best bet is (I hate saying this) to call the Microsoft Access support folks and seek their help.

The Wizard Won't Come Out of His Castle

This one is a more focused version of the preceding problem where Access 97 wouldn't start. Now the problem is localized to a particular wizard. The solution is the same: Look for the missing file, replace it from the master disks, and then see whether that solves the problem. If all else fails (which may happen), pick up a bag of nacho chips and call in your favorite nerd for some assistance.

The wizard files usually congregate in the main Access 97 folder, so at least you know where the file goes.

Chapter 27

Ten Tips from the Database Nerds

In This Chapter

▶ Cool ideas from that most uncool of all populations

*L*ike 'em or loathe 'em, the technical experts are always with you. Every-where you turn, you see someone who may know more about technology than you do. These folks sometimes look funny, frequently act strange, and can often seem amazingly disconnected from reality.

In their more lucid moments, though, the technical experts possess some nuggets of wisdom. This chapter is a distillation of good advice that I picked up over the years. Some of it is very focused, while other parts are downright philosophical. Such is life with the technical experts (but you knew that already).

Document As If Your Life Depends on It

Yes, it's a pain. Yes, it's a bother. Yes, *I* do it myself (kinda scary when a guy actually listens to his own advice). If you build a database, make sure that you document every little detail about it. Here's a list of items to start with:

- **General information about the database:** Include file locations, an explanation of what the database does, and information on how it works.

- **Table layouts, including field names, sizes, contents, and sample contents:** If some of the data comes from esoteric or temporary sources (like the shipping report that you shred right after data entry), note that fact in the documentation so that people know.

- **Report names, an explanation of the information on the report, and lists of who gets a copy of the report when it's printed:** If you need to run some queries before doing a report, document the process (or better yet, get a nerd to help you automate the whole thing). Documenting who receives the report is *particularly* important. Jot down the job title in the documentation as well as the current person in the position.

✔ **Queries and logic:** For every query, provide a detailed explanation of how the query works, especially if it involves multiple tables.

✔ **Miscellaneous details:** Provide information such as the backup process and schedule, where back-up tapes are located (you *are* doing backups, right?), and what to do if the computer isn't working. If your database runs a particularly important business function, such as accounting, inventory, point-of-sale, or order entry, make sure that some kind of manual process is in place to keep the business going if the computer breaks down — and remember to document the process!

One final thought: Keep the documentation up to date. Every few months, review your documentation to see whether some updates are needed. Documentation is only useful if it's up to date and if someone other than yourself can understand it. Likewise, make sure you (or your counterparts in the department) know where the documentation is located. If you have an electronic version, keep it backed up and have a printout handy.

Don't Make Your Fields Way Too Big

When you're building a table, take a moment to make your text fields the appropriate size for the data you're keeping in those fields. By default, Access 97 sets up text fields to hold 50 characters — a pretty generous setting, particularly if the field happens to be holding two-letter state abbreviations. Granted, 48 characters of space aren't anything to write home about, but multiply that space across a table with 100,000 customer addresses in it and you get 4.8MB of storage space that's very busy holding *nothing*.

Adjust the field size with the Field Size setting on the General tab in Design view.

Real Numbers Use Number Fields

Use number fields for *numbers,* not for text *pretending* to be a number. Computers perceive a difference between the postal code *47201* and the number *47,201.* The postal code is stored as a series of five characters that all happen to be digits, but the number is stored as an actual number. You can do math with it (just try that on a postal-code field, sometime) and all kinds of fun stuff.

When choosing the type for a new field with numbers in it, ask yourself a simple question: Are you *ever* going to make a calculation or do anything math-related with the field? If so, use a number type. If not, store the field as text and go on with your life.

Better Validations Make Better Data

Validations work hand in hand with masks to prevent bad data from getting close to your tables. Validations are easy to make, quick to set up, and ever vigilant (even when you're so tired you can't see straight). If you aren't using validations to protect the integrity of your database, you really should start. Flip to Chapter 7 and have a look at the topic.

Use Understandable Names

When building a table or creating a database, think about the names you use. Will you remember what they mean three months from now? Six months from now? Are they intuitive enough for someone else to look at the table and figure out what it does, long after your knowledge of Access 97 puts your career on the fast track?

Now that Windows 95 *finally* offers long filenames, please use them. You don't need to get carried away, but now you have no excuse for files called *97Q1bdg5*. Using *Q1 1997 Budget Rev 5* makes *much* more sense to everyone involved.

Take Great Care When Deleting

Whenever you're deleting records from a table, make sure that you're killing the *right* record, check again, and — only when you're sure — delete the original. Even then, you can still do a quick Ctrl+Z and recover the little bugger.

Why all the checking and double-checking? Because after you delete a record *and do anything else in the table,* Access 97 completely forgets about your old record. It's gone, just as if it never existed. If that record happened to be important and you don't have a current back-up file, you're out of luck. Sorry!

Keep Backups

There's no substitute for a current backup of your data, particularly if the data is vital to your company. Don't believe me? Let the phrase *no receivables* float through your mind for a while. How do you feel about backups now? I thought you'd see it my way.

Think First and Then Think Again

Apply this rule to any Access 97 step that contains the word *delete* or *redesign*. Think about what you're doing. Then think again. Software makes handling large amounts of data easier than ever before, but it also offers the tools to screw up your data on a scale not seen since the time of P.T. Barnum.

Thomas Watson, Sr., the president of IBM for years and years, said it best: "Think."

Get Organized and Keep It Simple

Although they may seem different at first blush, these two tips work together to promote classic nerd values like *a place for every gadget* and *my query ran faster than yours, so there*. By keeping your computer orderly and organizing your entire workspace, you have everything you need at hand. Get yourself a Barcalounger and a remote control, and you never need to leave the office again.

But you can get *too* organized. In fact, doing so is altogether too easy. Temper your desire to organize with a passion for doing work with as few steps as possible. On your computer, limit the number of folders and subfolders you use — a maximum of five levels of folders is *more* than enough for just about anybody. If you go much beyond five levels, your organization starts bumping into your productivity (and nobody likes a productivity loss, least of all the people who come up with those silly little slogans for the corporate feel-good posters).

Know When to Ask for Help

If you're having trouble with something, swallow your ego and ask for help. Saying *I don't know* and then trying to find out holds no shame. This rule is *especially* important when you're riding herd on thousands of records in a database. Small missteps are magnified and multiplied, so ask for help *before* the situation becomes dire.

Chapter 28

Ten Sights to See in Your Copious Free Time

In This Chapter

▶ Topics to look into as your expertise grows

▶ Ten ways to wow your coworkers

*Y*ou won't be a beginner forever. I know that sometimes you feel as though you will, but at some point one fateful day, you'll look up and realize that Access 97 *makes sense*. Don't worry — you didn't turn the corner into full-blown nerddom, you just got comfortable with the program — and that's a good thing.

Now you're ready to look ahead and see what else is out there. Access 97 includes a wide array of powerful capabilities, so you have plenty of room to explore. This chapter gives you ten places to start on your quest, along with resource ideas so that you can learn more. Good luck!

Programming for People Who Don't Program

Access 97 has a powerful almost-programming feature called *macros*. You don't need to know a bunch of complicated commands or weird-looking functions to use them, but that doesn't mean macros aren't powerful. You can use macros to change a menu, build a toolbar, display dialog boxes, and automate many different tasks in Access 97. Macros are *real* power — and they're within your reach.

To learn more about macros, press F1 or click on the Office Assistant. In the Office Assistant's dialog box, type **Tell me about macros** and press Enter. If you already know something about programming and want to do some *really* fancy work, type **Tell me about Visual Basic** and then look ahead to the next section.

For all the Access 97 nerd tricks, check out *Access 97 Programming For Windows For Dummies,* by Rob Krumm (published by IDG Books Worldwide, Inc.).

Serious Programming for Techies

Of course, a *real* programming language lies underneath Access 97; it's called *Visual Basic for Applications.* Believe me, VBA is a real, for-sure programming language, capable of writing real, for-sure applications.

If you're already familiar with Visual Basic for Windows, you know how flexible and powerful Visual Basic language is. The VBA version is specifically oriented toward writing programs that extend the use of Access 97. Using VBA is harder than writing a macro, but the rewards are much greater, too. Turn to the Office Assistant for more about Visual Basic for Applications, or check out *Access 97 Programming For Windows For Dummies* (which covers *both* macros and the Access 97 version of Visual Basic).

Integrating Access 97 with Other Programs

You can use Access 97 with other Windows applications in many ways. Because Access 97 is fully OLE2 compliant (that's a fancy way of saying that it can easily swap information with many other programs), other programs can call Access 97 to perform certain functions and vice versa. All the Office 97 applications are now Internet-aware, which means that they have special behind-the-scenes links that help you work with Net stuff.

A really good example of this integration is an Access 97 database that works with a World Wide Web page on the Internet. When someone selects a particular item on the Web page, the Web server sends a message to Access requesting information. Access runs a couple of queries and then hands the results over to an Access Visual Basic program that writes the answers up as a Web page, complete with all the correct HyperText Markup Language (HTML) tags. Talk about a cool thing!

Although I'm starting to sound like a broken record, *Access 97 Programming For Windows For Dummies* is a really great place to start getting into stuff like this. If the Internet and the World Wide Web are mysteries to you, check out *The Internet For Dummies,* 3rd Edition (by John R. Levine, Carol Baroudi, and Margaret Levine Young) to find out more.

Enlisting the Helpful Lookup Wizard

The Lookup Wizard is another wizard that's just waiting to give you a hand. When you're creating a table, the Lookup Wizard can build a special *lookup field* that pulls data from another Access 97 table. Lookups are a great way to accurately include items such as customer numbers or product ID numbers that are easily mistyped when you're entering them by hand. Using a lookup field ensures that *only* correct data ends up in your table. For more about the Lookup Wizard, consult the Office Assistant. (Even though he's not a Wizard, he's still a pretty helpful guy.)

Advanced Query Wizards Do Esoteric Things

As your databases get more complicated, you need bigger and better wizards to keep all the parts working just right. Two wizards that fill the bill are the Find Duplicates and Archive Wizards.

The Find Duplicates Wizard checks your database for entries that are significantly similar (for example, the address is identical but the company name is entered differently) and brings them to your attention. The Archive Wizard helps you cull old records from your table, keeping things neat and tidy around your databases.

And where can you learn more? Just ask Mr. Office Assistant for his thoughts about *query wizards.*

If You Think Forms Are Cool Now, Just Wait Until You See This!

Chapter 22 barely scratches the surface of what forms can do in Access 97. With so *much* more to know about forms, somebody could write an entire book called *The Art of Access Forms.* (Hey — that's a pretty cool idea. I may just do that!)

For example, forms based on queries provide up-to-the-minute information *every time* you open the form. Combining macros and forms creates powerful data entry, editing, and analysis tools. The possibilities are, as usual, endless.

Check the Office Assistant for more by asking about *forms* or *forms and macros.*

Go into Desktop Publishing with Access 97 and Word 7

Microsoft thoughtfully built some cool linkage between the new versions of its flagship products — Access and Word. With a mouse click and some Wizard-fiddling, your boring Access 97 table becomes a slick, professional, desktop-published catalog direct from the always fashion-conscious studios of Microsoft Word 7. This is integration you can *use,* not just imagine.

Check the Office Assistant for more information about *Word.*

Watch Excel and Access Conspire to Produce Statistics

When your data needs that special touch to produce a complicated statistical analysis, look to the built-in links between Access 97 and Excel 97. Probably the coolest feature of this linkage is the capability to flip an Access 97 table into the Excel Pivot Wizard and look at your data in ways you only dreamed of (and perhaps never dared to hope for). Of course, you need Excel on your computer to do these tricks, but what's a couple hundred bucks compared to the ultimately cool statistics awaiting you?

As you may expect, the Office Assistant knows all and sees all about using Access and Excel together. Ask about *Excel* and see what he says.

Dancing in the Streets and Shouting "OLE"

I mention the OLE feature in the section about integrating Access 97 with other Windows 95 programs. But OLE is powerful enough to deserve its own section. Through OLE (or *Object Linking and Embedding*), you can put an Access 97 database right into a Microsoft Word 7 document or easily add sounds to an Access 97 table. OLE is *very* flexible — almost mind-bogglingly so.

For a good introduction to OLE (pronounced "O-Lay" in nerddom), pick up a copy of *OLE For Dummies,* by John Mueller and Wallace Wang.

Mailing Stuff Directly from Access 97

If your company uses Microsoft Mail, you can send someone part of your database *directly* from the Access menu. This feature is just another example of Microsoft's commitment to leaving you absolutely no choice but to buy its products for everything you do. Instead of worrying about copying, pasting, and generally mucking around with your data, one menu selection and a couple of dialog boxes send a table or form winging its way through e-mail.

Guess where the info is — yup, that's right. The Office Assistant, keeper of all knowledge, knows about *mailing database objects*.

Appendix
Installing Access 97

● ●

*A*s great a product as Access 97 is (and it really is a pretty good one), it can't do anything without being installed on your computer. Granted, the box is kinda cute, but it's a little pricey to use simply as a decorator item. Installing the software is the only way to recoup your money on the investment. If there were another way out, I'd tell you.

Before installing Access 97, make sure that you have everything you need, computer-wise. By the way, these are *my* recommendations, not the official Microsoft specifications. To make Access 97 work reasonably well, you need the following:

✔ A 486 (running at 50 MHz or better) or Pentium-based computer

✔ At least 12MB of RAM, but 16MB (or more) is a far better idea

✔ Windows 95 (sorry — you can't use Windows 3.1 with Access 97)

✔ A CD-ROM drive for the installation process

As I write this, the details of how Access 97 will ship are a little fuzzy. According to my sources, it's definitely going to arrive on a CD-ROM, but I'm not sure whether floppy disks will still be an option. My best guess is that the stores will only carry the CD-ROM version, but floppies will be available directly from Microsoft. For your sake, I hope you got the CD-ROM, because I figure Access 97 will take something in the vicinity of 35 to 50 diskettes. Even on my most patient days, that's a *lot* of disk swapping.

These instructions also work fine if you have the Microsoft Office 97 Professional CD-ROM, which also includes Word, Excel, PowerPoint, and a host of nifty little mini-applications from the brightest (if not the most well-slept) minds in Redmond, Washington.

Enough chitchat — time to install the software so you can get something done today.

1. **Eject the music CD you're listening to and put the Access 97 disc in your CD-ROM drive instead.**

The moment is at hand. It's kinda like being at the top of the first hill on the roller coaster. The view is great, the prospects are scary, and it's too late to back out now. And to top it all off, you actually *paid* for the privilege of being here.

If you have the diskettes, find the one marked Setup and put it into your disk drive (usually drive A:).

2. **If a nice Office 97 installation window automatically appears, skip ahead to Step 4. Otherwise, click on the Start button and then select Run from the Start menu.**

On some machines, the CD automatically starts itself, thanks to a nifty feature called *AutoPlay*. If your machine behaves like mine does, you'll probably be doing the manual installation thing. In that case, the cute little Run dialog box appears on-screen, and you're ready to continue.

3. **In the Run dialog box, type the disk drive letter, the colon and backslash (:\), and finally the word** setup. **Click OK when you're ready to start the setup process.**

For CD-ROM installations, you usually enter **D:\SETUP** in the Run dialog box. For floppy installations, the entry is traditionally **A:\SETUP**.

4. **The setup program says a few warm words of welcome. Click on Continue to, um, continue.**

Access 97 displays the Name and Organization Information dialog box. It wants to get acquainted. Isn't that neighborly?

5. **Find the floppy disk labeled License Disk and put it into your disk drive. Click on OK when it's there.**

This is Microsoft's latest attempt to reduce software piracy. Considering the alternatives (like old-fashioned copy protection), it's okay with me. After proving that you're the program's rightful owner, the installation process continues.

6. **Type your name into the Name area and your company name into the Organization box. Click on OK when you're done, and then click on OK again to reassure Access 97 that what you typed is correct.**

This is part of the normal registration process. You aren't signing up for any mailing lists (at least not yet).

7. **Now the installation program wants yet *another* ID number from you. This time, it's your CD Key number. Look for a sticker on the back of the CD-ROM case and carefully type the number from the sticker into the CD Key text box. Double-check your work and then click on OK.**

If the Setup program says that your CD Key number is invalid, click OK to make the warning dialog box go away. Then look *very* carefully and retype the CD Key number.

In the very rare event that the Microsoft Product Support folks ever ask you for the CD Key number, you can quickly find it by running Access 97 and choosing Help⇨About from the main menu.

8. When the Setup program proudly displays the Product ID number, try to look impressed and then click on OK.

The installer takes a brief peek around your hard drive to see what it can find. When the Setup program is done, it reports its findings in the dialog box shown in Figure A-1.

Use the recommended folder names for the installation. Unless there's a *very* good technical reason for choosing something else, leave the folder names alone. This makes future technical support calls *much* easier on both you and the technician helping you.

9. Click on OK to continue.

The Setup choices dialog box appears, as shown in Figure A-2. If you want an *uncommon* installation, use the Custom button, which gives you a wild variety of choices on every niggling little part of Access 97. Don't select a Custom installation unless you have some very specific needs or are *really* bored.

10. Click on the Typical button for a common installation.

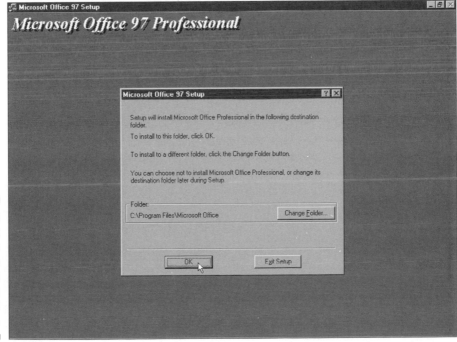

Figure A-1:
Don't change these settings without a darn good reason.

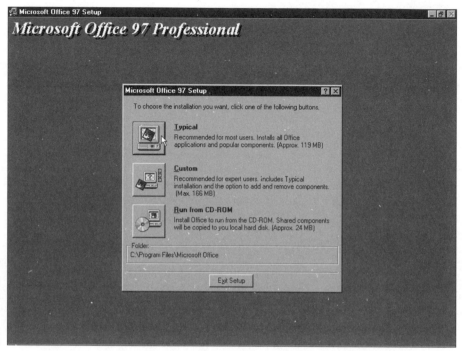

When Access 97 offers you a quick list of additional options, just click on Continue. The installation program takes a few moments to think (while leaving the screen disturbingly blank, I might add), but finally gets around to putting Access 97 on your computer.

In the name of enhanced entertainment value and shameless propaganda-mongering, the screen then displays a few advertising billboards during the Access 97 installation process (see Figure A-3 for an example).

When the files are all copied, the installer takes one last look around, makes some behind-the-scenes tweaks, and (drumroll please!) announces that Access 97 now resides on your computer (as shown in Figure A-4).

11. Click on OK to complete the Access 97 installation process.

Congratulations! Take a celebratory break and then meander back to Chapter 1 for a tour of the software.

If you have an Internet connection and want to get the most out of the new Access 97 online connectivity, double-click on the new Setup for Microsoft Internet Explorer 3.0 icon on the desktop; then follow the on-screen instructions.

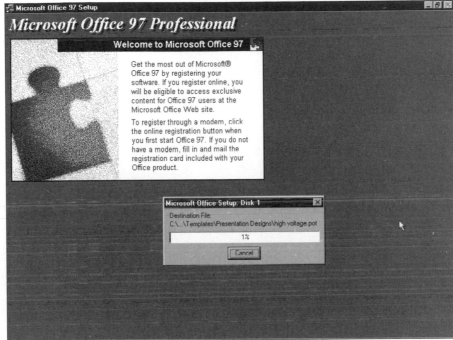

Figure A-3:
This
commercial
message is
courtesy of
Microsoft.

Figure A-4:
Whee — it's
done!

Index

(continued)

IDG BOOKS WORLDWIDE REGISTRATION CARD

Title of this book: **Access 97 for Windows® for Dummies®**

My overall rating of this book: ❑ Very good [1]   ❑ Good [2]   ❑ Satisfactory [3]   ❑ Fair [4]   ❑ Poor [5]

How I first heard about this book:

❑ Found in bookstore; name: [6]   ❑ Book review: [7]

❑ Advertisement: [8]   ❑ Catalog: [9]

❑ Word of mouth; heard about book from friend, co-worker, etc.: [10]   ❑ Other: [11]

What I liked most about this book:

What I would change, add, delete, etc., in future editions of this book:

Other comments:

Number of computer books I purchase in a year: ❑ 1 [12]   ❑ 2-5 [13]   ❑ 6-10 [14]   ❑ More than 10 [15]

I would characterize my computer skills as: ❑ Beginner [16] ❑ Intermediate [17] ❑ Advanced [18] ❑ Professional [19]

I use ❑ DOS [20]   ❑ Windows [21]   ❑ OS/2 [22]   ❑ Unix [23]   ❑ Macintosh [24]   ❑ Other: [25]_____

(please specify)

I would be interested in new books on the following subjects:

(please check all that apply, and use the spaces provided to identify specific software)

❑ Word processing: [26]   ❑ Spreadsheets: [27]

❑ Data bases: [28]   ❑ Desktop publishing: [29]

❑ File Utilities: [30]   ❑ Money management: [31]

❑ Networking: [32]   ❑ Programming languages: [33]

❑ Other: [34]

I use a PC at (please check all that apply): ❑ home [35]   ❑ work [36]   ❑ school [37]   ❑ other: [38] _____

The disks I prefer to use are ❑ 5.25 [39]   ❑ 3.5 [40]   ❑ other: [41]_____

I have a CD ROM: ❑ yes [42]   ❑ no [43]

I plan to buy or upgrade computer hardware this year: ❑ yes [44]   ❑ no [45]

I plan to buy or upgrade computer software this year: ❑ yes [46]   ❑ no [47]

Name: _____   Business title: [48] _____   Type of Business: [49] _____

Address (❑ home [50] ❑ work [51]/Company name: _____)

Street/Suite#

City [52]/State [53]/Zipcode [54]: _____   Country [55] _____

❑ **I liked this book!** You may quote me by name in future
IDG Books Worldwide promotional materials.

My daytime phone number is _____

IDG
BOOKS
WORLDWIDE

THE WORLD OF
COMPUTER
KNOWLEDGE®

 **YES!**

Please keep me informed about IDG Books Worldwide's
World of Computer Knowledge. Send me your latest catalog.

 **INFO WORLD** TECHNICAL BOOKS

 ...FOR DUMMIES™ BESTSELLING BOOK SERIES FROM IDG

 S-D Visual™

 ...SECRETS®

 Macworld® Books